The Gold Standard in Theory and History

THE

GOLD STANDARD

IN THEORY AND HISTORY

HG
297
.G63
198E

Edited by
BARRY EICHENGREEN

Methuen
New York and London

First published in 1985 by
Methuen, Inc.
29 West 35th Street, New York, NY 10001

Published in Great Britain by
Methuen & Co. Ltd
11 New Fetter Lane, London EC4P 4EE

Introduction and selection © 1985 Barry Eichengreen

Printed in Great Britain by
Richard Clay (The Chaucer Press) Ltd
Bungay, Suffolk

Library of Congress Cataloging in Publication Data

Main entry under title:
The Gold Standard in theory and history.
(UP: 896)
Bibliography: p.
Includes Index.
1. Gold standard—History. I. Eichengreen, Barry J.
HG297.G63   1985   332.4′222′09   85-10495

ISBN 0-416-39110-9 (pbk.)

British Library Cataloguing in Publication Data

The Gold Standard in theory and history.
1. Gold standard—History
I. Eichengreen, Barry
332.4′52′09   HG297

ISBN 0-416-39100-9

Contents

Acknowledgements

The editor and publisher would like to thank the following for permission to reproduce copyright material:
P.B. Whale and Tieto Limited, chapter 3; Donald N. McCloskey and J. Richard Zecher, chapter 4, which first appeared in Jacob A. Frenkel and Harry G. Johnson (eds), *The Monetary Approach to the Balance of Payments* (George Allen & Unwin); Robert J. Barro and Cambridge University Press, chapter 5, 'Money and the price level under the gold standard', which first appeared in *Economic Journal*, 1979; W.M. Scammell, chapter 6 (© Board of Editors of the Bulletin of Economic Research); Robert Triffin, chapter 7, from *Our International Monetary System: Yesterday, Today and Tomorrow*, by Robert Triffin. Copyright © 1968 by Random House, Inc., reprinted by permission of Random House, Inc.; A.G. Ford, chapter 8, 'Notes on the working of the gold standard', from *Oxford Economic Papers*, February 1960, vol. 12, no. 1, reprinted by permission of Oxford University Press; Ragnar Nurkse, chapter 11, which first appeared in *International Currency Experience*, League of Nations, 1944; chapter 12 first appeared in Milton Gilbert, *The Gold-Dollar System: Conditions of Equilibrium and the Price of Gold*, Essay in International Finance No. 70, November 1968. Copyright © 1968. Reprinted by permission of the International Finance Section of Princeton University; Richard N. Cooper, chapter 13 (© 1982 by the Brookings Institution, Washington, D.C.).

1

Editor's introduction[1]

Barry Eichengreen

The international monetary system is part of the institutional framework that binds national economies together. An ideally functioning system permits producers to specialize in goods in which the nation has a comparative advantage and savers to search beyond national borders for profitable investment opportunities. It does so by combining the virtues of stability and flexibility. Stability in the market for foreign exchange minimizes the volatility of import and export prices, permitting producers and consumers to exploit fully the advantages of international specialization. Flexibility in the operation of the international monetary system permits the divergent objectives of national economic authorities to be reconciled with one another.

The one point upon which critics of our present system of flexible exchange rates agree is that it fails to combine these virtues. It provides neither the stability conducive to international specialization nor the flexibility required for independent action. Turbulence in international financial markets continues to disrupt firms' production and investment decisions. It gives rise to seriously misaligned exchange rates which confer on certain national producers an arbitrary (if temporary) competitive advantage. The penetration of imports leads to protectionist measures which are not easily eliminated once exchange rate movements are reversed. At the same time, short-term capital flows undermine the ability of national authorities to pursue independent economic policies. Governments, finding themselves chronically unable to co-ordinate policies with one another, are tempted to restore their independence of action through the imposition of exchange controls which are then circumvented by the private sector at considerable cost.

Along with dissatisfaction with the system's operation come proposals for international monetary reform. The search becomes one for a model or precedent after which institutional reform might be patterned. It is here that the appeal of the gold standard is to be found. More precisely, it is an idealized vision of the gold standard that is appealing. In this idealization, the gold standard was a remarkably durable and efficient mechanism for insuring price and income stability, relieving balance-of-payments pressure, and reconciling the actions of national monetary authorities. Supposedly it combined these virtues because it worked automatically, limiting the scope for discretionary policy. Money supplies in each country were linked directly to domestic reserves of gold, and balance-of-payments adjustment was accomplished through international shipments of precious metal. Monetary authorities were restrained from indulging their preference for inflationary finance, and the relative stability of prices that resulted was conducive to steady income growth. Since the authorities in each country were subject to the same gold standard constraints, the system brought about a *de facto* harmonization of monetary policies without requiring explicit co-ordination. Thus seen, the gold standard is a tempting model of international monetary reform for those inclined towards policy predicated on rules rather than discretion.

This vision of the gold standard, like the unicorn in James Thurber's garden, is of course a mythical beast. Far from the normal state of affairs prior to the twentieth century, the gold standard existed on a global scale for scarcely a third of a century. Comparisons of price and income stability under the gold standard and under other monetary regimes yield ambiguous results and are extremely sensitive to the measures of stability used. Debtor and creditor countries seem to have had radically different experiences during the gold standard era. The gold standard did not prevent the international trans-mission of financial crises nor did it preclude the occasional forced suspension of convertibility. The discretionary actions of national monetary authorities featured prominently in the gold standard's actual operation both under normal circumstances and in periods of exceptional stress.

If we reject the myth of gold standard we are confronted with the question of how the system actually worked. Regrettably, there exists no comprehensive account of the gold standard's operation as an international monetary system. Elements of the answer can be found, however, in two very different literatures, those of economic theory and economic history. In the literature of economic theory we find formal models of the gold standard as a self-equilibrating system of markets. One class of models focuses on the mechanism by which balance-of-payments equilibrium is restored. While the best-known example is the price-specie-flow mechanism associated with David Hume (1752) (essay reproduced in this volume, pp. 39–48), there exist alternative models of how balance-of-payments equilibrium is restored under a gold standard regime. A second class of models formalizes the mechanism by which tendencies internal to the gold standard may moderate price-level fluctuations over long periods. The recent article by Barro (1979) (reproduced, pp. 81–99) provides an elegant statement of this stabilizing mechanism. These models are useful for gauging the internal consistency of accounts of the gold standard's operation. But by their stylized nature they inevitably abstract from other aspects of the gold standard mechanism, and they shed more light on the myth of the gold standard than on the historical reality.

In the literature of economic history we find in contrast detailed studies of aspects of the gold standard's operation. Some consider its impact on particular countries or, as in the work of Ford (1962) and de Cecco (1974), on the relations between countries. Others focus on the role of central banks or, as in the work of Clay (1957), particular central bankers. These studies appear to have little in common with the outlines of the gold standard myth or the theories of international finance. Although they provide a wealth of institutional and historical detail on particular episodes and individual markets, by their detailed and idiosyncratic nature contributions to this literature tend to discourage efforts to generalize about how the gold standard worked.

This state of affairs is frequently taken to indicate that our understanding of the gold standard remains imperfect. But, in fact, our knowledge of the gold standard is considerably more complete than is typically assumed. Most of the elements needed to paint a complete picture are readily at hand. Completing the picture only requires that we blend the contributions of economic theorists and economic historians. Like the blind men with the elephant, students of the gold standard have derived their views from an awareness confined to individual parts of the beast. Theorists have restricted their attention to aspects of the adjustment mechanism. Only rarely have they been inspired in their theoretical enquiries by the insights of historical scholars. Historians have typically confined their attention to instances of the gold standard's operation. Only rarely have they attempted to generalize on the basis of their studies or been guided in their historical enquiries by the insights of economic theorists.

Interaction between these two sets of scholars and integration of these two literatures are precisely what is needed to generate fresh insights into how the gold standard worked. To demonstrate the 'intellectual gains from trade', the present volume brings together selections on the international gold standard from the literatures of history and economics. The book is directed at students of both economic history and international finance in the hope that their understanding of the gold standard will be enriched by exposure to the contributions of scholars in a related field.

*

The three basic features of a gold standard regime are (i) interconvertibility

interconvertibility

between domestic money and gold at a fixed official price, (ii) freedom for private citizens to import and export gold, and (iii) a set of rules relating the quantity of money in circulation in a country to that country's gold stock. An international gold standard exists when a number of countries adhere to these principles. With each country willing to convert its domestic currency into a fixed weight of gold and with the price of gold set on world markets subject only to the margins covering shipping and insurance costs, an international gold standard establishes fixed exchange rates between national currencies. Balance-of-payments settlements are effected though international transfers of gold, and balance-of-payments equilibrium is obtained through the impact of gold flows on internal conditions.

The international gold standard is sometimes portrayed as the normal state of affairs prior to World War I. Yet a gold standard regime embodying the basic features listed above prevailed on a global scale only for a third of a century, from 1880 to 1914. At the end of the Napoleonic Wars, the currencies of the world were based with few exceptions on silver rather than gold. Britain was an important exception, having been on a full legal gold standard from 1821 and on a *de facto* gold standard from 1717, when Sir Isaac Newton, then Master of the Mint, set too high a silver price for the gold guinea. With the Mint price of silver lower than its international market price, Britain's newly reminted full-bodied silver coins were quickly driven from circulation.[2]

During the Napoleonic Wars, Britain experienced a severe inflation which necessitated the suspension of convertibility. To prevent a recurrence of inflation, a law of 1819 required the Bank of England to make its notes redeemable in gold at the market price prevailing in May 1821.[3] This placed the Bank of England in a curious position, since it was still a private, profit-oriented institution, albeit one with special privileges and obligations as banker to the government. A quarter of a century later, the Bank Charter Act of 1844 sought to clarify the Bank's position, dividing the institution into an Issue Department vested with the responsibility of backing the note circulation with gold, and a Banking Department charged with the profit-making activities of the Bank and functioning as the vehicle for market intervention.

Until the 1880s only Britain maintained a full-fledged gold standard for any length of time. The United States and France remained officially on bimetallic standards. By law, each country offered to convert its currency into specified amounts of either gold or silver. In effect, each attempted to operate a commodity price stabilization scheme, using reserves of gold and silver as buffer stocks to stabilize the relative price of two metals. Their experiences illustrated the pitfalls of attempting to use small buffer stocks to stabilize prices in large markets. In the United States, the Mint ratio established by the Coinage Act of 1792 was 15 ounces of silver to an ounce of gold, which closely approximated the then prevailing market price. In the course of subsequent decades, a great increase in Mexican and South American silver production caused the relative price of silver to gold to decline to approximately $15\frac{1}{2}$ to 1. With gold undervalued at the Mint, silver was brought there for coinage and gold was shipped abroad where its price was higher (the opposite of the effect of Isaac Newton's undervaluation of silver – cf. p. 4). For much of the period 1792–1834, the US was effectively on a silver standard. The Coinage Act of 1834 changed the Mint ratio to approximately 16 to 1 in an attempt to bring gold coins back into circulation. But gold discoveries in Russia, Australia and California beginning in 1848 depressed the market price of gold relative to the 1834 Mint ratio. By 1851, a silver dollar was worth 104 cents on the open market. With silver now rarely used in transactions, the US was in effect on a gold standard until convertibility was suspended with the outbreak of the Civil War.

Over the first three-quarters of the nineteenth century, France experienced similar difficulties. Although the country was legally on a bimetallic standard from 1803, little gold circulated internally until the late 1840s since the Mint ratio of $15\frac{1}{2}$ to 1 was lower than the market ratio. Once mid-century gold discoveries depressed the market price of gold, gold replaced silver in internal circulation.

From the beginning of the 1870s, a succession of countries adopted full-fledged gold standards. The first step in the erection of an international gold standard was taken by Germany in 1871. Although Germany had previously derived some advantage from its silver standard in trade with Eastern Europe, by 1870 most of that region had suspended convertibility. The indemnity Germany received in 1871–3 as victor in the Franco-Prussian War provided the resources needed to carry out a currency reform. A new gold-based currency unit, the mark, was adopted, and Germany used her indemnity to purchase gold on a substantial scale. With German gold purchases following [*After Franco-Prussian War*] silver discoveries in Nevada and other mining territories, bimetallic countries were faced with a precipitous decline in the relative price of silver. Their response was to suspend silver coinage and convertibility, starting with Holland, Denmark, Norway and Sweden, and spreading to France and the associated countries of the Latin Monetary Union (Belgium, Switzerland, Italy and Greece). Gold became the monetary standard in every European country except those which retained inconvertible paper. In 1879 the international gold standard reached across the Atlantic, when the United States ended the Greenback Period by restoring gold convertibility, and into Asia when Russia and Japan adopted convertibility. Austria-Hungary and Italy did not legally adopt gold convertibility but from the turn of the century pegged their currencies in terms of gold.[4]

There were important differences in the manner in which these countries adhered to the central features of the gold standard regime. One might differentiate countries by the extent to which gold coin circulated internally. Gold coin formed an important part of currency circulation only in England,

France, Germany, the United States, Russia (after 1879), Australia, South Africa and Egypt. One might distinguish countries on a full gold standard where convertibility was automatic (Britain, Germany and the US) from countries on a 'limping' gold standard where convertibility was at the authorities' option (France, Belgium and Switzerland).[5]

One might also differentiate countries according to their 'cover system', which linked the quantity of currency and coin in circulation to the country's gold reserve. There existed three main types of cover system: the fiduciary system, the proportional system, and a combination of the two. The fiduciary system allowed the authorities to create a certain quantity of unbacked currency (the fiduciary issue) while requiring remaining currency to be fully backed with gold. This was the cover system used by England, Finland, Japan, Norway and Russia. The proportional system treated all currency alike but permitted the central bank to maintain a ratio of gold to currency issue of less than 100 per cent. This was the mode of coverage used by Belgium, Holland and Switzerland. Cover systems which combined features of these two rules were adopted by Germany, Austria-Hungary, Italy and Sweden.[6] In some countries additional flexibility was built into the system by permitting the note issue to exceed the legal limit upon payment of a tax or by permitting reserves to fall below their legal minimum upon the Finance Minister's authorization. Although the central banks of Finland, Germany, Italy, Japan, Sweden and (in a sense) Britain did not have a monopoly of note issue in the final decades of the nineteenth century, in all of these countries the circulation of other bank notes was relatively small and declining.

*

The appeal of the gold standard can be traced to the belief that it provides price and exchange-rate stability. The advantage of exchange-rate stability, as Gregory (1932) put it, is that international trade and investment can be conducted with minimal risk of capital losses due to exchange rate fluctuations. Of the fact that the classical gold standard provided exchange-rate stability there can be little dispute. Only a small number of countries were forced off the gold standard in the period 1880–1914. The major devaluations of the period were those of Portugal, Argentina, Italy, Chile, Bulgaria and Mexico. Exchange-rate stability did not extend to China, El Salvador or Honduras, which remained on silver and whose currencies therefore fluctuated in terms of gold, nor did it encompass Spain and the Latin American countries whose currencies remained inconvertible for extended periods. None the less, the extent of exchange-rate stability under the classical gold standard is impressive in comparison with the most recent decade.

Just as exchange-rate stability was said to promote mutually advantageous international transactions, so price-level stability was said to encourage domestic specialization and long-term planning. Since at least Ricardo (1816) it has been argued that the obligation to maintain convertibility provided a check on inflationary finance. By limiting the discretion of monetary authorities, gold standard discipline minimized the danger that the value of financial assets would be eroded by inflation. Even those such as Viner (1937) who remained sceptical that the gold standard would produce long-run price stability predicted that a system of inconvertible currencies would yield considerably worse results. They advanced this argument even while recognizing that the authorities retained a significant measure of discretion under a gold standard regime (a point taken up below).

Whether the gold standard's operation tended to stabilize prices over the longer term is a distinct question. Mill (1865) first described the mechanism through which this tendency could occur. His assumption was that the flow supply of newly mined gold should be responsive to relative prices. As the world economy expanded and the demand for money grew, downward pressure would be placed on the world price level. As the prices of other commodities fell in terms of the *numéraire* commodity gold, new supplies of gold should be elicited by its rising value. Another interpretation of this mechanism is that a falling price level reduces the costs of the gold-mining industry relative to the value of its product, causing additional resources to be devoted to mining and more output to be forthcoming. Similarly, to the extent that deflation causes the price of jewellery to fall in terms of gold coin, jewellery will be presented at the Mint for conversion into coin, increasing the quantity of coin in circulation and moderating the downward pressure on prices (see Barro, 1979).

In the nineteenth and twentieth centuries, fluctuations in world monetary gold reserves have been dominated by mining activity. Even Mill, who emphasized the stabilizing function of mining, recognized that time was required before a mining response would occur. Others emphasized the randomness of gold discoveries rather than their responsiveness to relative prices. Alfred Marshall (1923) for one was dubious that long-run price stability would be provided by a system dependent on the 'hazards of mining'.

Ultimately, these questions of price and income stability can only be settled on an empirical level. The problem is one of agreeing upon an appropriate basis for comparison. Disagreement starts with the years which are properly denoted those of the gold standard and on appropriate measures of stability. Typically, comparisons are made between the period 1880–1913 and that following World War II, although it is sometimes objected that the Bretton Woods System is properly viewed as a quasi-gold-standard regime.[7] Bordo (1981) has compared rates of inflation, unemployment and income growth in the two periods for the United Kingdom and the United States. The rate of change of wholesale prices appears to have been more moderate under the gold standard than during more recent periods. In contrast, comparisons of per capita income growth and unemployment indicate that the gold standard had no obvious superiority over recent monetary arrangements; if anything, the opposite is true. Even the relatively low inflation rates of the classical gold standard era can be cast in a less favourable light, since they are the product of averaging together two decades of deflation prior to 1893 and two subsequent decades of inflation.

Some observers would argue that the variability of inflation and income growth rates (rather than the trend) provides a superior measure of stability. Such comparisons are appropriate if one takes the view that it is not inflation or deflation but their variability that interferes with decision-making. Similarly, it might be argued that the operation of the monetary standard has relatively little impact on average rates of income growth but important implications for the stability with which growth proceeds. Bordo (1981) computes various measures of inflation and income growth variability.[8] On the basis of his variability measures, it is difficult to determine the superiority of either monetary regime. For Britain, Bordo finds that the standard deviation of prices was somewhat lower under the gold standard regime; for the US it was slightly higher. In both countries, rates of real-income growth were more variable under the gold standard.

A related argument is that, rather than the total variation in prices and incomes, only the proportion of that variability that could not be predicted by market participants was relevant for economic welfare. Consider the predictability of prices. Had individuals been able to accurately predict prices under the gold standard regime, then they could adapt their behaviour to anticipated inflation or deflation without incurring the costs of prediction errors. The historian's problem is how to estimate the predictability of a time series. Cooper (1982) (reproduced, pp. 251–67) attempts to infer price predictions from *ex post* real interest rates. He finds that under the gold standard *ex post* real interest rates rose during deflationary periods and fell during inflationary periods as if individuals failed to anticipate changes in prices. A limitation of this approach is that no attempt is made to correct for other factors which may have caused shifts in *ex ante* real interest rates. Moreover, during the 1950s and 1960s interest rates also failed to adjust to changes in inflation, a tendency which is especially evident once tax effects are taken into account. Thus, on the basis of *ex post* real interest rates, few conclusions can be drawn concerning the superior predictability of prices under either monetary regime.

Another approach to evaluating price predictability under the alternative monetary regimes is to estimate forecasting equations for prices and to compare the mean squared errors of the forecasts. The advantage of this approach is that it considers prices directly rather than attempting to infer price forecasts from interest rates. Its disadvantage is that it is based on an 'as if' assumption – namely, it requires the assumption that agents behaved as if they had knowledge of the forecasting equation. Moreover, the results of such exercises can always be questioned since there are innumerable forms which such an equation might take.[9]

*

In the absence of any clear-cut superiority in terms of price or income stability, the outstanding feature of the classical gold standard appears to have been its association with exchange-rate stability. Those few exchange-rate adjustments which did occur were the result of balance-of-payments crises. The question therefore is why there were so few balance-of-payments crises during the period 1880–1913; in other words, why did the balance-of-payments adjustment process work so smoothly under the classical gold standard?
It could be argued that the successful maintenance of fixed exchange rates had little to do with the gold standard *per se*. Exchange-rate stability could have been nothing more than a reflection of the underlying stability of financial conditions. In fact, however, the period 1880–1913 was one of recurrent financial instability. Monetary disturbances associated with banking difficulties recurred in successive episodes centred on the years 1884, 1890, 1893, and 1907. These difficulties were transmitted internationally through capital flows and dealings in foreign exchange.[10] Thus, the instability of the underlying financial environment renders all the more remarkable the dearth of convertibility crises.
To understand the successful maintenance of fixed exchange rates in the decades before World War I, we must analyse the balance-of-payments adjustment mechanism under a gold standard regime. How the adjustment process worked prior to 1913 is 'the ritual question' posed by students of the gold standard (to adopt the phrase of de Cecco, 1974). A glance at the literature appears to reveal many competing models of the adjustment process. In competition with the price-specie-flow mechanism of Hume (1752) we have the spending approach of Whale (1937) (reproduced, pp. 49–61) and Ford (1962), the capital-flows approach described by Whale (1937) and Scammell (1965) (reproduced, pp. 103–19), and the monetary approach to balance-of-payments adjustment as emphasized by McCloskey and Zecher (1976) (reproduced, pp. 63–80). Superficially, there would appear to exist profound disagreement on the question of the adjustment process. But in fact the competing models of the adjustment mechanism are entirely compatible and need only to be combined to provide a reasonably complete picture of how the gold standard worked.
The classic model of gold standard adjustment is the price-specie-flow mechanism of David Hume (1752).[11] The simplest way to understand this

[handwritten notes] Good in theory NOT in practice due to "arbitrage + law of one price"

mechanism is in terms of a stylized model of a world economy in which two categories of commodities are traded. We will denote these categories consumer goods and gold. What then is the effect of a disturbance to this economy, say a one-time addition to the domestic stock of gold?[12] At the initial prices, increased gold holdings give rise to an excess supply of gold and an excess demand for consumer goods. Prices must adjust to restore equilibrium to both markets. The assumption upon which simple treatments of the price-specie-flow mechanism are based is that transactions occur initially among domestic residents. As residents simultaneously attempt to sell gold and acquire consumer goods, the price of consumer goods rises in terms of gold (equivalently, the domestic gold price falls). The price of consumer goods in terms of gold is now higher at home than abroad; equivalently, gold is more expensive abroad. Domestic residents have an incentive to obtain consumer goods from abroad where they are relatively inexpensive. Similarly, foreign residents have an incentive to obtain their gold from the domestic country, where its price is low in terms of consumer goods. Under the (admittedly artificial) assumption that these events occur sequentially, the effects of the gold discovery now begin to leak overseas. A surplus of consumer goods is shipped to the domestic country, and a surplus of gold is shipped to the foreign country. In the absence of adjustments on the production side (which are introduced below), foreign residents must reduce their spending on consumer goods to make a surplus available for export. Similarly, domestic residents must increase their spending relative to production to absorb a surplus of imports. Seen in terms of the external accounts, the home country runs a balance-of-payments deficit whose corollary is its loss of gold.

This detailed description of the price-specie-flow mechanism illustrates a basic point that is all too frequently overlooked or misunderstood. It demonstrates that disputes over whether balance-of-payments equilibrium is restored through 'adjustments in commodity markets', 'adjustments in gold markets', or 'adjustments in spending' are fundamentally misguided. Adjustments in commodity markets and adjustments in gold markets are two sides of the same coin. In a simple two-commodity model there exists only one relative price, so a rise in one commodity price is the same phenomenon as a fall in the other. In other words, when one market clears, so must the other, as a result of Walras's law. It is simply not meaningful to ask whether adjustment takes place in one market or the other, or to debate whether the gold market or other commodity markets were 'more important' in the adjustment mechanism.[13]

Hume was fully aware that his stylized account of the price-specie-flow mechanism was useful as an analytical exercise but not as a description of reality. Transactions do not generally occur sequentially, first within and then between national markets. International arbitrage in markets for both gold and consumer goods creates a powerful incentive for the maintenance of the international 'law of one price'. McCloskey and Zecher (1976), following a long tradition, argue this point forcefully. Except for tariff barriers and international transport costs, they assert, there is no reason for prices to differ by wider margins internationally than among regions of a national economy. The incentives for arbitrage are the same within and between nations. But this recognition leaves the theorist in a quandary: once arbitrage creates a tendency for prices to be equated across markets, the balance-of-payments adjustment process can no longer operate through Humeian relative price effects.[14]

This is the challenge taken up in a series of investigations including the path-breaking work of Whale (1937). Whale questioned each aspect of the classical interpretation of how the gold standard worked, noting in particular that commodity price changes occurred so rapidly that few if any relative price movements could be observed during the adjustment process, and that the elimination of payments imbalances was conspicuously accompanied by interest-rate differentials and international capital flows. His response was to introduce a third market into the basic model of the adjustment process. Appending a financial market with international trade in assets to the simple two-sector model permitted him to analyse other channels through which adjustment might occur. In our stylized model, residents of both countries now hold stocks of consumer goods, gold and a single interest-bearing financial asset. What then is the effect in this more general model of a one-time addition to the domestic gold stock? It is useful to repeat our previous 'thought experiment', assuming initially that transactions take place first among domestic residents before introducing international arbitrage in the short run. (Nothing essential depends on what is only an expositional device.) The initial excess supply of gold has as its counterpart an excess demand for consumer goods and securities.[15] The domestic prices of consumer goods and securities rise; equivalently, the domestic gold price falls. Residents of the country where the gold discovery has taken place now have an incentive to obtain their consumer goods and securities from abroad where both are relatively inexpensive, while residents abroad have an incentive to obtain their gold from the domestic country. The domestic country's exports of gold equal in value its imports of consumer goods and securities. Thus, with trade in financial assets, the trade balance deficit no longer equals the gold outflow; rather, the balance-of-payments deficit equals the international transfer of gold. The payments deficit is the sum of the trade balance deficit and the capital outflow, where 'capital outflow' is another name for domestic purchases of foreign securities. It is irrelevant whether we describe this mechanism in terms of price or interest-rate effects, since security prices and securities' rates of return are inversely related. Saying that security prices are higher at home than abroad following the gold discovery is no different from saying that interest rates are lower at home than abroad. In this model capital flows from the country where interest rates are low to the country where they are high, until security prices and interest rates are again equalized internationally.

The point of this excursion through alternative models of the adjustment process is to demonstrate that interpretations of the international adjustment mechanism which emphasize changes in commodity prices, changes in spending, changes in interest rates or changes in capital flows are entirely compatible with one another. They simply focus attention on different junctions of the same interconnected markets. Some descriptions place great weight on international divergences in the prices of traded goods (Hume, 1752). Others emphasize parallelism in commodity price movements, focusing instead on changes in spending and movements in relative interest rates (Marshall, 1926; Whale, 1937; Triffin, 1968; Scammell, 1965). Still others argue that arbitrage was equally pervasive in commodity and asset markets, precluding persistent international divergences in either prices or interest rates. They emphasize the importance of changes in spending in the adjustment process (McCloskey and Zecher, 1976).[16] Yet these authors should be seen not as presenting alternative models but simply as attaching different values to certain critical parameters. Their differences boil down to the disputed answers to a set of empirical questions. How quickly did arbitrage tend to equalize the prices of traded commodities? How extensive was the international exchange of financial assets? Were securities closer substitutes for gold or for (other) commodities? The questions all concern how much weight to attach to different aspects of the same adjustment mechanism.

*

Absent from this discussion has been any mention of banking, either private or central. Of course, the affairs of banking impinged on the gold standard, and vice versa, throughout the period in question. The monetary regime of 1880–1913 was not a gold coin standard. Central banks maintained an excess of gold reserves with which they could alter the ratio of currency circulation to gold backing. Financial institutions which practised fractional reserve banking could create money and near monies by accepting deposits and extending loans. Whale (1937) points to the existence of a long-standing debate over the monetary aggregate relevant to the adjustment process. One early school of thought embraced what might be called the quantity theory assumption. High-powered money and in particular currency and coin in circulation were thought relevant to the adjustment process. Banks' deposit and loan practices were seen to have little impact on the spending and saving decisions determining the balance of payments. A subsequent school embraced what might be called the interest-elasticity assumption. Under this assumption, the impact of interest-rate changes on banking practice was an important component of the adjustment process. This suggests focusing on the broader monetary aggregates and on the manner in which 'the reaction of the banking system to a change in its reserves ... called for a multiple change in the terms on which the banks lent, or the discount rate ....'[17] This approach has the capacity to address the links between gold reserves and monetary aggregates. These links were of great importance in many countries; in England, for example, by the end of our period the ratio of gold reserves to the aggregate liabilities of the banking system was probably less than 5 per cent.[18] In the presence of fractional reserve banking, a one-time addition to the gold stock which forces up security prices and reduces interest rates permits banks to pay lower interest rates on deposits and at the same time makes their lending activities less profitable. Given the fall in the profitability of lending, banks will hold a higher ratio of precautionary reserves to liabilities, reducing the deposit multiplier. The implication for the gold standard adjustment mechanism is that a gold discovery, by reducing interest rates, will cause the money multiplier to fall, partially offsetting the increase in the monetary base and requiring a smaller gold outflow before balance-of-payments equilibrium is restored. On this basis, Whale (1937) and Ford (1962) suggest that the reactions of the banking system were a critical component of the adjustment mechanism.

[margin note: Problem of gold discovery]

In emphasizing the reactions of the banking sector, Whale was attempting to redress a balance which had swung heavily toward a preoccupation with the actions of central banks. Central-bank policy is the concern of those who argue that the classical gold standard was a managed system. In this view, gold flows were minimal and convertibility crises were averted because of central banks' stabilizing influence. Central banks had a range of instruments at their disposal, including discount rates, open market operations, and gold devices (direct intervention in the gold market and changes in the regulations governing convertibility). These might be used to reinforce, indeed to anticipate, the impact of specie flows on domestic markets. In theory these reinforcing actions might achieve adjustment without requiring any gold movements whatsoever.

For many years, textbook treatments of the classical gold standard portrayed central banks as obeying 'rules of the game'. Under these 'rules', the authorities were to intervene so as to reinforce the impact on domestic money and credit markets of incipient gold flows. For example, a central bank losing gold was to raise its discount rate, increasing the cost to the banking sector of rediscounting at the central bank and inducing banks to hold a larger ratio of precautionary reserves to liabilities, thereby reducing the money multiplier. This reduction in the money multiplier would reinforce the impact of incipient gold flows on domestic financial markets. The central bank might also intervene with open market sales of securities, further reducing the monetary base and permitting balance to be restored to the external accounts with a minimum of actual gold flows.

An extensive literature addressed the question of whether central banks obeyed these 'rules of the game'. Nurkse (1944) (reproduced, pp. 201–25) noted widespread violations of the 'rules' between the two world wars, and he attributed the instability of the interwar gold standard partly to sterilization by central banks. Implicit in his discussion was the premise that the 'rules' had been obeyed in earlier decades. Yet Bloomfield (1959) upon replicating Nurkse's calculations for the period 1880–1914 found that violations of the 'rules' were numerically every bit as frequent during the classical gold standard era.[19]

Such discussions are predicated upon the assumption that central banks recognized 'rules of the game'. Yet the phrase, if not the concept, appears first only in the literature of the interwar period. The phrase 'rules of the game' gained currency after it was used by Keynes (1925) and then by Sir Robert Kindersley, a director of the Bank of England, in evidence before the Macmillan Committee in February 1930. Yet even, indeed especially, those who used the term acknowledged the role played by discretionary action under a gold standard regime. As the *Report* of the Macmillan Committee (1931) (reproduced, pp. 185–99) put it, 'The management of an international gold standard is an art and not a science.'

Central bankers had the discretion to decide whether or not to act, when to act, what kind and how much action to take, and what instrument or instruments to use. The scope for discretion is especially clear in the case of the Bank of England. The only 'rule of the game' that was articulated prior to 1914 was the rule stated by Walter Bagehot, Editor of *The Economist* for a quarter of a century and author of *Lombard Street* (1873). Bagehot's Rule was to raise Bank Rate to stem an external gold drain and to lend freely in response to an internal drain; in the event of both internal and external drains, the Bank was to raise its discount rate to high levels but to continue to provide liquidity. Yet even Bagehot's Rule permitted the authorities discretion in deciding the timing of a Bank Rate increase.

Sayers (1936, 1957) and Scammell (1965) have documented three distinct stages in the development of the Bank of England's operating procedures. During the 1870s, techniques of monetary control remained rudimentary. While the discount rate was changed frequently, open market operations were not always used to make the discount rate effective (i.e. to ensure that it affected the cost of credit by inducing discounting at the central bank) and considerable reliance was still placed on the automatic expansion and contraction of the monetary base following international gold movements. In the 1880s the Bank of England began to supplement Bank Rate with gold devices, or intervention in the gold market.[20] After 1890 less reliance was placed on the gold devices, and Bank Rate policy came into its own as the

Bank of England mastered the task of co-ordinating discount-rate change
with open market operations.

In a typical response to a gold outflow, the Bank of England might at first do
nothing, given the possibility that the outflow was temporary or reversible.
But if losses continued, the Bank might attempt to protect the reserve by using
the gold devices. If these failed to stem its losses, the Bank would raise Bank
Rate and make it effective in the market. Of course, these initiatives might be
taken in a different order and in various combinations. It is not surprising
therefore that no mechanical relationship can be observed in the short run
between gold reserves and discount rates.

Sayers (1957) characterizes the Bank of England as using a powerful Bank
Rate weapon to defend convertibility on the basis of a 'thin film of gold'. Other
central banks, notably the Bank of France and Bank of Belgium, made
considerably less use of this instrument. In the case of the Bank of France, the
luxury of larger reserves may have permitted it to tolerate wider swings in its
financial position. White (1933) has suggested further that the Bank of
France's reserve required less active management because of 'the sluggishness
of French industrial life'.[21] But it is not clear that either explanation is
applicable to the Bank of Belgium. As Scammell (1965) argues, the relative
fixity of these continental discount rates must be attributable largely to
conservative gold export policies. Continental central banks were prepared to
actively discourage attempts to obtain gold for export. German, French and
Swedish authorities all relied extensively on moral suasion. As Cassel (1936,
p. 12) remarks, in countries other than England

> free and unlimited redeemability was by no means guaranteed ... if anybody
> wanted large sums of gold, particularly for export, he was most likely to be
> met with objections. A prominent Swedish banker once told me that if he
> had asked the Riksbank for any considerable sum of gold he would have
> been refused.

An active discount policy or impediments to gold export were required
because of the conventions of proportional reserve backing and fiduciary
circulation. They grew increasingly important with the rise of the practice of
backing the currency with reserves of convertible foreign exchange. Rather
than accumulating barren metal, central banks augmented their portfolios
with interest-bearing securities that might be readily converted into gold.
According to Lindert (1969), by 1910 the ratio of official foreign-exchange
reserves to gold had reached 25 per cent. The practice was less prevalent on the
continent than elsewhere; in 1913 the fifteen European central banks held
approximately 12 per cent of their reserves in foreign exchange. The countries
of the periphery relied to a much greater extent on convertible foreign
exchange. Scammell (1965) has gone so far as to argue that the prewar

actually a sterling standard, with Britain perpetually
...account surpluses to supply other countries with sterling
...n in fact ran only two current-account deficits in the cen-
...1913. There is a suggestive parallel between British behaviour
...classical gold standard and American deficits in the 1950s and 1960s,
...d of which had as their counterpart the accumulation of dollar
...s by the central banks of the rest of the world. The Bretton Woods
System suffered from speculative pressures in the 1960s, once dollar reserves
abroad exceeded US gold reserves, raising the question of whether the same
fate would have befallen the classical gold standard had World War I not
intervened. There are reasons to downplay the dangers of such a collapse in the
first decades of the twentieth century, since foreign-exchange reserves were
then more widely diversified across currencies than in the 1960s. The
dominance of sterling in aggregate foreign-exchange reserves stemmed largely
from its importance in India and Japan. On the continent, according to
Lindert's estimates, reserves of French francs and German marks outweighed
sterling reserves.[22]

*

Perhaps the most popular explanation for the gold standard's smooth
operation is that it was a managed system, and that it was managed by the
Bank of England. London was unrivalled as the most important financial
centre of the era. In the hierarchy of financial markets it was followed by
Berlin, Paris, Vienna, Amsterdam, Brussels, Zurich and New York. The next
tier was occupied by the less active markets of the Scandinavian countries.
London's pre-eminence provided the Bank of England with singular leverage
over international flows of capital and gold, endowing it with the capacity to
exercise leadership in the management of the international monetary system.
London's influence over international capital flows was so powerful that no
other centre could afford to ignore events occurring there. When Bank Rate
was raised in London, many central banks had no choice but to respond by
creating further stringency in domestic credit markets so as to minimize the
loss of gold. Implicit in this interpretation is the idea that policies were
harmonized internationally through this leader–follower interaction. Parallel movements in discount rates or other instruments of policy supposedly
ensured the maintenance of external balance while the Bank of England in its
leadership role adjusted the overall thrust of credit policy to ensure internal
balance at home and abroad.

There are a number of problems with this interpretation of the gold
standard as a managed system. For example, it is far from clear whether the

adjustment to shocks would have been facilitated by parallel movements in discount rates. If shocks affected primarily the balance of payments, adjustment would be smoothest when surplus countries lowered their discount rates at the same time as deficit countries raised theirs, not when all countries moved in parallel. Nor can one sustain the thesis that the Bank of England formulated policy with the stability of the world economy in mind; in fact the Bank was narrowly concerned with its reserve position and paid only occasional attention to internal conditions even at home. To rescue the argument it has been suggested that the classical gold standard was co-operatively managed. Scammell (1965) speaks of the growth of an international financial fraternity, which was manifested in part in co-operation among the central banks of the leading countries. It is true that the Bank of England, the Bank of France and several of their counterparts engaged in certain co-operative actions, such as extending loans, negotiating swap arrangements and earmarking gold. But co-operation among central banks remained at best sporadic prior to 1914. It is difficult to support the argument that policy co-ordination was responsible for the international system's stability.

Another explanation offered for the classical gold standard's stability is that freedom of trade facilitated balance-of-payments adjustment (see Scammell, 1965). Yet it is never adequately explained why an absence of tariffs would facilitate smooth adjustment. Imposing a tariff will tend to raise a country's price level, holding all other influences constant, and, by increasing the demand for money balances, will tend to draw gold toward the country where protection is adopted. But this is a one-time effect which would follow a tariff's imposition or revision without necessarily hindering subsequent reserve flows in response to other factors affecting the balance of payments. This explanation encounters the further objection that trade was far from free in the period 1880–1914. While Britain left imports largely unrestricted, from the early 1880s the other important trading nations all had broad-based tariffs in place.[23]

It has been suggested that the gold standard operated smoothly over a relatively long period of time because capital movements automatically generated stabilizing demands for goods. In this view, an exogenous rise in foreign lending would stimulate construction in the capital-importing region whose investors would turn for imports of capital goods to the country from whence the funds were drawn. Hence a capital outflow, instead of weakening the balance of payments, would be neutralized by a rise in commodity exports to the capital-importing region. Ford (1962) provides some evidence of this mechanism at work in relations between Britain and Argentina. Unfortunately, this view finds little support in other case studies of the period. Overall, the links between British external investment and overseas demands for British goods are tenuous at best (see Edelstein, 1981). Similarly, the evidence suggests that only a small portion of French foreign investment was spent on French commodity exports (see White, 1933).

We appear to be left with no explanation for what is termed the gold standard's 'smooth operation'. Perhaps the resolution is that this 'smooth operation' is itself an illusion. The gold standard may have operated smoothly for the countries at the centre. But countries on the periphery of the North Atlantic capital market had rather different experiences, marred by convertibility crises, devaluations and internal dislocations. The hierarchical structure of international capital markets may help to explain this asymmetry. For example, when London raised its discount rate, capital was drawn from continental financial centres in the next rank of the financial hierarchy. When these centres raised their discount rates, capital was drawn from countries on the next financial tier. By the time countries on this next tier raised their discount rates, capital was being drawn from colonies, protectorates, and countries with underdeveloped financial markets, which lacked the power to neutralize this movement. It is no coincidence, then, that the convertibility crises of the period were concentrated in the periphery. From the periphery's viewpoint, the operation of the gold standard was anything but smooth.

That countries with underdeveloped financial markets were less able to influence the direction of capital flows is but one strand in the centre–periphery argument advanced by the gold standard's critics. These critics suggest that a change in short-term capital movements induced by discount policy at the centre had a disproportionate impact on the level of activity in developing countries. Capital tended to be drawn back toward centre countries during worldwide recessions, moderating the downturn at the centre but exacerbating it at the periphery. Certain authors, notably Triffin (1968), have pointed to still other asymmetries in the gold standard's operation. Triffin argues that, because of London's singular importance as a source of credit for financing international transactions in foodstuffs and raw materials, Britain through the impact of Bank Rate overseas was more than compensated for the economic costs of stringent credit conditions at home. The argument is that a temporary credit stringency swung the terms of trade in Britain's favour by increasing the cost to foreign producers of holding stocks of primary products. The higher cost of holding inventories would cause stocks to be dumped on world markets. Since elasticities of demand for foodstuffs and raw materials – the commodities which were Britain's principal imports – were exceptionally low, with stocks dumped on world markets their prices would have to·fall relative to those of other goods. Thus, a balance-of-payments deficit, by eliciting a rise in the Bank of England's discount rate, would lead to an improvement in Britain's international terms of trade in the course of the adjustment process. Note that the anticipated movement in the terms of trade is in the opposite direction from that predicted by models of the price-specie-flow mechanism, in which a gold outflow depresses domestic prices relative to those abroad and causes a deterioration in the terms of trade.

Empirical support for this theory of the adjustment mechanism is scanty and unconvincing. Contemporary observers of the London market asserted that the volume of commercial bills discounted to finance inventory carrying costs was remarkably insensitive to interest-rate movements. Kenen (1960) and Moggridge (1972) have examined the same time series for relative prices and discount rates and reached opposite conclusions on the validity of this Triffin Effect. Like the other centre–periphery asymmetries posited in the literature, evidence on this question is only beginning to be explored.

*

Convertibility was suspended either *de facto* or *de jure* with the outbreak of World War I. The belligerents engaged in deficit spending financed by money creation to mobilize resources for war. Where the suspension of convertibility was unofficial, citizens were discouraged by appeals to patriotism from attempting to convert currency into gold. Where no explicit prohibitions were placed on gold exports, the difficulties of obtaining insurance and shipping space discouraged international specie flows. By the conclusion of hostilities, persistent inflation had rendered infeasible the continued maintenance of prewar parities, and the gold standard was suspended in favour of freely floating exchange rates. Only the United States, where inflation had been relatively moderate and gold reserves were abundant, maintained convertibility at the prewar rate.

The monetary history of the 1920s can be understood as a record of strenuous and ultimately futile efforts to restore the international gold standard. From the outset there existed widespread agreement on the desirability of returning to gold. The *First Interim Report* of the Cunliffe Committee (1918) provides a representative statement of this view. While this Committee was established to consider financial options for the United Kingdom, the assumptions upon which it proceeded were remarkably similar to those prevailing abroad. The Committee entertained no alternative to restoring sterling's gold standard parity at the prewar rate of exchange. Resurrecting the prewar parity was seen not merely as desirable but as essential to ensure the financial stability required for reconstruction.

The Cunliffe Committee's *Report* is notable also for its description of how the gold standard was supposed to have worked. The *Report* placed great weight on the distinction, originally drawn by Mill, between temporary and permanent disturbances to the balance of payments. Bank Rate should be raised, the Committee recommended, in response to permanent disturbances, but the Bank of England should react passively to temporary disturbances so long as its reserve did not fall 'in a degree considered dangerous'. Thus, the discretionary element in central bank management was given explicit recognition. The importance attached to discretion reflected an awareness that central bank policy had internal repercussions which might adversely affect trade and industry. The members of the Cunliffe Committee were keenly aware that high interest rates stabilized the reserve position not merely by attracting foreign capital but also by depressing output and employment. Thus, contrary to criticisms that appear in much of the historical literature, the Committee was in fact aware of the existence of a short-run trade-off between internal and external balance. None the less, its members remained convinced that the gold standard was essential for the provision of stability conducive to long-run growth and prosperity.

Not until 1925 did Britain succeed in returning to gold. [24] The decision to return was taken despite the advice of Keynes, who wrote in his *Tract on Monetary Reform* (1923) and elsewhere of a trade-off between internal and external balance which implied that restoring the prewar gold parity would entail a costly loss of output and employment. From 1931 until recently, the return to gold was generally viewed as a grave mistake made by the Chancellor of the Exchequer, Winston Churchill, who was misled by his advisers. It has been suggested that the interests of British industry were willingly sacrificed to the interests of finance, though there were those who hoped that American prices would rise sufficiently to relieve Britain of the burden of deflation. The work of Sayers (1970) and Moggridge (1969, 1972) has done much to revise this view. While never questioning that the return to gold was a mistake, they show that Keynes in fact had access to the Chancellor as well as to other policymakers, who simply found his arguments unpersuasive. They indicate the difficulties with the argument that the interests of industry were sacrificed to those of finance, when the return to gold was portrayed (however unconvincingly) as employment policy and received industry's active support. As for the claim that the authorities anticipated a rise in American prices, the documents reveal that they hoped for little more than price stability abroad. Officials simply accepted the financial community's lower estimate of the economic costs associated with the adjustment.

Other countries besides Britain attached comparable importance to the restoration of prewar parities. Swedish policymakers engineered a severe deflation and restored their prewar parity at the beginning of the 1920s. At the same time it was argued that countries which had experienced persistent inflation might be well-advised to opt for convertibility at a depreciated rate of exchange. [25] Several nations, including France and Belgium, ultimately adopted this alternative. For example, following *de facto* stabilization of the French franc in 1926 at a fraction of its prewar gold value, there ensued nearly two years of debate over the merits of restoring the prewar parity. Ultimately, the difficulties of reducing real wages and the implications of increasing the real value of the public debt militated against appreciation, and the franc was officially stabilized at the prevailing rate of exchange.

Some 50 nations participated in the international gold standard during the interwar years. Resurrection of the international system has usually been dated from Britain's return to gold in 1925, while its demise is usually associated with sterling's devaluation in the autumn of 1931. Even before sterling's devaluation, Australia and a number of Latin American countries had been forced off gold, while Germany and Austria had imposed strict exchange controls to prevent depreciation. By the end of 1931 some two dozen nations had followed Britain off gold. As these episodes demonstrated, the interwar gold standard was susceptible to convertibility crises and thus failed to embody the principal virtue of the prewar monetary system. Moreover, the interwar system was far from conducive to price and income stability, as the difficulties of the 1920s culminating in the onset of the Great Depression dramatically illustrated.

There is no shortage of explanations for the unsatisfactory performance of the interwar gold standard system. The definitive account of the system's malfunction is the Report of the Macmillan Committee (1931). This Committee, set up to inquire into the relations of industry to finance, numbered among its members John Maynard Keynes. Keynes played a prominent role in drafting the Report; his imprint is visible in the Committee's willingness to address what it called 'the question of whether adherence to an international standard may involve the payment of too heavy a price in the shape of domestic instability'.[26] A reasonably complete list of the important explanations for the interwar gold standard's malfunction would include the following (see also Gregory, 1932 and Cassel, 1936):

(a) Sterilization operations by central banks impeded the adjustment process (see also Nurkse, 1944). Specifically, asymmetries in the response of surplus and deficit countries shifted the burden of adjustment onto those with relatively weak external positions. Central banks put increasing weight on stabilizing domestic prices, output and employment as opposed to balancing the external accounts, causing them to intervene in ways which disrupted the international adjustment mechanism.[27] Central Banks

(b) Gold stocks proved insufficient in quantity for the system's smooth operation. The low level of reserves relative to incomes constrained monetary growth, generated deflation, and forced central banks to defend currency convertibility on the basis of slender reserves.

(c) The downward rigidity of wages and costs impeded the adjustment to deflationary pressures. Hence the shortage of gold caused falling output and employment rather than falling wages and prices. The unemployment which resulted created budgetary difficulties for the authorities, further undermining confidence in the currency.

(d) Central banks indulged their tendency to supplement gold with foreign-currency reserves. A growing amount of money was pyramided on a limited quantity of gold, causing convertibility crises to spread internationally once questions of confidence were raised (see however point (b) above).

(e) The available gold was distributed internationally in an uneven fashion. By 1931 the United States and France possessed between them some 60 per cent of the world's monetary gold. These two countries' tendency to hoard gold transmitted deflationary pressures abroad, forcing central banks to defend convertibility with even smaller reserves.

(f) Unlike the prewar system, which had been focused on London, the interwar gold standard was organized around two competing financial centres: London and New York. This, according to Nurkse (1944), was its 'special source of weakness'. Co-operation among central banks could have alleviated the problem, but after 1928 the authorities grew less willing to co-ordinate intervention in response to imbalances in the external accounts or to engage in co-operative reflationary efforts. In addition, New York in formulating interest-rate policy grew increasingly preoccupied by the effects of the American stock market boom.

(g) The rise of trade barriers starting in the late 1920s disrupted the adjustment process, interfering with the ability of deficit countries to restore balance by increasing exports and causing the concentration of gold reserves in the most protectionist countries.

While these explanations are by no means mutually exclusive nor always internally consistent, together they provide a compelling picture of an international monetary system disturbed by misaligned exchange rates, insufficient and unhelpfully distributed reserves, and the growth of reserve currency backing, and at the same time incapable of responding to disturbances due to rigidities in wage structure, rising tariffs and the failure of co-operation. A problem with this picture is that it overlooks the extent to which the same conditions prevailed before the War. For example, it is argued that difficulties arose in the interwar period once the links between gold reserves and money supplies were loosened. However, as Triffin (1968) notes, paper currency and bank deposits accounted for nearly 90 per cent of money circulation and gold only 10 per cent even before the War. There was nothing new about asymmetries in the response of surplus and deficit countries to imbalances in the external accounts. As Cassel (1936, p. 3) described the prewar situation, 'Creditor countries were in a position to accumulate, if they chose to do so, disproportionate gold stocks without using them for any other purpose than for exercising political influence or merely for satisfying national pride in the possession of gold.'

Cassel and other commentators recognized that the deflationary bias resulting from an international struggle for gold was not unknown in the prewar era. 1925 was not the first time central banks had raised their discount rates simply in order to attract gold. It is true that central bank co-operation provided a mechanism for relieving the competition for gold if the authorities could arrange a co-ordinated reduction in discount rates. However, it is difficult to argue that a decline of co-operation was the crucial difference between the classical and interwar systems. If anything, central bank co-operation was more extensive in the period between the wars than had been the case earlier.[28] This is not to imply, however, that even more extensive co-operation could not have alleviated some of the problems of the interwar years.

Similar objections can be raised in response to the other explanations. That wages exhibited inflexibility downward in the 1920s is beyond doubt, but it is not evident that wages were more flexible before 1913 (see Macmillan Committee, 1931; Gregory, 1932). The only period of extensive wage flexibility was the short span from 1920 to 1922 when wages fell by roughly 40 per cent in both Britain and the United States. But in these years British wages were indexed under the provisions of the sliding-scale agreements adopted during the War, and these agreements progressively fell out of favour as the decade progressed. The relevant comparison would appear to be between 1920–2 and surrounding decades, not between the prewar and interwar periods (see Triffin, 1968).

Explanations based on the composition or distribution of reserves encounter similar objections. The acquisition of foreign-currency reserves was no new practice; according to Lindert's (1969) estimates, the ratio of official foreign-exchange reserves to gold was as high in 1913 as in 1925. While the practice was encouraged at the Genoa Conference in 1922 and continued to spread thereafter, it is inappropriate to contrast too sharply the interwar 'gold-exchange standard' with the 'gold standard' of prewar years. Similarly, there was nothing new about an uneven distribution of international gold reserves; in earlier decades French and American gold requirements had been proportionally double those of Britain.

Finally, the theory that tariff barriers impeded adjustment encounters the two objections mentioned above; first, it is not clear why tariffs should contribute to financial instability; and second, tariff protection had also been prevalent in the decades before the War.

Given these objections, what are we left with as an explanation for the interwar gold standard's instability? There is no question that by the 1920s markets had grown increasingly integrated and sensitive to balance-of-payments disturbances. Destabilizing short-term capital flows – flows of 'hot money' as they were known – could be ignited by seemingly minor incidents at home or abroad. The Austrian convertibility crisis of 1931 was initiated by the failure of a single, albeit overwhelmingly important, commercial bank, the Credit Anstalt. The proximate cause of the run on sterling was not so much the underlying weakness of the balance of payments as the impact on confidence of continental bank failures and rumours of unrest in the British navy.[29] Yet the volatility of capital flows is a symptom, not a source, of international financial instability. After all, the sensitivity of capital flows to interest differentials is credited with exercising a stabilizing influence prior to World War I. The question is therefore why in the 1920s short-term capital suddenly started to flow in destabilizing directions.

The answer lies in how changes in the environment affected the attitudes and expectations of investors. One difference between the prewar and interwar periods with implications for the attitudes of investors was the extent to which economic policymakers were influenced by internal and external conditions. While the contrast should not be overdrawn, it is none the less fair to say that after 1919 policymakers' commitment to defend the gold reserve and gold parity was increasingly tempered by other considerations. Even if Bloomfield's (1959) evidence on the extent of sterilization in the period 1880–1913 suggests that violations of the 'rules of the game' were numerically no more frequent between the wars than they had been before, they still may have been qualitatively different and more fundamentally disruptive in character, and thus may have had more far-reaching effects. The extent to which internal and external targets weighed in the calculations of policymakers varied among nations, but major weight was attached to internal variables in nearly every case. Investors were fully cognizant of governments' growing hesitancy to sacrifice other objectives on the altar of exchange-rate stability; so to avoid the capital losses associated with devaluation they began to bet against convertibility. There may be some validity to the notion that the world economy was subjected to larger shocks in the 1920s, although it is difficult to design a metric by which the size of shocks might be measured. Yet even were the shocks identical, policymakers' preferences for a different position on the trade-off between attainable values of internal and external variables would have caused them to choose more convertibility crises as the price of moderating internal fluctuations. Knowledge of this new preference then affected speculators' actions, which further altered the trade-off between internal and external balance with which the authorities were confronted.

*

With the collapse of the interwar gold standard the world entered into a renewed period of floating exchange rates. This episode differed from the 'clean float' of the early 1920s in that exchange rates came to be actively managed. The United States broke with gold in 1933. In March President Roosevelt restricted foreign-exchange dealings and gold and currency movements, and in April he issued an executive order requiring individuals to deliver their gold coin, bullion and certificates to Federal Reserve Banks. By setting progressively higher dollar prices for gold, the Administration engineered a series of devaluations. The dollar price of gold was finally stabilized in January 1934 at $35 an ounce, leaving the dollar with 59 per cent of its former gold content. By 1936, when France and the other countries of the Gold Bloc had suspended convertibility, only the US maintained a link between domestic currency and gold. But with international gold flows restricted and the $35 gold price a matter of convenience rather than law, American monetary arrangements embodied none of the basic elements of the gold standard. The other major currencies of the world floated against the dollar, and hence the price of gold in their respective currencies varied from day to day.

Well before the close of World War II, the United States and Britain opened consultations on postwar monetary reconstruction. The negotiations which culminated in the Bretton Woods Agreement have been extensively analysed elsewhere.[30] What concerns us here is the role of gold in the monetary regime in force through 1971. The Bretton Woods System has been characterized as a 'much diluted form of a gold exchange standard' (Dam, 1982, p. 133). The US dollar continued to be pegged to gold at $35 an ounce. Although changes in the dollar price of gold were permissible under Bretton Woods, they were seen by most observers as undesirable and bordered on the inconceivable. Other countries were required to declare a par value against the dollar or gold, and while America's gold reserves were comprised by its gold stock, other countries enjoyed the option of holding reserves in either dollars or gold. Thus, gold played a number of related roles in the postwar gold-dollar standard, as Bretton Woods was sometimes called. With the dollar pegged to gold and other currencies pegged to the dollar, gold remained the ultimate unit of account. (Other observers suggested that gold derived its unit-of-account function from its link with the dollar.) Since the principal gold owners (and producers) opposed the metal's total demonetization, gold remained a reserve asset – in the immediate postwar period, the most important form of reserves. Finally, gold provided part of the endowment of the newly constituted International Monetary Fund. Founding members of the Fund were required to contribute gold in the amount of 25 per cent of their quotas or 10 per cent of their net official gold and dollar holdings, whichever was less.

The differences between the gold-dollar standard and the classical gold standard were manifold. Gold coins did not circulate, restrictions remained on gold imports and exports, national currencies could no longer be converted at central banks, and citizens of the United States and other countries could not even own gold for most purposes. Non-dollar currencies could be devalued or revalued in response to 'fundamental' balance-of-payments disequilibria. The thrust of these new arrangements was to loosen further the already elastic links between gold reserves and money supplies. If the classical gold standard is interpreted as a system for pegging exchange rates to one another by defining them in terms of fixed weights of gold and for tying domestic money supplies to gold reserves (and it can be so defined if neither requirement is interpreted too rigidly), then the gold-dollar standard established at Bretton Woods really incorporated only the first of these features. Keynes exaggerated only slightly when he suggested that, in the new system, gold was nothing more than a 'convenient common denominator'.[31]

In fact, the role of gold under Bretton Woods was slightly more than that. It can be considered under two categories: liquidity and adjustment. The liquidity issue bears a strong resemblance to interwar arguments about the insufficiency of gold. Liquidity under the Bretton Woods System denoted *highly liquid* international reserves of gold, convertible foreign currency, and unconditional IMF credit. These reserves were needed in times of stress to defend a currency's dollar (and gold) parity. Although reserve requirements might not rise proportionately, the monetary expansion needed for economic growth none the less required steadily increasing reserves. Reserves might be obtained in a variety of ways. Outside the US they might be obtained by running payments surpluses against America and accumulating dollar assets, the dollar being far and away the world's most desirable reserve currency.[32] Less straightforwardly, reserves might be obtained from newly mined gold or from an agreement by all Bretton Woods countries, including the United States, to uniformly raise the domestic-currency price of gold. In practice, the balance-of-payments deficits of the United States, especially in the 1960s, were the main source of incremental liquidity. Additional dollar holdings provided more than half the 22 per cent increase in international reserves between 1960 and 1967.[33] Most newly produced gold disappeared into private hoards or was employed in industry rather than supplementing official reserves.

The persistent payments deficits of the United States were criticized by America's trading partners. The French in particular indicted the US for abusing its special role under the Bretton Woods System and after 1965 engaged in sporadic efforts to convert their dollar holdings into gold. Essentially they argued that the US obtained seigniorage by providing reserves to the rest of the world. This seigniorage might be used to increase spending on other nations' goods, purchase foreign companies, or finance military adventures. Gilbert (1968) (reproduced, pp. 229–49) and Kenen (1969) among others countered that the US had not sought this position but had been pushed into it by the demand abroad for additional reserve assets denominated in dollars.[34]

The persistence of American payments deficits indicated to some the limitations of the adjustment mechanism. Gilbert (1968) lists the channels through which adjustment might be promoted, the most important being changes in monetary and fiscal policies and changes in par values. There is some question of whether 'inappropriate' fiscal and monetary policies were responsible for the American payments deficits; in any case, governments were less willing than ever to accept external constraints on domestic demand-management policies. Thus, if US payments deficits were to be eliminated, the mechanism would have to be changes in par values. Yet throughout the Bretton Woods era countries were singularly unwilling to adjust the peg. Between the 1949 and 1967 devaluations of sterling, the only parity adjustments by industrial economies were the 1957–8 devaluation of the French franc and the relatively small 5 per cent revaluations in 1961 of the German mark and the Dutch guilder. Devaluation undermined national prestige and called into question the competence of policymakers, while revaluation threatened the competitiveness of domestic industry. The adjustable peg proved not to be very adjustable. Much like the gold standards of earlier periods, economies were saddled for considerable periods with inappropriate exchange rates, and adjustment was shifted in an asymmetrical fashion onto deficit countries.[35]

Triffin (1960) argued that this system contained the seeds of its own destruction. Foreign accumulations of dollars provided the main source of incremental liquidity, but once total foreign dollar holdings exceeded US gold reserves, as was the case from 1960, the system was vulnerable to collapse at any time. Foreign governments, whose own dollar holdings exceeded US gold stocks by the mid-1960s, were entitled to bring their dollars to the Federal Reserve for conversion, but if they did the US would be unable to maintain the system's linchpin, the $35 gold price. The 'Triffin Paradox' was that the system relied on dollars for liquidity, but that the very accumulation of dollars abroad was undermining confidence in the dollar's convertibility.

There existed three possibilities for the world economy to avoid a liquidity squeeze: a higher gold price achieved by a dollar devaluation and currency realignment abroad, creation by the IMF of new supplementary sources of liquidity, or abandonment of fixed parities in favour of generalized floating. Each of the options ultimately implied a reduced role for gold in the international monetary system, either directly or through its likely impact on market participants' expectations. Floating exchange rates, which effectively eliminated gold's special position, found some favour among academics but were viewed by policymakers as undesirable. Gilbert (1968) argued for a substantial increase in the dollar price of gold. Others felt that gold discipline was an all-or-nothing matter; if the US tampered with the dollar price of gold, future gold pegs would not be credible. Kenen (1969) and others argued for the creation of supplementary reserves by the IMF. Keynes had had such an idea in mind when, during wartime consultations, he proposed the creation of an international clearing union to provide unconditional drawing rights. However, the IMF that emerged from Bretton Woods was empowered to manage only a fixed pool of gold, dollars and other currencies which might be purchased by participants under certain restrictive conditions. While quotas were increased periodically and were in fact doubled between 1945 and 1960, the liquidity problem was far from solved. IMF credit, like other forms of reserves, retained a link with gold, and some European countries opposed as inflationary all proposals to create new liquidity until the US deficit was eliminated.

In the end the course adopted was attempting to muddle through. Exchange controls and moral suasion were used to discourage central-bank conversion of American financial assets into gold but could not in the end prevent the deterioration of confidence in the dollar. By the end of 1970 official dollar claims of foreigners were more than twice US gold reserves, and the suspension of convertibility was increasingly anticipated. The straw that supposedly broke the camel's back was a British request in August 1971 that the Federal Reserve swap a portion of the Bank of England's dollar holdings for sterling, which was perceived in the US as the beginning of a general run on the dollar. On Sunday 15 August the US gold window was officially closed. The exchange-rate alignments associated with the 1971 Smithsonian Agreement proved to be only a temporary expedient. With the gold window closed, the gold-dollar system of the postwar period drew to an end, and the international economy was perched on the edge of a new era of generalized floating.

*

The system of floating exchange rates with which we have lived for more than a decade has operated to no one's satisfaction. Hence the appeal of an international gold standard envisaged as restoring stability and automaticity to the international monetary mechanism. The practice of targeting monetary aggregates has failed to lessen inflation because, according to some, of the allure of discretionary intervention. Hence the appeal of convertibility as a legal means of limiting the scope for discretion.

That the gold standard was less than automatic and that its record in providing stability was less than glowing is not troublesome to its proponents. They argue that a gold standard carefully designed to eliminate discretion would also eliminate problems of financial instability. Critics of these proposals question whether policymakers used to discretion would permit their hands to be tied under a rules-based regime. Alternatively, were policymakers suddenly to be converted to the virtues of rules, there exist alternatives to pegging the domestic price of gold which appear to hold out greater promise for purchasing-power stability (see Cooper, 1982).

One should not overlook the special problems of attempting to resurrect the gold standard in the final years of the twentieth century. In theory, one of the gold standard's virtues is that the supply of new gold is responsive to changes in price. This is the case in Barro's (1979) model of the gold standard, where the mining industry is treated as perfectly competitive. At present, however, the vast majority of new gold supplies come from two sources: the highly centralized industries of South Africa and the Soviet Union. The mining industry can scarcely be characterized as perfectly competitive and, as the Report of the US Gold Commission (1982) has shown, in recent years price elasticities of supply have actually been negative. Leaving aside the political implications of dependence on these two sources of supply, there seems little assurance that gold production will tend to stabilize prices.

The other major problem in implementing convertibility is that of choosing an appropriate official price for gold. Since World War II the growth of real income has far outstripped the growth in the value of the world's stock of monetary gold. At current market prices central-bank stocks of gold would not provide credible backing for a convertible system. The two alternatives open to the authorities are to bring about a deflation of prices on an order never experienced in modern times or to set an official gold price several times prevailing market prices. A dramatic reduction in the price level is inconsistent with the target of price stability valued by the gold standard's advocates and would be unacceptable for precisely the same reasons that France ultimately chose not to restore the prewar exchange rate in 1928. Raising the official price of gold sufficiently above the present market price would render reserves adequate to back money currently in circulation. However, by inducing private holders of gold to present it to the central bank, the policy of setting an official price above present market prices would lead to an expansion of the money supply and quite possibly to an inflation rivalling any recently seen. In response to this dilemma it has been suggested that the authorities might be empowered to vary periodically the official price of gold. But since then the system would embody discretion rather than automaticity, it would be bereft of its central feature.

Resurrecting the gold standard would appear to involve significant costs, serious uncertainties, and dubious benefits. But if the historical record provides little support for the theorist's vision of the gold standard as an ideal monetary regime, it contains valuable lessons for those contemplating the reform of our international monetary system.

Notes

1 I acknowledge with thanks comments on previous drafts from Alec Cairncross, Carlos Diaz-Alejandro, Trevor Dick, Peter Kenen, Charles Kindleberger, Ian McLean, Jacques Melitz, Joel Mokyr, Peter Oppenheimer and William Parker. Their encouragement and advice made the publication of this collection possible.
2 This is an example of the operation of Gresham's law.

3 The contemporary debate over the monetary standard is conveniently reviewed by Viner (1937).

4 The restoration of convertibility did not put an end to monetary controversies in the United States. See for example Friedman and Schwartz (1963).

5 Detail on the different systems can be found in Bloomfield (1959).

6 Again, see Bloomfield (1959). Various arguments were made in favour of the English system of fiduciary coverage and the continental system of proportional coverage. It has been argued that the English system permits less contraction of the money supply in the wake of a gold outflow. However, given banks' practice of holding excess gold reserves and the authorities' ability to adjust periodically the size of the fiduciary issue, it is difficult to substantiate any association between coverage system and money-supply elasticity.

7 See for example Bordo (1981), Cooper (1982) and Reynolds (1983). Typically, the interwar gold standard is omitted from these comparisons for being peculiar and short-lived.

8 The statements in the text are based on comparisons of the standard deviations of the variables.

9 A good example of this line of research is Callahan (1984).

10 A recent case study of international transmission is provided by Kindleberger (1983).

11 An analysis very similar to Hume's, which contains elements not only of the price-specie-flow mechanism but of the role of changes in spending in the adjustment process and of the law of one price, appears in Cantillon (1755).

12 This is the opposite of the exercise considered by Hume himself, who begins, 'Suppose four-fifths of all the money in Great Britain to be annihilated in one night'.

13 The reader familiar with the literature on the monetary approach to the balance of payments will recognize the similarity of the arguments here to those advanced by Whitman (1975) to reconcile the monetary, absorption and elasticities approaches to the adjustment process.

14 This assumes away, of course, the existence of nontraded goods. Under the demanding assumptions of the Heckscher-Ohlin model of international trade, it is possible to show that if product prices are equalized internationally, so are factor prices. See for example Ethier (1983). Since factors of production are assumed not to be traded internationally, in this model the same forces which tend to equalize the prices of traded goods internationally will tend to equalize the prices of nontraded goods internationally. Another way of thinking about this is that, in the Heckscher-Ohlin model, product-price equalization causes factor-price equalization; since by assumption nontraded goods are produced subject to the same technology and costs are the same everywhere, nontraded goods prices will be the same everywhere. In models which relax the assumption of factor-price equalization or identical technologies, it is possible for the adjustment process to work through changes in the relative price of nontraded goods. This is one of the adjustment mechanisms (along with spending effects) emphasized by Bertil Ohlin and the view of the adjustment mechanism criticized by McCloskey and Zecher (1976). Whatever the validity of the various arguments, it should be noted that neither Ohlin nor Taussig was directly concerned with the gold standard adjustment mechanism in the passages criticized by McCloskey and Zecher. Ohlin was concerned with the German Transfer Problem rather than the gold standard *per se*, while Taussig in the article cited was discussing the gains from trade and their relationship to the structure of incomes. Elsewhere, Taussig (1927) analysed balance-of-payments adjustment under a gold standard, focusing on changes in the

terms of trade rather than changes in the relative prices of nontraded goods, a view none the less equally at variance with the one advanced by McCloskey and Zecher.

15 Behind this statement lies the assumption that gold, securities and consumer goods are gross substitutes for one another. Cases of complementarity could be analysed similarly but would yield less intuitive results.

16 Some models in a Keynesian spirit permit output to react endogenously to disturbances and take spending as a function of income. See Meade (1951). Other models in a monetarist spirit take output as exogenous while assuming that spending is a stable function of real money balances. See McCloskey and Zecher (1976). Models of the monetary approach to the adjustment process frequently incorporate not only the assumption that spending is a stable function of real balances but also the further assumption that markets clear in the sense that arbitrage enforces the law of the one price and that full employment is continuously maintained. Arguably, it is the first of these assumptions that most clearly distinguishes the monetary approach from other models of the adjustment mechanism.

17 Whale (1937), p. 19.

18 Bloomfield (1959), p. 21.

19 In particular, Bloomfield verified the predicted inverse relationship between reserve ratios and discount rates for England, Germany, Austria-Hungary, Belgium, the Netherlands, and Russia. In the case of France, the inverse correlation was less marked because the discount rate was left unchanged for long periods of time. Finally, he found no evidence of an inverse correlation for Finland, Norway, Denmark or Switzerland.

20 The 'gold devices' included paying more than the statutory amount for gold bars and varying the purchasing price of certain foreign coins. In addition, the Bank of England could influence conditions in the gold market by extending interest-free advances to gold importers to subsidize the cost of the time gold was in transit between markets. On the history of these devices, see US National Monetary Commission (1910), Sayers (1936), Scammell (1965) and Moggridge (1972). Similarly, the Bank of France could, at its option, legally redeem its notes either in gold coin or five-franc silver pieces. Since the market value of the silver content of five-franc pieces was less than the nominal value of the coin, the Bank could use this mechanism to discourage attempts to export specie. See White (1933).

21 In the period before 1890, it has been argued, the volume of bank deposits, loans and advances may not have been sufficient for the Bank of France to intervene so as to influence the money multiplier without severely distorting market conditions. See Whale (1937), p. 22.

22 For instance, at the end of 1913, Russia, one of the principal reserve currency countries, held $222 million in francs, $53 million in marks, and $24 million in sterling (Lindert, 1969). Russia had unusually close financial ties with France, but the example is still revealing.

23 See Gourevitch (1977). The assertion that tariffs impede adjustment could be predicated on the assumption that, in tariff-ridden economies, an international transfer of given size requires a larger change in the terms of trade. However, the argument has not been developed. Some authors who mention the disruptive effects of tariffs are mainly concerned with the international distribution of gold and its relation to protection. This issue of gold distribution is taken up below.

24 Britain along with other countries had moved from a gold coin standard to a gold bullion standard. Gold coins no longer circulated internally, and the nation's bullion reserves were concentrated at the central bank. In Britain the time-honoured right to take gold to the Mint and have it coined was abolished, this right

having been made the exclusive privilege of the Bank of England, which was no longer required to sell gold on demand except in pure bars of 400 (Troy) ounces.

25 For example, these were the recommendations of the committee of experts at the Genoa Conference in 1922. See Clarke (1973).

26 In drafting the Report, Keynes extended his analysis of the conflict between internal and external balance as first presented in the *Tract* (1923) and elaborated in the *Treatise* (1930).

27 For example, in an early post-mortem, Cassel (1932, p. 71) criticized the sterilization of gold inflows by France and the United States, asserting that 'the breakdown of the Gold Standard was the result of a flagrant mismanagement of this monetary mechanism'.

28 The possibilities for using central-bank co-operation to relieve the international struggle for gold are further analysed by Clarke (1967) and Eichengreen (1984).

29 See Cairncross and Eichengreen (1983).

30 See the accounts provided by Gardner (1956) and Horsefield (1969).

31 Quoted in Dam (1982), p. 96.

32 The role of sterling as a reserve asset should not be neglected, but that role was confined to a geographically circumscribed group of countries with close trading links to the United Kingdom.

33 Statistics can be found in the International Monetary Fund's *International Financial Statistics* (various issues).

34 The fact that the US paid interest on dollar assets held by foreign countries was not seen as a compelling counterargument on the grounds that the dollar's special reserve role permitted the payment of interest at artificially low rates.

35 The asymmetry is perhaps most evident in developing countries, where devaluation was commonplace but revaluation was unknown.

References

Bloomfield, Arthur I. (1959), *Monetary Policy under the International Gold Standard, 1880–1914*, New York, Federal Reserve Bank of New York.

——(1963), *Short-term Capital Movements under the Pre-1914 Gold Standard*, Princeton Studies in International Finance, no. 11, Princeton, Princeton University Press.

Bordo, Michael David (1981), 'The classical gold standard: some lessons for today', *Federal Reserve Bank of St Louis Review* (May).

——(1984), 'The gold standard: the traditional approach', in Bordo and Schwartz (1984).

Bordo, Michael D. and Anna J. Schwartz (1984) (eds), *A Retrospective on the Classical Gold Standard*, Chicago, University of Chicago Press.

Brown, William Adams (1940), *The International Gold Standard Reinterpreted, 1914–1934*, New York, National Bureau of Economic Research.

Cagan, Phillip (1982), *Current Problems of Monetary Policy: Would the Gold Standard Help?* Washington, D.C., American Enterprise Institute.

Cairncross, Alec and Barry Eichengreen (1983), *Sterling in Decline: The Devaluations of 1931, 1949 and 1967*, Oxford, Blackwell.

Callahan, Colleen M. (1984), 'Movements in aggregate price uncertainty in the United States', unpublished manuscript, University of North Carolina.

Cantillon, Richard (1755), *Essai sur la nature du commerce en général*, ed by H. Higgs (1931), reprinted by A.M. Kelley, New York, 1964.

Cassel, Gustav (1932), *The Crisis in the World's Monetary System*, Oxford, Clarendon Press.

——(1936), *The Downfall of the Gold Standard*, Oxford, Clarendon Press.

Clapham, J.H. (1944), *The Bank of England: A History*, Cambridge, Cambridge University Press.

Clarke, S.V.O. (1967), *Central Bank Cooperation, 1924–1931*, New York, Federal Reserve Bank of New York.

——(1973), *The Reconstruction of the International Monetary System: The Attempts of 1922 and 1933*, Princeton Studies in International Finance, no. 33, Princeton, Princeton University Press.

Clay, Sir Henry (1957), *Lord Norman*, London, Macmillan.

Dam, Kenneth (1982), *The Rules of the Game*, Chicago, University of Chicago Press.

de Cecco, Marcello (1974), *Money and Empire*, Oxford, Blackwell.

Dornbusch, Rudiger and Jacob Frenkel (1984), 'The gold standard and the Bank of England in the crisis of 1847', in Bordo and Schwartz (1984).

Dutton, John (1984), 'The Bank of England and the rules of the game under the international gold standard: new evidence', in Bordo and Schwartz (1984).

Edelstein, M. (1981), 'Foreign investment and empire, 1860–1914', in R. Floud and D. McCloskey (eds), *The Economic History of Britain since 1700*, Cambridge, Cambridge University Press, 1981, 2, 70–98.

Eichengreen, Barry (1984), 'Central bank cooperation under the interwar gold standard', *Explorations in Economic History* (January).

Ethier, Wilfred (1983), *Modern International Economics*, New York, Norton.

Fellner, William (1981), 'Gold and the uneasy case for responsibly managed fiat money', in *Essays in Contemporary Economic Problems*, Washington, D.C., American Enterprise Institute.

Fetter, Frank W. (1965), *Development of British Monetary Orthodoxy, 1797–1875*, Cambridge, Mass., Harvard University Press.

Flood, Robert P. and Peter M. Garber (1984), 'Gold monetization and gold discipline', *Journal of Political Economy* (February).

Ford, A.G. (1962), *The Gold Standard 1880–1914: Britain and Argentina*, Oxford, Clarendon Press.

Fraser, H.F. (1933), *Great Britain and the Gold Standard*, London, Macmillan.

Friedman, Milton and Anna Schwartz (1963), *A Monetary History of the United States, 1867–1960*, Princeton, Princeton University Press.

Gardner, Richard N. (1956), *Sterling–Dollar Diplomacy*, Oxford, Clarendon Press.

Goodhart, C.A.E. (1972), *The Business of Banking 1891–1914*, London, Weidenfield & Nicolson.

Gourevitch, P.A. (1977), 'International trade, domestic coalitions and liberty: the crisis of 1873–1896', *Journal of Interdisciplinary History* (Autumn).

Gregory, T.E. (1932), *The Gold Standard and its Future*, London, Methuen, reprinted by Arno Press, New York, 1979.

Hawtrey, Ralph G. (1927), *The Gold Standard in Theory and Practice*, London, Longmans, Green.

Horsefield, J.K. (1944), 'The origins of the Bank Charter Act, 1844', *Economica* (November).

——(1969), *The International Monetary Fund 1945–1965*, Washington, D.C., International Monetary Fund.

Kemp, Tom (1971), 'The French economy under the franc Poincaré', *Economic History Review* (February).

Kenen, Peter B. (1960), *British Monetary Policy and the Balance of Payments*, Cambridge, Mass., Harvard University Press.

——(1969), 'The international position of the dollar in a changing world', *International Organization*, 3.

Keynes, John Maynard (1923), *A Tract on Monetary Reform*, London, Macmillan.

——(1925), *Essays in Persuasion*, London, Macmillan.

——(1930), *A Treatise on Money*, London, Macmillan.

Kindleberger, Charles (1973), *The World in Depression, 1929–1939*, Berkeley, University of California Press.

——(1983), 'International propagation of financial crises: the experience of 1888–93', forthcoming.

League of Nations (1932), *Interim Report of the Gold Delegation* and *Report of the Gold Delegation*, Geneva, League of Nations, 1930. II. 26 and C. 502. M. 243, 1932, reprinted by Arno Press, New York, 1978.

Lewis, W.A. (1948), *Economic Survey, 1919–1939*, Geneva, League of Nations.

——(1978), *Growth and Fluctuations, 1870–1913*, Boston, Allen & Unwin.

Lindert, Peter H. (1969), *Key Currencies and Gold, 1900–1913*, Princeton Studies in International Finance, no. 24, Princeton, Princeton University Press.

Marshall, Alfred (1923), *Money, Credit and Commerce*, London, Macmillan.

——(1926), *Official Papers*, London, Macmillan.

Meade, James (1951), *The Theory of International Economic Policy*, London, Oxford University Press.

Mill, J.S. (1865), *Principles of Political Economy*, reprinted by A.M. Kelley, New York, 1961.

Moggridge, Donald (1969), *The Return to Gold, 1925*, Cambridge, Cambridge University Press.

——(1972), *British Monetary Policy, 1924–1931*, Cambridge, Cambridge University Press.

Morgenstern, Oskar (1959), *International Financial Transactions and Business Cycles*, Princeton, Princeton University Press.

Paul, Ron and Lewis Lehrman (1982), *The Case for Gold*, Washington, D.C., The Cato Institute.

Pippinger, John (1984), 'Bank of England operations, 1893–1913', in Bordo and Schwartz (1984).

Ramon, G. (1929), *Histoire de la Banque de France*, Paris, B. Grasset.

Reynolds, Alan (1983), 'Why gold?', *The Cato Journal*, 31 (Spring).

Ricardo, David (1816), 'Proposals for an economical and secure currency; with observations on the profits of the Bank of England as they regard the public and the proprietors of bank stock', in Piero Sraffa (ed.), *The Works and Correspondence of David Ricardo*, IV, Cambridge, Cambridge University Press, 1951.

Sayers, R.S. (1936), *Bank of England Operations 1890–1914*, London, P.S. King.

——(1957), *Central Banking After Bagehot*, Oxford, Clarendon Press.

——(1970), 'The return to gold, 1925', in Sidney Pollard (ed.), *The Gold Standard and Employment Policies Between the Wars*, London, Methuen.

——(1976), *The Bank of England, 1891–1944*, Cambridge, Cambridge University Press.

Taussig, F.W. (1927), *International Trade*, New York, Macmillan.

Triffin, Robert (1960), *Gold and the Dollar Crisis*, New Haven, Yale University Press.

——(1968), *Our International Monetary System: Yesterday, Today and Tomorrow,* New York, Random House.

US National Monetary Commission (1910), *Interviews on the Banking Systems of England, Scotland, France, Germany, Switzerland and Italy,* Washington, D.C., US Government Printing Office.

US Gold Commission (1982), *Report to the Congress of the Commission on the Role of Gold in the Domestic and International Monetary Systems,* Washington, D.C., US Government Printing Office.

Viner, Jacob (1937), *Studies in the Theory of International Trade,* New York, Harper, reprinted by A.M. Kelley, New York, 1975.

Whale, P.B. (1937), 'The working of the prewar gold standard', *Economica* (February).

——(1944), 'A retrospective view of the Bank Charter Act, 1844', *Economica* (August).

White, H.D. (1933), *The French International Accounts, 1880–1913,* Cambridge, Mass., Harvard University Press.

Whitman, Marina V.N. (1975), 'Global monetarism and the monetary approach to the balance of payments', *Brookings Papers on Economic Activity,* 3.

Part I

The gold standard in theory

Introduction

One of the most durable questions in economic theory is how the gold standard worked, especially how the adjustment process worked to restore balance-of-payments equilibrium. The most influential model of the adjustment process is the price-specie-flow mechanism associated with David Hume, developed by him in the first selection presented in Part I. Hume's model emphasizes, but not to the exclusion of other factors, the role of relative price movements in restoring the equality of exports and imports. The model advanced by P.B. Whale in the second selection shifts the focus to the role of interest rates and international capital flows in the adjustment process, and minimizes the importance of actual gold movements, the factor highlighted by Hume. In the third selection, Donald McCloskey and J. Richard Zecher again shift the focus, this time to money supply and money demand, criticizing the Humeian view that adjustment worked through relative price effects and highlighting instead the impact of changes in wealth and real money balances on the level of spending. Robert Barro, in the fourth selection, takes a long-run view of the gold standard, demonstrating how changes in the overall price levels could in theory have been neutralized by offsetting changes in the world supply of monetary gold.

2

On the balance of trade

David Hume*

It is very usual, in nations ignorant of the nature of commerce, to prohibit the exportation of commodities, and to preserve among themselves whatever they think valuable and useful. They do not consider, that, in this prohibition, they act directly contrary to their intention; and that the more is exported of any commodity the more will be raised at home of which they themselves will always have the first offer.

It is well known to the learned, that the ancient laws of Athens rendered the exportation of figs criminal; that being supposed a species of fruit so excellent in Attica, that the Athenians deemed it too delicious for the palate of any foreigner. And in this ridiculous prohibition they were so much in earnest, that informers were thence called *sycophants* among them, from two Greek words, which signify *figs* and *discoverer*. There are proofs in many old acts of parliament of the same ignorance in the nature of commerce, particularly in the reign of Edward III. And to this day, in France, the exportation of corn is almost always prohibited; in order, as they say, to prevent famines; though it is evident, that nothing contributes more to the frequent famines, which so much distress that fertile country.

The same jealous fear, with regard to money, has also prevailed among several nations; and it required both reason and experience to convince any people, that these prohibitions serve to no other purpose than to raise the exchange against them, and produce a still greater exportation.

*From *Essays, Moral, Political and Literary*, vol. 1, London, Longmans, Green, 1898, pp. 330–41, 343–5, abridged. This essay was first published in 1752.

detrimental to hoard gold

These errors, one may say, are gross and palpable: But there still prevails, even in nations well acquainted with commerce, a strong jealousy with regard to the balance of trade, and a fear that all their gold and silver may be leaving them. This seems to me, almost in every case, a groundless apprehension; and I should as soon dread, that all our springs and rivers should be exhausted, as that money should abandon a kingdom where there are people and industry. Let us carefully preserve these later advantages; and we need never be apprehensive of losing the former.

It is easy to observe, that all calculations concerning the balance of trade are founded on very uncertain facts and suppositions. The custom-house books are allowed to be an insufficient ground of reasoning; nor is the rate of exchange much better; unless we consider it with all nations, and know also the proportions of the several sums remitted; which one may safely pronounce impossible. Every man, who has ever reasoned on this subject, has always proved his theory, whatever it was, by facts and calculations, and by an enumeration of all the commodities sent to all foreign kingdoms.

The writings of Mr Gee struck the nation with an universal panic, when they saw it plainly demonstrated, by a detail of particulars, that the balance was against them for so considerable a sum as must leave them without a single shilling in five or six years. But luckily, twenty years have since elapsed, with an expensive foreign war; yet is it commonly supposed, that money is still more plentiful among us than in any former period.

Nothing can be more entertaining on this head than Dr Swift, an author so quick in discerning the mistakes and absurdities of others. He says, in his *Short View of the State of Ireland*, that the whole cash of that kingdom formerly amounted but to 500,000*l*.; that out of this the Irish remitted every year a neat million to England, and had scarcely any other source from which they could compensate themselves, and little other foreign trade than the importation of French wines, for which they paid ready money. The consequence of this situation, which must be owned to be disadvantageous, was, that, in a course of three years, the current money of Ireland, from 500,000*l*. was reduced to less than two. And at present, I suppose, in a course of thirty years it is absolutely nothing. Yet I know not how, that opinion of the advance of riches in Ireland, which gave the Doctor so much indignation, seems still to continue, and gain ground with every body.

In short, this apprehension of the wrong balance of trade, appears of such a nature, that it discovers itself, wherever one is out of humour with the ministry, or is in low spirits; and as it can never be refuted by a particular detail of all the exports, which counterbalance the imports, it may here be proper to form a general argument, that they may prove the impossibility of this event, as long as we preserve our people and our industry.

Suppose four-fifths of all the money in Great Britain to be annihilated in one night, and the nation reduced to the same condition, with regard to specie, as in the reigns of the Harrys and Edwards, what would be the consequence? Must not the price of all labour and commodities sink in proportion, and everything be sold as cheap as they were in those ages? What nation could then dispute with us in any foreign market, or pretend to navigate or to sell manufactures at the same price, which to us would afford sufficient profit? In how little time, therefore, must this bring back the money which we had lost, and raise us to the level of all the neighbouring nations? Where, after we have arrived, we immediately lose the advantage of the cheapness of labour and commodities; and the farther flowing in of money is stopped by our fulness and repletion.

Again, suppose, that all the money of Great Britain were multiplied fivefold in a night, must not the contrary effect follow? Must not all labour and commodities rise to such an exorbitant height, that no neighbouring nations could afford to buy from us; while their commodities, on the other hand, became comparatively so cheap, that, in spite of all the laws which could be formed, they would be run in upon us, and our money flow out; till we fall to a level with foreigners, and lose that great superiority of riches, which had laid us under such disadvantages?

Now, it is evident, that the same causes, which would correct these exorbitant inequalities, were they to happen miraculously, must prevent their happening in the common course of nature, and must for ever, in all neighbouring nations, preserve money nearly proportionable to the art and industry of each nation. All water, wherever it communicates, remains always at a level. Ask naturalists the reason; they tell you, that, were it to be raised in any one place, the superior gravity of that part not being balanced, must depress it, till it meet a counterpoise; and that the same cause, which redresses the inequality when it happens, must for ever prevent it, without some violent external operation.[1]

Can one imagine, that it had ever been possible, by any laws, or even by any art or industry, to have kept all the money in Spain, which the galleons have brought from the Indies? Or that all commodities could be sold in France for a tenth of the price which they would yield on the other side of the Pyrenees, without finding their way thither, and draining from that immense treasure? What other reason indeed is there, why all nations, at present, gain in their trade with Spain and Portugal; but because it is impossible to heap up money, more than any fluid, beyond its proper level? The sovereigns of these countries have shown, that they wanted not inclination to keep their gold and silver to themselves, had it been in any degree practicable.

But as any body of water may be raised above the level of the surrounding element, if the former has no communication with the latter; so in money, if the communication be cut off, by any material or physical impediment (for all laws alone are ineffectual), there may, in such a case, be a very great inequality of money. Thus the immense distance of China, together with the monopolies of our India companies, obstructing the communication, preserve in Europe the gold and siver, especially the latter, in much greater plenty than they are found in that kingdom. But, notwithstanding this great obstruction, the force of the causes abovementioned is still evident. The skill and ingenuity of Europe in general surpasses perhaps that of China, with regard to manual arts and manufactures; yet are we never able to trade thither without great disadvantage. And were it not for the continual recruits, which we receive from America, money would soon sink in Europe, and rise in China, till it came nearly to a level in both places. Nor can any reasonable man doubt, but that industrious nation, were they as near us as Poland or Barbary, would drain us of the overplus of our specie, and draw to themselves a larger share of the West Indian treasures. We need not have recourse to a physical attraction, in order to explain the necessity of this operation. There is a moral attraction, arising from the interests and passions of men, which is full as potent and infallible.

How is the balance kept in the provinces of every kingdom among themselves, but by the force of this principle, which makes it impossible for money to lose its level, and either to rise or sink beyond the proportion of the labour and commodities which are in each province? Did not long experience make people easy on this head, what a fund of gloomy reflections might calculations afford to a melancholy Yorkshireman, while he computed and magnified the sums drawn to London by taxes, absentees, commodities, and found on comparison the opposite articles so much inferior? And no doubt, had the *Heptarchy* subsisted in England, the legislature of each state had been continually alarmed by the fear of a wrong balance; and as it is probable that the mutual hatred of these states would have been extremely violent on account of their close neighbourhood, they would have lorded and oppressed all commerce, by a jealous and superfluous caution. Since the union has removed the barriers between Scotland and England, which of these nations gains from the other by this free commerce? Or if the former kingdom has received any increase of riches, can it reasonably be accounted for by any thing but the increase of its art and industry? It was a common apprehension in England, before the union, as we learn from L'abbe du Bos,[2] that Scotland would soon drain them of their treasure, were an open trade allowed; and on the other side the Tweed a contrary apprehension prevailed: With what justice in both, time has shown.

What happens in small portions of mankind, must take place in greater. The provinces of the Roman empire, no doubt, kept their balance with each other, and with Italy, independent of the legislature; as much as the several counties of Great Britain, or the several parishes of each county. And any man who travels over Europe at this day, may see, by the prices of commodities, that money, in spite of the absurd jealousy of princes and states, has brought itself nearly to a level; and that the difference between one kingdom and another is not greater in this respect, than it is often between different provinces of the same kingdom, Men naturally flock to capital cities, sea-ports, and navigable rivers. There we find more men, more industry, more commodities, and consequently more money; but still the latter difference holds proportion with the former, and the level is preserved.[3]

Our jealousy and our hatred of France are without bounds; and the former sentiment, at least, must be acknowledged reasonable and well-grounded. These passions have occasioned innumerable barriers and obstructions upon commerce, where we are accused of being commonly the aggressors. But what have we gained by the bargain? We lost the French market for our woollen manufactures, and transferred the commerce of wine to Spain and Portugal, where we buy worse liquor at a higher price. There are few Englishmen who would not think their country absolutely ruined, were French wines sold in England so cheap and in such abundance as to supplant, in some measure, all ale, and home-brewed liquors: But would we lay aside prejudice, it would not be difficult to prove, that nothing could be more innocent, perhaps advantageous. Each new acre of vineyard planted in France, in order to supply England with wine, would make it requisite for the French to take the produce of an English acre, sown in wheat or barley, in order to subsist themselves; and it is evident, that we should thereby get command of the better commodity.

There are many edicts of the French king, prohibiting the planting of new vineyards, and ordering all those which are lately planted to be grubbed up: So sensible are they, in that country, of the superior value of corn, above every other product.

Mareschal Vauban complains often, and with reason, of the absurd duties which load the entry of those wines of Languedoc, Guienne, and other southern provinces, that are imported into Brittany and Normandy. He entertained no doubt but these latter provinces could preserve their balance, notwithstanding the open commerce which he recommends. And it is evident, that a few leagues more navigation to England would make no difference; or if it did, that it must operate alike on the commodities of both kingdoms.

There is indeed one expedient by which it is possible to sink, and another by which we may raise money beyond its natural level in any kingdom; but these cases, when examined, will be found to resolve into our general theory, and to bring additional authority to it.

I scarcely know any method of sinking money below its level, but those institutions of banks, funds, and paper-credit, which are so much practised in this kingdom. These render paper equivalent to money, circulate it throughout the whole state, make it supply the place of gold and silver, raise proportionably the price of labour and commodities, and by that means either banish a great part of those precious metals, or prevent their farther increase. What can be more short-sighted than our reasonings on this head? We fancy, because an individual would be much richer, were his stock of money doubled, that the same good effect would follow were the money of every one increased; not considering, that this would raise as much the price of every commodity, and reduce every man, in time, to the same condition as before. It is only in our public negotiations and transactions with foreigners, that a greater stock of money is advantageous; and as our paper is there absolutely insignificant, we feel, by its means, all the ill effects arising from a great abundance of money, without reaping any of the advantages.[4]

Suppose that there are 12 millions of paper, which circulate in the kingdom as money, (for we are not to imagine, that all our enormous funds are employed in that shape) and suppose the real cash of the kingdom to be 18 millions: Here is a state which is found by experience to be able to hold a stock of 30 millions. I say, if it be able to hold it, it must of necessity have acquired it in gold and silver, had we not obstructed the entrance of these metals by this new invention of paper. *Whence would it have acquired that sum?* From all the kingdoms of the world. *But why?* Because, if you remove these 12 millions, money in this state is below its level, compared with our neighbours; and we must immediately draw from all of them, till we be full and saturate, so to speak, and can hold no more. By our present politics, we are as careful to stuff the nation with this fine commodity of bank-bills and chequer-notes, as if we were afraid of being over-burthened with the precious metals.

It is not to be doubted, but the great plenty of bullion in France is, in a great measure, owing to the want of paper-credit. The French have no banks: Merchants bills do not there circulate as with us: Usury or lending on interest is not directly permitted; so that many have large sums in their coffers: Great quantities of plate are used in private houses; and all the churches are full of it. By this means, provisions and labour still remain cheaper among them, than in nations that are not half so rich in gold and silver. The advantages of this situation, in point of trade as well as in great public emergencies, are too evident to be disputed.

The same fashion a few years ago prevailed in Genoa, which still has place in England and Holland, of using services of China-ware instead of plate; but the senate, foreseeing the consequence, prohibited the use of that brittle commodity beyond a certain extent; while the use of silverplate was left unlimited. And I suppose, in their late distresses, they felt the good effect of this ordinance. Our tax on plate is, perhaps, in this view, somewhat impolitic.

Before the introduction of paper-money into our colonies, they had gold and silver sufficient for their circulation. Since the introduction of that commodity, the least inconveniency that has followed is the total banishment of the precious metals. And after the abolition of paper, can it be doubted but money will return, while these colonies possess manufactures and commodities, the only thing valuable in commerce, and for whose sake alone all men desire money.

What pity Lycurgus did not think of paper-credit, when he wanted to banish gold and silver from Sparta! It would have served his purpose better than the lumps of iron he made use of as money; and would also have prevented more effectually all commerce with strangers, as being of so much less real and intrinsic value.

It must, however, be confessed, that, as all these questions of trade and money are extremely complicated, there are certain lights, in which this subject may be placed, so as to represent the advantages of paper-credit and banks to be superior to their disadvantages. That they banish specie and bullion from a state is undoubtedly true; and whoever looks no farther than this circumstance does well to condemn them; but specie and bullion are not of so great consequence as not to admit of a compensation, and even an overbalance from the increase of industry and of credit, which may be promoted by the right use of paper-money. It is well known of what advantage it is to a merchant to be able to discount his bills upon occasion; and every thing that facilitates this species of traffic is favourable to the general commerce of a state. But private bankers are enabled to give such credit by the credit they receive from the depositing of money in their shops; and the bank of England in the same manner, from the liberty it has to issue its notes in all payments. There was an invention of this kind, which was fallen upon some years ago by the banks of Edinburgh; and which, as it is one of the most ingenious ideas that has been executed in commerce, has also been thought advantageous to Scotland. It is there called a Bank-credit; and is of this nature. A man goes to the bank and finds surety to the amount, we shall suppose, of a thousand pounds. This money, or any part of it, he has the liberty of drawing out whenever he pleases, and he pays only the ordinary interest for it, while it is in his hands. He may, when he pleases, repay any sum so small as twenty pounds, and the interest is discounted from the very day of the repayment. The advantages, resulting from this contrivance, are manifold. As a man may find surety nearly to the amount of his substance, and his bank-credit is equivalent to ready money, a merchant does hereby in a manner coin his houses, his household furniture, the goods in his warehouse, the foreign debts due to him, his ships at sea; and can, upon occasion, employ them in all payments, as if they were the current money of the country. If a man borrow a thousand pounds from a private hand, besides that it is not always to be found when required, he pays interest for it, whether he be using it or not: His bank-credit costs him nothing except during the very moment in which it is of service to him: And this circumstance is of equal advantage as if he had borrowed money at much lower interest. Merchants, likewise from this invention, acquire a great facility in supporting each other's credit, which is a considerable security against bankruptcies. A man, when his own bank-credit is exhausted, goes to any of his neighbours who is not in the same condition; and he gets the money, which he replaces at his convenience.

After this practice had taken place during some years at Edinburgh, several companies of merchants at Glasgow carried the matter farther. They associated themselves into different banks, and issued notes so low as ten shillings, which they used in all payments for goods, manufactures, tradesmen's labour of all kinds; and these notes, from the established credit of the companies, passed as money in all payments throughout the country. By this means, a stock of five thousand pounds was able to perform the same operations as if it were six or seven; and merchants were thereby enabled to trade to a greater extent, and to require less profit in all their transactions. But whatever other advantages result from these inventions, it must still be allowed that, besides giving too great facility to credit, which is dangerous, they banish the precious metals: and nothing can be a more evident proof of it, than a comparison of the past and present condition of Scotland in that particular. It was found, upon the recoinage made after the union, that there was near a million of specie in that country: But notwithstanding the great increase of riches, commerce, and manufactures of all kinds, it is thought, that, even where there is no extraordinary drain made by England, the current specie will not now amount to a third of that sum.

But as our projects of paper-credit are almost the only expedient, by which we can sink money below its level; so, in my opinion, the only expedient by which we can raise money above it, is a practice which we should all exclaim against as destructive, namely, the gathering of large sums into a public treasure, locking them up, and absolutely preventing their circulation. The fluid, not communicating with the neighbouring element, may, by such an artifice, be raised to what height we please. To prove this, we need only return to our first supposition, of annihilating the half or any part of our cash; where we found, that the immediate consequence of such an event would be the attraction of an equal sum from all the neighbouring kingdoms. Nor does there seem to be any necessary bounds set, by the nature of things, to this practice of hoarding. A small city, like Geneva, continuing this policy for ages, might engross nine tenths of the money of Europe. There seems, indeed, in the nature of man, an invincible obstacle to that immense growth of riches. A weak state, with an enormous treasure, will soon become a prey to some of its poorer, but more powerful neighbours. A great state would dissipate its wealth in dangerous and ill-concerted projects; and probably destroy, with it, what is much more valuable, the industry, morals, and numbers of its people. The fluid, in this case, raised to too great a height, bursts and destroys the vessel that contains it; and mixing itself with the surrounding element, soon falls to its proper level. [...]

From these principles we may learn what judgment we ought to form of those numberless bars, obstructions, and imposts which all nations of Europe, and none more than England, have put upon trade; from an exorbitant desire of amassing money, which never will heap up beyond its level, while it circulates; or from an ill-grounded apprehension of losing their specie, which never will sink below it. Could any thing scatter our riches, it would be such mpolitic contrivances. But this general ill effect, however, results from them, hat they deprive neighbouring nations of that free communication and exchange which the Author of the world has intended, by giving them soils, climates, and geniuses, so different from each other.

Our modern politics embrace the only method of banishing money, the using of paper-credit; they reject the only method of amassing it, the practice of hoarding; and they adopt a hundred contrivances, which serve to no purpose but to check industry, and rob ourselves and our neighbours of the common benefits of art and nature.

All taxes, however, upon foreign commodities, are not to be regarded as prejudicial or useless, but those only which are founded on the jealousy above-mentioned. A tax on German linen encourages home manufactures, and thereby multiplies our people and industry. A tax on brandy increases the sale of rum, and supports our southern colonies. And as it is necessary, that imposts should be levied, for the support of government, it may be thought more convenient to lay them on foreign commodities, which can easily be intercepted at the port, and subjected to the impost. We ought, however, always to remember the maxim of Dr Swift, That, in the arithmetic of the customs, two and two make not four, but often make only one. It can scarcely be doubted, but if the duties on wine were lowered to a third, they would yield much more to the government than at present: Our people might thereby afford to drink commonly a better and more wholesome liquor; and no prejudice would ensue to the balance of trade, of which we are so jealous. The manufacture of ale beyond the agriculture is but inconsiderable, and gives employment to few hands. The transport of wine and corn would not be much inferior.

But are there not frequent instances, you will say, of states and kingdoms, which were formerly rich and opulent, and are now poor and beggarly? Has not the money left them, with which they formerly abounded? I answer, If they lose their trade, industry, and people, they cannot expect to keep their gold and silver: For these precious metals will hold proportion to the former advantages. When Lisbon and Amsterdam got the East-India trade from Venice and Genoa, they also got the profits and money which arose from it. Where the seat of government is transferred, where expensive armies are maintained at a distance, where great funds are possessed by foreigners; there naturally follows from these causes a diminution of the specie. But these, we may observe, are violent and forcible methods of carrying away money, and are in time commonly attended with the transport of people and industry. But where these remain, and the drain is not continued, the money always finds its way back again, by a hundred canals, of which we have no notion or suspicion. What immense treasures have been spent, by so many nations, in Flanders, since the revolution, in the course of three long wars! More money perhaps than the half of what is at present in Europe. But what has now become of it? Is it in the narrow compass of the Austrian provinces? No, surely: It has most of it returned to the several countries whence it came, and has followed that art and industry, by which at first it was acquired. For above a thousand years, the money of Europe has been flowing to Rome, by an open and sensible current but it has been emptied by many secret and insensible canals: And the want of industry and commerce renders at present the papal dominions the poorest territory in all Italy.

In short, a government has great reason to preserve with care its people and its manufactures. Its money, it may safely trust to the course of human affairs without fear or jealousy. Or if it ever give attention to this latter circumstance, it ought only to be so far as it affects the former.

Notes

1 There is another cause, though more limited in its operation, which checks the wrong balance of trade, to every particular nation to which the kingdom trades. When we import more goods than we export, the exchange turns against us, and this becomes a new encouragement to export; as much as the charge of carriage and insurance of the money which becomes due would amount to. For the exchange can never rise but a little higher than that sum.

2 *Les Intérêts d'Angleterre Malentendus.*

3 It must carefully be remarked, that throughout this discourse, wherever I speak of the level of money, I mean always its proportional level to the commodities, labour, industry, and skill, which is in the several states. And I assert, that where these advantages are double, triple, quadruple, to what they are in the neighbouring states, the money infallibly will also be double, triple, quadruple. The only circumstance that can obstruct the exactness of these proportions, is the expense of transporting the commodities from one place to another; and this expense is sometimes unequal. Thus the corn, cattle, cheese, butter, of Derbyshire, cannot draw the money of London, so much as the manufactures of London draw the money of Derbyshire. But this objection is only a seeming one: For so far as the transport of commodities is expensive, so far is the communication between the places obstructed and imperfect.

4 We observed in Essay III [not included here] that money, when increasing, gives encouragement to industry, during the interval between the increase of money and rise of the prices. A good effect of this nature may follow too from paper-credit; but it is dangerous to precipitate matters, at the risk of losing all by the failing of that credit, as must happen upon any violent shock in public affairs.

3

The working of the prewar gold standard

P.B. Whale*

imp.
interest rates
+
international capital flows

In discussions concerning the postwar gold standard and the possibility of restoring an efficient international monetary system, it is natural to take the operation of the gold standard in prewar times as a kind of standard. It is therefore of more than historical interest to know exactly how the prewar gold standard did work.

The most generally accepted view on this matter – the classical explanation, as it may be conveniently termed – may be summarized as follows. A condition of balance of payments disequilibrium led, if more than temporary, to an international gold movement: the gold movement induced changes in the volume of monetary circulation in the countries concerned, a contraction here and an expansion there: the changes in circulation brought about the changes in incomes and prices required to adjust the balance of trade. In establishing a connection between the gold movement and the change in the volume of circulation, it is necessary to take account of the nature of the currency system involved. As credit means of payment, bank liabilities in the form of notes and deposits, have long been the most important forms of money in the more advanced countries, the effect of a gold movement there depended on the reaction of the banking system to a change in its reserves; and in so far as a given change in reserves called for a *multiple* change in the bank liabilities, the process normally involved a change in the terms on which the banks lent, or the discount rate.

Humes
model

Δ in reserves = Δ discount etc

Economica, February 1937, pp. 18–32.

We shall not be concerned here to discuss the part played by price and income changes in maintaining international equilibrium. Our concern is with the process by which these price and income changes were brought about. As there appears to be some difference of opinion as to which points in the foregoing explanation are really important, it may be well to state that in this discussion the two following will be regarded as crucial:

1 The view that general changes in incomes and prices only occur as a result of changes in the volume of circulation. This may be termed the Quantity Theory assumption. (It will be noticed that if the Quantity Theory means this, it is not a truism.)

2 The view that in a modern economy these changes in circulation are brought about by changes in discount or interest rates. This means of course that the maintenance of the gold standard requires from time to time a disturbance in the processes of saving and investing in particular countries: if true, it provides an important argument against the gold standard system.[1]

It may be noticed that I do not regard the part played by actual gold movements as crucial. Already, before the War, foreign balances were coming to be used as reserves in place of gold, and some writers make a great deal of this change. It may certainly have had the effect of making adjustments more 'one-sided', but apart from this, it does not appear to me to necessitate any important modification of the theory, at any rate so long as the exchange reserves are treated in the same way as gold reserves. I shall however have something to say about the practice of basing money on foreign balances in one particular connection (see below).

*

It is noteworthy that Taussig, although in a way he has been the leading exponent of the classical explanation, has often warned his readers that the evidence gives the theory very doubtful support. Further, I think it may be said that on the whole the attempts at historical verification undertaken by the younger members of the Harvard School have increased rather than diminished the doubts. (This is least true perhaps of Professor Viner's book, but Viner does not share my view as to which points are 'crucial'.)

In fairness, certain circumstances may be mentioned which would tend in any case to make verification difficult.

1 The distribution of newly mined gold obviated to a certain extent the necessity for gold movements between non-producing countries. A country

could suffer a *relative* loss of gold through failing to acquire its normal share in the new supplies.

2 Similarly, in the adjustment of price relations between two countries, it would not be necessary for their discount rates actually to move in *opposite* directions, if there were at the same time a general upward or downward trend in rates.

But when account has been taken of these, certain difficulties remain.

1 The point which has troubled Taussig most is that in many cases the adjustments appeared to have occurred more immediately and with less friction than his theory would lead one to expect.

2 The dependence of international price adjustments on national discount policies raises the question whether discrepancies in interest rates might not lead to inconvenient capital movements. This has often been discussed as a theoretical issue. The evidence collected by Professors Andrew and Beach, to which further reference will be made presently, appears to show that in fact gold movements to and from both the United States and Britain before the War are more easily connected with relations of interest rates than with relations of price levels.

3 The prewar policy of certain leading central banks hardly seems to have been conformable to the requirements of a gold standard operating in the manner envisaged by the classical explanation. It is notorious that both the Bank of France and the National Bank of Belgium consistently pursued the policy of keeping their discount rates low and steady.[2] It may be said that the Bank of France was able to avoid varying its discount rates because the country was only on a limping standard. But this point cannot be substantiated unless it can be shown that the exchange value of the franc fell below the gold export point for appreciable periods. Other special circumstances might be adduced in the case of France (e.g. the limited importance of credit money, in later years the size of the metallic reserve). But it is doubtful if they would apply to Belgium also, and the fact that both these countries were able to maintain their exchange parities through changing circumstances, while their discount rates only followed the movements of rates elsewhere in a diminished degree, is certainly remarkable. The case of the Bank of England is different, for that institution certainly did have to take active measures, including the variation of its discount rate, for the protection of its gold reserve. But the object of discount policy may be to control capital movements, and the recent studies of Mr Sayers and Professor Beach show that the Bank often preferred other devices to the use of its discount rate in order to avoid disturbing internal credit conditions. In fact the Bank seems to have been

reluctant to raise the discount rate unless internal trade could stand it or actually needed a curb (i.e. from the point of view of internal stability). In short, then, none of these central banks really observed 'the rules of the game'; and yet the system worked.

4 It is sometimes asked why a different process of adjustment should be necessary in the relations between different countries from that which may be supposed to operate in the relations between different parts of the same country. The fairly obvious answer is that within any country, at any rate if it has a unitary banking system, the common money in the hands of the public can be shifted from one part to another, whereas between countries direct monetary transfers mean movements of the *reserves* on which a multiple superstructure of credit is based. But on this view Scotland with its separate banking system should be related to England as a foreign country rather than as a different part of Britain. Admittedly the reserves of the Scottish banks take the form of London balances rather than gold holdings. But is there evidence that price equilibrium between England and Scotland is maintained by the Scottish banks varying their interest rates in response to changes in their reserves?

These are my main grounds for doubts, but two other cases may be mentioned which, although they do not belong to the prewar working of the gold standard, none the less serve to test the theory underlying the classical view on that matter.

5 I am told, by Mr Ashton, that serious difficulties were often experienced in Lancashire in the late eighteenth century owing to the shortage of local means of payment, and that various expedients had to be resorted to in consequence. Now according to orthodox theory the local price level should have adjusted itself to the actual supply of means of payment; and if this meant that the price level was unduly low in relation to other parts of the country, the favourable balance of trade should have brought in supplies of money to raise the price level. But this did not happen apparently; the local price level was determined more directly by the national system of prices. Might not the national price level be similarly determined by the world system of prices?

6 The fall of prices in France in 1920, when the franc was still inconvertible, presents an interesting case. In the spring of that year certain measures of a deflationary tendency were adopted. The discount rate of the Bank of France was raised; taxation was increased to improve the budgetary position; and provision was made for annual reductions of the indebtedness of the government to the central bank. I do not think it can be denied that there was a connection between these measures and the ensuing fall in prices. It is possible to argue that the fall was simply the result of internal deflation. On the other hand, having regard to the magnitude of the effect and the comparative

inefficacy of similar deflationary measures at other times, it may be more plausible to connect the fall in French prices with the fall in world gold prices which took place at the same time. On this view the significance of the French measures was that by restoring confidence in the currency for a time they prevented the exchange from depreciating; with the exchanges comparatively steady, the French price system became subject to world influences. This at any rate is the interpretation favoured by most French economists.

*

The crucial points in the classical explanation were challenged long ago by the writers of the Banking School. But the members of this school were unable to offer a satisfactory alternative explanation; and it is mainly the absence of this, I think, which accounts for the continued predominance of the classical view. The purpose of what follows is to provide an alternative hypothesis.

We may begin with a line of thought first developed, I believe, by Mr Harrod in his *International Economics*.[3] Mr Harrod points out that a decline in the effective demand for a country's exports automatically curtails the incomes of the exporters, and through these, the incomes of those who sell to the exporters, and so on. Further it is shown that, in the absence of a counteracting influence, the contraction of incomes must proceed just far enough to restore the balance of trade; for the contracting tendency is only exhausted by people being induced to economize on foreign trade goods (imports or home-produced goods which can find an export market). A counteracting influence is present, however, in the fact that individuals will reduce their money balances, either because they wish for a time to maintain their expenditure despite the reduction of their incomes, or because with reduced incomes they no longer consider it necessary to keep so large a balance. This 'setting free' of money tends to restore incomes; and incomes not being contracted sufficiently, there is a deficit in the balance of trade and gold flows out. A recent German writer, Dr Maier, treats gold flows somewhat similarly as a result of an excess of money balances at the equilibrium level of incomes.[4]

Whether one regards gold flows as the result of 'setting free' balances rather than as the direct consequence of the falling off of exports, also whether or not one agrees with Mr Harrod that the first process of income contraction is *instantaneous*, both seem to depend on a matter of convention. If one adopts the convention that incomes are earned and spent in the same period, these views appear to be correct; if one adopts the convention that incomes are earned in one period (Mr Robertson's 'day') and spent in the next, they are not. But there is no need to pursue this point. In relation to our practical issues, this analysis seems at first sight to make very little difference. So far as the final adjustment of incomes is brought about by gold flows (or for that matter by changes in exchange reserves), the process may be that outlined in the classical theory; gold flows affect reserves and the credit system has to adapt itself to changes in reserves by altering the terms of lending.

But there is another possibility which gives this analysis great practical significance. This is that as each industry, from the export industry onwards, experiences a decline in the value of its output, there will be a reduction of bank loans and a cancellation of credit money. The balances which would otherwise be released to restore incomes would thus be extinguished and the 'counteracting influence' noticed above removed. Gold movements and changes in reserves will occur, but they may on this view be accompaniments and not causes of the change in the volume of credit. The argument does not of course show that the changes in the volume of credit and in reserves will naturally tend to be proportional to one another. This may not matter if there is some flexibility in reserve ratios; or the reserves may be adjusted to the credit volume, as suggested in the next section. In any case the extent to which the reserves control the volume of credit is on this view greatly reduced.

The significant point of difference between this and the classical view is that according to this the change in the volume of credit comes about, as it were, spontaneously, without being induced by a change in interest rates. Some might seek to minimize this point by arguing that in these circumstances the 'natural rate' of interest falls, so that the maintenance of the same 'money' rate is equivalent to a rise. Certainly, to use the old terminology, investment falls short of savings. But I think there is a difference between a change in the demand for loans due to a change in the aggregate demand for products, and one due to a change in the relationship between the market rate of interest and the marginal productivity of capital schedule. Take the case of an increase in the marginal productivity of capital, interest rates remaining the same (or a fall in interest rates, marginal productivity remaining the same); and assume, as is most appropriate in applying the natural rate of interest concept, that resources are fully employed. The outcome will be an increase of borrowing for the purpose of making production more capitalistic, and, assuming no change in voluntary saving, an immediate distortion, in the Austrian terminology, of the structure of production. On the other hand, if borrowing is increased as a result of an increase in aggregate effective demand from outside, it is the direction of the new demands which will determine the re-allocation of resources, and the bidding up of the prices of factors and materials by the borrowers will effect primarily a *horizontal* change in industry. It is true that this is not the whole story. Since factories and instruments of production are often not convertible from one purpose to another, the expansion of any industry, even if accompanied by the decline of another, is likely to call for new investment, to raise, in short, the schedule of marginal productivity of capital. Hence if interest rates remain the same, there will be some distortion of the structure of production, not so much because the capital developments in connection with the expanding industry are inappropriate as because there will be insufficient curtailment of capital development in other directions. When this concession is made, however, I think there remains a substantial difference between the two types of case. And apparently it is not necessary to make a corresponding concession in the case of a decline in aggregate demand. It is true that in this case the production of capital goods is likely to fall off more than that of consumption goods during the period in which total output is declining, because all changes in total output tend to be reflected disproportionately in the production of capital goods. But this is analytically distinct from the kind of distortion envisaged in the Austrian theory. Once costs have been adjusted and full employment regained, the change in the direction of employment which is likely to be involved will have the same effect as in the opposite case (an increase in foreign demand) in raising the demand for capital. Hence it cannot be said that in this case the failure to *lower* interest rates introduces 'structural distortion'.

In any case, leaving aside these abstruse questions of capital theory, adjustments in the volume of credit through changes in demand at the same rate of interest are likely to be more immediate than those induced by changes in the rate, and the complications resulting from discrepancies of interest rates between countries are avoided.

*

Our theory must also take account of the possibility that gold movements, instead of being the determinants of the supply of money, may themselves be determined by monetary requirements. According to the strict quantity theory the demand for money is always adjusted to the supply through changes in its value, and monetary requirements must be the same as the actual supply. I do not need to discuss whether this is true for an isolated community; the suggestion is that in a regime of fixed exchange rates the monetary requirements of a particular country may be altered by changes in prices or trade activity independently of any prior change in the supply of money. If then the national supply of money is inelastic, owing, for example, to reserve requirements, an increase in monetary requirements will tend to raise interest rates, by curtailing the offer of funds for investment or increasing the demand for loans if the need is for larger bank balances, by curtailing bank reserves if the need is for cash in the narrower sense. Higher interest rates may promote a gold inflow through a movement of short-term capital. (The same relationship between price levels, interest rates and monetary requirements can be seen, I think, in seasonal movements. Seasonal variations in monetary requirements appear to affect interest rates more than price levels.)

Evidence of this kind of relationship between gold movements and the monetary system is provided by the work of Professor A. Piatt Andrew and Professor Beach on the cyclical gold movements of the United States and the United Kingdom respectively. In both cases it has been found that gold flowed in during periods of active trade and rising prices, and flowed out in the opposite phase of the cycle. These facts are explicable on the orthodox theory only on the assumption that the countries concerned lagged behind the rest of the world in cyclical movements. It is highly improbable that this was the case with both the United States and the United Kingdom. The more reasonable interpretation is that these gold movements depended in the first instance on the relation of interest rates. Further evidence of concomitant movements of gold into and out of internal circulation confirms the view that it was the monetary requirements determined by a given price level which provided the underlying cause of the international gold movements. Presumably the countries which acted as the counter-parties to Britain and America in these movements were in a position to allow a considerable fluctuation in their gold reserves.

In the foregoing argument it is not intended to deny that the rate of interest exercised a controlling influence over the movement of prices and the general course of the trade cycle. High interest rates were doubtless of crucial importance in bringing booms to an end. What is contended is that in these particular cases the raising of interest rates did not have the effect of producing a *relative* reduction of prices in certain countries. High rates in London led rather to a world fall in prices, partly because of the sympathetic movement of rates elsewhere, partly because of the effect on British entrepôt trade and British long-term foreign investment.

The restriction of the argument to certain cases is also important. Professor Beach's study of British gold movements relates to the period from 1880 to 1914. It is possible that he would have obtained different results if he had taken an earlier period. The data have not, I think, been systematically studied, but one has the impression that in several of the earlier nineteenth-century booms the expansion of credit in England outpaced any similar movement in other countries, with the result that there occurred an adverse balance of payments and a foreign drain. (I gather from his review in the *Statistical Journal* that Mr Hawtrey considers that this may sometimes have happened in the course of the period studied by Professor Beach.) This is all in accordance with the classical line of thought, but it is also reconcilable with our alternative hypothesis. According to the argument of the preceding section, a change in the direction of demand which tends to turn the balance of trade against a country exercises at the same time a corrective deflationary influence. In the case of an inappropriate increase in home demand due to internal credit expansion, the effect on the balance of trade – the 'leakage' of demand abroad – should curtail the tendency for demand to expand cumulatively. But if the original impulse to credit expansion continues to operate, the trade balance may remain unfavourable; and gold may continue to flow out until the loss of reserves compels action to be taken. If the markets of the country are very closely linked with foreign markets, the loss of reserves by the ordinary banks should lead to an almost immediate correction of the expansive impulse, except in so far as a sympathetic movement is generated in the other countries; for example there would appear to be little danger of a persistent tendency for credit to expand faster in Canada than in the United States. On the other hand, if the independent home market is relatively large, the original expansion may go on for some time and give rise to secondary expansions, before the full effect on the balance of payments is felt. In this case then there is need for anticipatory action and central bank intervention may be called for.

Our argument does not dispose, therefore, of the need for a national regulation of credit in order to prevent or correct an undue expansion in comparison with other countries. This regulation involves, directly or indirectly, the adjustment of interest rates; but in this case it can be said, I think, that the money rates are merely being kept in line with the natural rate,[5] and any movement of capital which results can be ascribed to an increase in the demand for capital.

*

There remains to be considered the process of adjustment in connection with capital movements, assuming that the importing country requires additional real capital and not merely additional supplies of means of payment, as in the case considered at the beginning of the previous section.[6]

A transfer of capital involves in itself a redistribution of spending power, and this is likely to be accompanied by a change in the direction of demand. This is the basis for the view that the 'transfer' process involves a change in the terms of trade. So far as this happens, there will have to be a change in the relationship between the price and income structures of the countries concerned; the factors of production will have become more valuable in some countries, less valuable in others. But this change will be of the same kind as that required by any other change in the direction of demand, and all that has been said above about the process of adjustment applies equally here.

The redistribution of spending power itself, however, apart from any change in the direction of demand and the terms of trade, may require a redistribution of money or means of payment. This is a point with respect to which there are certain differences of opinion. Some writers (Iversen, White, for example) hold that there must first be a redistribution of money, although it may be only a temporary one, in order that the redistribution of spending power shall take place at all. Others (including the present writer) think that the making of a foreign loan or investment itself shifts spending power *pro tanto*, but that this shift requires to be *accompanied* by a monetary redistribution if the process of transfer is to be smooth.[7] Nurkse would apparently reject both these views and see no necessity for monetary changes apart from changes in the terms of trade.

Assuming that the primary shift in spending power does call for a monetary transfer, the question arises as to how this may be brought about. Most obviously it may be effected by a movement of gold; and if gold reserves are ample in the lending country, the process may be a simple and natural one. The lending community makes its surrender of wealth to the borrowers partly in the form of money, transferring this by means of a movement of gold. But if the gold movement necessitates a multiple contraction of credit in order to preserve the minimum reserve ratio in the lending country (accompanied perhaps by a multiple expansion of credit in the borrowing country), several complications arise. The change in money supplies will be excessive: interest rates will be distorted to bring about the credit changes: and the changes in interest rates will impede the international movement of capital. In some cases, of course, interest rates may be raised in the lending country with the deliberate object of checking the movement of capital and gold abroad. It is when interest rates are raised in these ways and not as simple consequence of the transference of real capital, that it may be said that the demand for capital abroad has the effect of raising rates above the natural level.

There is, however, another way in which these monetary transfers may be brought about: that is, by creating additional money in the borrowing country on the basis of money held in the lending country. There is evidence, I think, that this was commonly done by the banks in many of the countries in which Britain invested – the Dominions and British colonies, the South American countries and Japan. The lending country is in this way spared the loss of gold, yet the borrowing country gets increased supplies of money. If the banks in the borrowing country treat their foreign (or overseas) balances as being exactly equivalent to gold reserves, and proceed to make them the basis for a multiple expansion of their notes or deposits, the complications mentioned above will not, it is true, be entirely avoided. But they may be content to allow their foreign balances to increase relatively to their deposits; and I believe that the evidence again shows that the banks in the countries mentioned did commonly act in this way, restrained presumably by some instinctive recognition that any greater expansion of credit would soon have to be reversed.

The character of the process is also affected by whether the banks of the borrowing country continue to hold their external funds in liquid form or convert them into interest-earning assets held in the lending centre. The ideal arrangement would appear to be for these banks to create local deposits of an amount exactly equal to their increased external balances and to hold these balances completely idle. This would give the closest possible approximation to the interregional shifts of circulation which take place within any one country. But the possibility that the external balances, instead of being 'sterilized', will be invested, must be reckoned with. What this means is that spending power will not be directly reduced in the lending country by the full amount of the foreign (overseas) loans; that part of the surrender of wealth which would otherwise have taken the form of a surrender of money will not take place at all. If we can assume that all other countries (not merely the borrowing country) are prepared to base their money on that of the lending country, this failure to contract spending power in the latter can be compensated by a greater expansion of credit in the borrowing country, leading to a certain expansion in 'neutral' countries also. That is to say, relative values will be the same as in the 'ideal' process but money prices will be on a higher level. In this inflationary form the process of adaptation will probably be easier at the time of an increase of foreign lending, but correspondingly greater difficulties will be experienced in the debtor countries when the flow of one-sided payments has to be reversed, that is, when debt repayments and interest charges come to exceed new loans. So far as the condition mentioned above is not fulfilled and there are neutral or third-party countries (possibly also some borrowers) which are not willing to base their money on that of the lending country, it seems inevitable that the latter should lose gold.

*

It must be emphasized that the suggestions made in the preceding discussion – particularly the suggestion of a more direct adaptation of the volume of credit to what is required by international price relations than is contemplated in the classical theory – are no more than tentative. They provide a hypothetical view of the working of the gold standard which is more in accordance with my own impressions with regard to the historical facts than the accepted view; but it is admitted that my view requires a more exhaustive testing, with regard both to the cases in which the gold standard has worked successfully and to those in which it has broken down, before it can claim acceptance.

In the meantime it may be useful to indicate certain consequences which would follow if my view were correct.

1 Since gold movements (or more generally, changes in reserves) and discount-rate adjustments are displaced from their central position in the process of international price adjustment, the question of 'observing the rules of the game', as this is ordinarily understood, loses much of its importance. Indeed in some cases it will appear desirable that gold movements (charges in reserves) should not be accompanied by a multiple change in the volume of credit money;[8] and if the ordinary banks maintain a constant ratio between their liabilities and their balances at the central bank, this may require

some offsetting of gold movements by the latter. With respect to discount-rate variations, it is possible that the abnormal size of international short-term capital movements in recent years has been due in part to the excessive use of this method of regulating the international position.

2 Whilst central bank policy is still important in certain respects, a new importance is given to the policy of the ordinary banks. If it is essential that the volume of credit should speedily adapt itself to changes in trade conditions, a new justification is found for the otherwise rather discredited theory that notes and deposits should be covered by 'self-liquidating' loans. (Perhaps the instincts of the Banking School were right on this point, too.) But the restriction of loans to the provision of working capital is not enough. For, as the reader has probably been objecting, it is quite possible that manufacturers faced with a declining demand will seek to increase their working capital in the form of stocks of unsold goods, at least for a time; and so far as the banks allow them to borrow for this purpose, the volume of credit will change in the wrong direction. (It is similarly possible that an improvement in trade will lead at first to a repayment of bank loans, but this is not very likely unless stocks have been abnormally large.) The behaviour of the banks in face of changing trade prospects is therefore of critical importance in my view, and what matters is not so much the rates of interest which they charge as their willingness to lend at all in certain cases. It would seem more probable that the banks would behave in the right way (from this point of view) if they are faced with gradual changes than if they are confronted suddenly with a situation seriously out of adjustment, e.g. by stabilization of the currency at too high a value.

3 It has not been found necessary to refer in the preceding discussion to the question of income and cost rigidities. This only becomes relevant if we are considering not merely the rectification of the balance of payments but also the maintenance of full employment. One of the factors which is often supposed to be responsible for wage rigidity – the payment of unemployment allowances from public funds – may, however, have a bearing on the former issue. So far as the maintenance of the expenditure of the workers in depressed industries is not mere transfer of expenditure, it must tend both to affect the volume of imports directly and to impair the cumulative process of income contraction.

Notes

1 cf. C.H. Walker, 'The working of the pre-war gold standard', *Review of Economic Studies*, vol. I, no. 3.
2 Except in the case of the former for a period in the 1850s and 1860s.
3 Roy Harrod, *International Economics*, London, Nisbet, 1933. Mr Harrod has

developed his ideas further in *The Trade Cycle*, Oxford, Clarendon Press, 1936. The present article was completed before I had opportunity to study his later work – hence the absence of any reference to it in the text.

4 Karl Freidrich Maier, *Goldwanderungen*, Jena, G. Fischer, 1935.

5 I admit that in the case in which there is general unemployment of productive factors, this does not mean any more than the rate which equalizes saving and investment at the existing level of incomes. But at least the maintenance of this rate is different from fixing a rate at which there is (or would be) an excess of saving with the existing level of incomes.

6 The transition which has already been made to the present tense will warn the reader of the hypothetical character of the argument.

7 See my article in *Economica* of February 1936.

8 This apart from the obvious case of temporary movements of gold.

4

How the gold standard worked, 1880–1913[1]

Donald N. McCloskey and J. Richard Zecher *

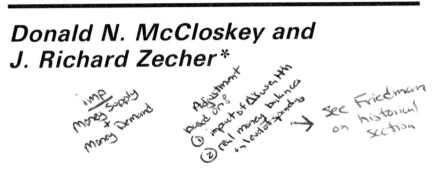

The monetary theory and its implications for the gold standard

Each intellectual generation since the mercantilists has revised or refined the understanding of how the balance of payments is kept in equilibrium under a system of fixed exchange rates, and all these understandings find a place in the historical literature on the gold standard of the late nineteenth century. It is difficult, therefore, to locate the orthodox view on how the gold standard worked, for it is many views. If one can find historical and economic writings describing the gold standard (and other systems of fixed exchange rates) in the manner of Hume, as a price-specie-flow mechanism, involving changes in the level of prices, one can also find writings describing it in the manner of Marshall, involving changes in the interest rate, or of Taussig, involving changes in the relative price of exportables and importables, or of Ohlin, involving changes in income. The theoretical jumble is made still more confusing by a number of factual anomalies uncovered lately.[2] Among other difficulties with the orthodox views, it has been found that the gold standard, even in its heyday, was a standard involving the major currencies as well as gold itself, and that few, if any, central banks followed the putative 'rules of the game'.

This essay reinterprets the gold standard by applying the monetary theory

*From Jacob A. Frenkel and Harry G. Johnson (eds.), *The Monetary Approach to the Balance of Payments*, London, Allen & Unwin, 1976, pp. 184–6, 192–208, abridged.

of the balance of payments to the experience of the two most important countries on it, America and Britain. Before explaining, testing and using the theory in detail, it will be useful to indicate a few of the ways in which accepting it will change the interpretation of the gold standard of the late nineteenth century. The most direct implication is that central bankers did not have control over the variables over which they and their historians have believed they had control. The theory assumes that interest rates and prices are determined on world markets, and therefore that the central bank of a small country has little influence over them and the central bank of a large country has influence over them only by way of its influence over the world as a whole.

A case in point is the Bank of England. It is often asserted, as Keynes put it, that

> During the latter half of the nineteenth century the influence of London on credit conditions throughout the world was so predominant that the Bank of England could almost have claimed to be the conductor of the international orchestra. By modifying the terms on which she was prepared to lend, aided by her own readiness to vary the volume of her gold reserves and the unreadiness of other central banks to vary the volumes of theirs, she could to a large extent determine the credit conditions prevailing elsewhere.[3]

When this musical metaphor is examined in the light of the monetary theory it loses much of its charm. If it is supposed, as in the monetary theory, that the world's economy was unified by arbitrage, and if it is supposed further that the level of prices in the world market was determined, other things equal, by the amount of money existing in the world, it follows that the Bank's potential influence on prices (and perhaps through prices on interest rates) depended simply on its power to accumulate or disburse gold and other reserves available to support the world's supply of money. By raising the interest rate (the Bank Rate) at which it would lend to brokers of commercial bills, the Bank could induce the brokers or whoever else in the British capital market was caught short of funds to seek loans abroad, bringing gold into the country and eventually into the vaults of the Bank. If it merely issued bank notes to pay for the gold the reserves available to support the supply of money would be unchanged, for Bank of England notes were used both at home and abroad as reserves. Only by decreasing the securities and increasing the gold it held – an automatic result when it discouraged brokers from selling more bills to the Bank and allowed the bills it already held to come to maturity – could the Bank exert a net effect on the world's reserves. In other words, a rise in the Bank Rate was effective only to the extent that it was accompanied by an open market operation, that is, by a shift in the assets of the Bank of England out of securities and into gold. The amounts of these two assets held by the Bank, then, provide extreme limits on the influence of the Bank on the world's money supply. Had the Bank in 1913 sold off all the securities held in its banking department it would have decreased world reserves by only 0.6 per cent; had it sold off all the gold in its issue department, it would have increased world reserves by only 0.5 per cent.[4] Apparently the Bank was no more than the second violinist, not to say the triangle player, in the world's orchestra. The result hinges on the assumption of the monetary theory that the world's economy was unified, much as each nation's economy is assumed to be in any theory of the gold standard. If the assumption is correct the historical inference is that the Bank of England had no more independent influence over the prices and interest rates it faced than, say, the First National Bank of Chicago has over the prices and interest rates it faces, and for the same reason.

A related inference from the monetary theory is that the United Kingdom, the United States, and other countries on the gold standard had little influence over their money supplies. Since money, like other commodities, could be imported and exported, the supply of money in a country could adjust to its demand and the demand would depend on the country's income and on prices and interest rates determined in the world market. The creation of money in a little country would have little influence on these determinants of demand and in consequence little influence over the amount actually supplied. How 'little' America and Britain were depends on how large they were relative to the world market, and in a world of full employment and well-functioning markets the relevant magnitude is simply the share of the nation's supply of money in the world's supply. One must depend on an assumption that the money owned by citizens of a country was in rough proportion to its income, for the historical study of the world's money supply is still in its infancy.[5] In 1913 America and Britain together earned about 40 per cent of the world's income, America alone 27 per cent.[6] A rise in the American money supply of 10 per cent, then, would raise the world's money supply on the order of 2.7 per cent; the comparable British figure is half the American. Clearly, in the jargon of international economics, America and Britain were not literally 'small countries'. Yet 2.7 per cent is far from the 10 per cent implied by the usual model, that of a closed monetary system, and the British figure is far enough from it to make it unnecessary for most purposes in dealing with the British experience to look closely into the worldwide impact of British policy.

Finally, the monetary theory implies that it matters little whether or not central banks under the gold standard played conscientiously the 'rules of the game', that is, the rule that a deficit in the balance of payments should be accompanied by domestic policies to deflate the economy. The theory argues that neither gold flows nor domestic deflation have effects on prevailing prices, interest rates and incomes. The inconsequentiality of the rules of the game may perhaps explain why they were ignored by most central bankers in the period of the gold standard, in deed if not in words, with no dire effects on the stability of the system. [...]

Did international markets work well?

If arbitrage – or, more precisely, a close correlation among national price levels brought about by the ordinary working of markets – can be shown to characterize the international economy of the late nineteenth century, many of the conclusions of the monetary theory will follow directly and the rest will gain in plausibility. In the monetary theory, the international market short-circuits the effects of domestic policy on American prices, and the expansion of the domestic supply of money spills directly into a deficit in the balance of payments.

It is essential, therefore, to examine the evidence for this short-circuiting. As a criterion of its effectiveness, we use the size of the contemporaneous correlations among changes in the prices of the same commodities in different countries. We have chosen a sample of the voluminous information on prices for examination here.[7] The statistical power of the tests is not as high as one might wish, for even if two nations shared no markets they could none the less exhibit common movements in prices if they shared similar experiences of climate, technological change, income growth or any of the other determinants of prices. In the long run, indeed, the other theories of the balance of payments imply some degree of correlation among national prices. For this reason we have resisted the temptation to improve the correlations by elaborate experimentation with lags and have concentrated on contemporaneous correlations, that is, on correlations among prices in the same year. If international markets worked as sluggishly as the other theories assume, there would be little reason to expect contemporaneous correlations to be high.

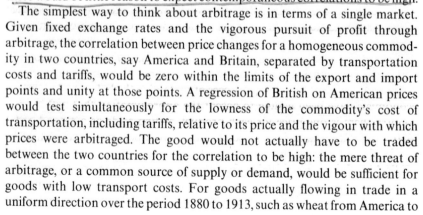

The simplest way to think about arbitrage is in terms of a single market. Given fixed exchange rates and the vigorous pursuit of profit through arbitrage, the correlation between price changes for a homogeneous commodity in two countries, say America and Britain, separated by transportation costs and tariffs, would be zero within the limits of the export and import points and unity at those points. A regression of British on American prices would test simultaneously for the lowness of the commodity's cost of transportation, including tariffs, relative to its price and the vigour with which prices were arbitraged. The good would not actually have to be traded between the two countries for the correlation to be high: the mere threat of arbitrage, or a common source of supply or demand, would be sufficient for goods with low transport costs. For goods actually flowing in trade in a uniform direction over the period 1880 to 1913, such as wheat from America to

Britain, one would expect the correlation to be perfect and the slope of the corresponding regression to be unity, no matter what the cost of transport or the level of tariffs, so long as these did not change. They both did change, of course, as exemplified by the failure of the German price of wheat to fall as far as the British or American during the 1880s, as the Germans imposed protective duties on wheat imports.[8] None the less, the average correlation among the changes in American, British and German prices of wheat is high, about 0.78. A regression of the annual change in British prices on the change in American prices (Britain had no tariffs on wheat, but the cost of ocean transport was falling sharply in the period) yields the following result (all the variables here and elsewhere in this section are measured as annual absolute changes; the figures below the coefficients in parentheses are standard errors; the levels of the variables have been converted to an index in which the average levels are equal to one).[9]

$$BWT = 0.0076 + 0.646\,AWT \qquad R^2 = 0.58$$
$$(0.0012)\ \ (0.102) \qquad\qquad D.-W. = 2.02$$

One would expect errors in the independent variable to affect this and the later regressions, biasing the slope towards zero (there were changes in the source of the American wheat price, for example, and after 1890 it is a New York price alone). The value of 0.646 would be a lower bound on the true slope and the value implied by a regression of the American on the British price (1.124) an upper bound. The two bounds bracket reasonably closely the value to be expected theoretically, namely, 1.0, and the constants in both regressions (which represent the trend in the dependent price over time) are insignificantly different from zero. Not surprisingly, in short, wheat appears to have had a unified world market in the late nineteenth century; *a fortiori*, so did gold, silver, copper, diamonds, racehorses and fine art.

This conclusion can be reinforced from another direction. For wheat the reinforcement is unnecessary, for few would doubt the international character of the wheat market, but it is useful to develop here the line of argument. Because of transport costs, information costs and other impediments to a perfect correlation among changes in national prices, any use of the notion of a perfectly unified market must be an approximation, within one country as well as between two countries. For purposes of explaining the balance of payments economists have been willing to accept the approximation that within each country there is one price for each product, setting aside as a second-order matter the indisputable lack of perfect correlation between price changes in California and Massachusetts or between price changes in Cornwall and Midlothian. It is reasonable, therefore, to use the level of the contemporaneous correlation between the prices of a good in different regions within a country as a standard against which to judge the unity of the market for that good between different countries. If the correlations between the prices of wheat in America, Britain and Germany were no lower than those between the prices of wheat in, say, different parts of Germany, there would be no grounds for distinguishing between the degree of unity in the national German market and in the international market for wheat. This was in fact the case. The average correlation between changes in the prices of wheat in pairs of German cities (Berlin, Breslau, Frankfurt, Konigsberg, Leipzig, Lindau and Mannheim) from 1881 to 1912 was 0.85, quite close to the average correlation for the three countries over the same period of 0.78.

One could proceed in this fashion through all individual prices, but a shorter route to the same objective is to examine correlations across countries between pairs of aggregate price indexes. Contrary to the intuition embodied in this thought, however, there is no guarantee, at any rate none that we have been able to discover, that the correlation of the indexes is an unbiased estimator of the average degree of correlation among the individual prices or, for that matter, that it is biased in any particular direction.[10] In other words, barriers to trade could be high or low in each individual market without the aggregate correlation necessarily registering these truths. None the less, putting these doubts to one side, we will trust henceforth to the intuition.

The pioneers of the method of index numbers, Laspeyres, Jevons and others writing in the middle of the nineteenth century, produced indexes of wholesale prices – believable indexes of retail prices began to be produced only in the 1890s and implicit GNP deflators, of course, much later – and in consequence wholesale price indexes dominated empirical work on the balance of payments in the formative years of the theory. The contemporaneous correlation between annual changes in British and American wholesale prices 1880–1913 is 0.66, high enough in view of the differences in weights in the indexes and in view of the low correlation of annual changes implied by the lags operating in the orthodox theories to lend support to the postulate of a unified world market.

It is at this point, however, that supporters of the orthodox theory begin to quarrel with the argument, as did Taussig with those bold enough to suggest that world markets in more than merely traded goods were integrated in the late nineteenth century, or as did the many doubters of the theory of purchasing power parity with those who used wholesale prices to indicate the appropriate rates of exchange after World War I. The standard objection has been that wholesale price indexes are biased samples from the distribution of correlations because they consist largely of easily traded goods, ignoring nontraded services and underrepresenting nontraded goods. A large lower tail of the distribution, it is said, is left off, leading to a false impression that national price levels are closely correlated.

A point that must be made at once, however, is that traded goods, in the sense of goods actually traded and goods identical to those actually traded, were not a small proportion of national income. Historians and economists have usually thought of the openness of economies in terms of the ratio of actual exports or imports to national income, and have inferred that the United States, with a ratio of exports to national income of about 0.07 in the late nineteenth century, was relatively isolated from the influence of international prices and that the United Kingdom, with a ratio of 0.28, was relatively open to it. Yet in both countries consumption of tradable goods, defined as all goods that figured in the import and export lists, was on the order of half of national income.[11] If any substantial part of the national consumption or production of wheat, coal or cloth entered international markets in which the country in question was a small supplier or demander, the prices of these items at home would be determined exogenously by prices abroad. Wholesale indexes, if they do indeed consist chiefly of traded goods, are not so unrepresentative of all of national income as might be supposed.

But what of the other, nontradable half of national income? Surely, as James Angell wrote in 1926, 'for non-traded articles there is of course no direct equalisation [of price] at all'.[12] The operative word in this assertion is 'direct', for without it the assertion is incorrect. The price of a good in one country is constrained not only by the direct limits of transport costs to and from world markets but by the indirect constraints arising from the good's substitutability for other goods in consumption or production. This was clear to Bertil Ohlin, who asked,

> To what extent are interregional discrepancies in home market prices kept within narrow limits not only through the potential trade in these goods that would come into existence if interregional price differences exceeded the costs of transfer, but also through the actual trade in *other* goods?[13]

It is not surprising to find Ohlin asking such a question, for the analytical issue is identical to the one that gave birth to that errant child of the Heckscher–Ohlin theory, factor–price equalization. The price of the milk used as much as the wage of the labour used is affected by the international price of butter and cheese. A rise in the price of a traded good will cause substitutions in production and consumption that will raise the prices of nontraded goods. To put the point more extremely than is necessary for present purposes, in a general equilibrium of prices the fixing of any one price by trade determines all the rest. The adjustment to the real equilibrium of relative prices, which must be achieved eventually, can be slow or quick. The monetary theory assumes that it is quick.

If it were in fact slow, one would expect the contemporaneous correlation between prices for countries on the gold standard to fall sharply as more comprehensive price indexes, embodying nontraded goods, are compared. This is not the case. The correlation between the annual changes in the GNP deflators 1880–1912 for America and Britain is 0.60, to be compared with the correlation for wholesale prices alone of 0.66. The regressions of the annual changes of American on British deflators and British on American were (standard errors in parentheses; levels of the price variables converted to indexes with their averages as the base):

$AP = 0.0002 + 0.961\ BP$ $R^2 = 0.35$, $D.-W. = 1.98$. Standard error
(0.0050) (0.266)   of the regression as a percentage of the average level of the American price $= 2.5\%$

$BP = 0.0017 + 0.33\ AP$ $R^2 = 0.34$, $D.-W. = 1.92$. Standard error
(0.0028) (0.089)   of the regression as a percentage of the average level of the British price $= 1.4\%$

The correlations of the German GNP deflator with the American (0.40) and the British (0.45) are considerably lower, but this may be simply a reflection of the inevitable frailties of Walther Hoffman's pioneering effort to produce such a deflator, or, perhaps, a reflection of the sharp rises in German tariffs. More countries have retail price indexes (generally with weights from working-class budgets) than have reliable GNP deflators, and these statistics tell a story that is equally encouraging for the postulate of arbitrage. The correlation matrix of annual changes in retail prices for the United States, the United Kingdom, Germany, France and Sweden is shown in table 4.1. The British–American correlation (0.57) is again not markedly below the correlation of the wholesale indexes, despite the importance of such nontraded goods as housing in the retail indexes.[14]

The correlation of American with British retail prices is probably not attributable to the trade in food offsetting a lower correlation between nontraded goods, for the simple correlation between American and British food prices in the years for which it is available (1894–1913) is lower, 0.49 compared with 0.57. Against this encouraging finding, however, must be put a less encouraging one. The average correlation between the changes in food prices in five regions of the United States (North Atlantic, South Atlantic,

Table 4.1 Simple correlations between annual changes in retail prices, 1880–1912

	USA	UK	Germany	France	Sweden
USA	1.00	0.57	0.28	0.24	0.38
UK		1.00	0.53	0.42	0.57
Germany			1.00	0.45	0.62
France				1.00	0.32
Sweden					1.00

North Central, South Central and the West) for 1891–1913 is very high, 0.87, contrasted with the British–American correlation of only 0.49. If food prices were as well arbitraged between as inside countries the British–American correlation would have to be much higher than it is. Still, even with perfect unity in the market for each item of food, one would not expect countries with substantially different budget shares to exhibit close correlations in the aggregate indexes. The lower correlation between Britain and the United States than between regions of the United States, then, may well reflect international differences of tastes and income rather than lower arbitrage.

If one proceeds in this fashion further in the direction of less traded goods the results continue to be mixed, although on balance giving support to the postulate of unity in world markets. The most obvious nontraded good is labour. The correlation between changes in wages of British and American coal miners 1891–1913 is 0.42 but the correlation between those of British and American farm labourers is only 0.26. Both are lower than the correlations between changes in the wages of the two employments in each country, 0.65 in Britain and 0.53 in America. The correlation between the annual changes in Paul Douglas's index of hourly earnings of union men in American building and the changes in A.L. Bowley's index of wages in British building from 1891 to 1901 is negligible, only 0.10. On the other hand, the average correlation among bricklayers' hourly wages in four cities (Boston, Cincinnati, Cleveland and Philadelphia) selected from the mass of data for 1890–1903 in the 19th Annual Report of the US Commissioner of Labour is only 0.14. The correlations for changes in wages between countries are low, in other words, but there is reason to believe that they are nearly as low within a geographically large country like the United States as well.

The same is true for an unambiguously nontraded commodity, common brick. That it is nontraded, that is, a poor substitute for traded goods, and that it enters into the production of nontraded commodities is evident from the negligible correlation between changes in its average price in Britain and America. Yet from 1894, when the statistics first become available, to 1913, the average correlation between prices of common brick at the plant in seven scattered states of the United States (California, Georgia, Illinois, New York, Ohio, Pennsylvania and Texas) was only 0.11, and even between three states in the same region (New York, Ohio and Pennsylvania) it was only 0.13. This degree of correlation may be taken as an indicator of the correlation between regions of the United States attributable to a common experience of general inflation, technological change and growth of income rather than to the unity of markets. It is small. In any case, common brick is a good at the lower end of the distribution of goods by their correlations, and there is little evidence of greater integration of markets within than between countries.

All these tests can be much expanded and improved, and we plan to do so in later work.[15] What has been established here is that there is a reasonable case, if not at this stage an overwhelming one, for the postulate of integrated commodity markets between the British and American economies in the late nineteenth century, vindicating the monetary theory. There appears to be little reason to treat these two countries on the gold standard differently in their monetary transactions from any two regions within each country.

Money, gold and the balance of payments

If international arbitrage of prices and interest rates was thoroughgoing and if the growth of real income in a country was exogenous to its supply of money, then the country's demand for money can be estimated by relatively straightforward econometric techniques. The balance of payments – identified here with flows of gold – predicted by the monetary theory can then be estimated as the difference between the growth in the country's total predicted demand for money and the growth in its actual domestic supply. If, further, the actual flow of gold closely approximates the flow implied by the estimated change in the demand for money minus the actual change in the domestic supply of money, the monetary theory of the gold standard warrants serious consideration. In fact, to a remarkable degree the monetary theory for the United States and the United Kingdom from 1880 to 1913 passes this final test.

In table 4.2 are presented the average movements of the British and American variables to be explained (the movements, that is, in money supplies and in that part of the money supply attributable to international flows of gold) and the average movements of the variables with which the monetary theory would explain them (the movements in prices, interest rates and incomes affecting the demand for money and the movements in that part of the money supply attributable to domestic forces). The average percentage change in the money supply was decomposed in a merely arithmetical way (described in the footnote to the table) into a part reflecting how the money supply would have behaved if all gold flows into or out of the country had been allowed to affect it (by way of the multiple effects of reserves on the money supply) and a residual reflecting all other influences. Arithmetically speaking, the causes of changes in British and American money supplies differed sharply; virtually all the change in Britain was attributable to international flows of gold while virtually all the change in America was attributable to other, domestic sources of new money. Economically speaking, the differences are less sharp. Although over these three decades on average the rate of change of the money supply was far larger in America than in Britain, the difference is adequately explained in terms of the monetary theory by the faster growth of American income, given the similarity (in accord with the findings of the last

Table 4.2   Average annual rates of change 1882–1913 of American and British money supplies (domestic and international), incomes, prices and interest rates (percentages; standard errors in parentheses)

		United Kingdom	United States
1	Money supply attributable to gold flows	2.22 (2.41)	−0.09 (2.89)
2	Money supply attributable to other influences	0.12 (2.51)	5.77 4.56
3	Total money supply	2.35 (1.78)	5.68 (5.21)
4	Real income	1.84 (2.33)	3.69 (5.35)
5	Implicit price deflator	0.24 (1.75)	0.23 (3.09)
6	Long-term interest rates (absolute change in basis points)	2.9 (2.0)	−2.3 (15.0)

Sources:
Line 1. The rate of change of the money supply attributable to gold flows was calculated as:

$$100 \left[\log \left(M_{t-1} + \frac{M_t}{H_t} R_t \right) - \log M_{t-1} \right]$$

where M is the total money supply, H is 'high-powered money' (M_t/H_t, therefore, is the so-called 'money multiplier') and R is the annual net flow of gold. The figures on money supply and high-powered money for the United Kingdom were taken from Sheppard (1969), p. 16; and for the United States from Friedman and Schwartz (1963), pp. 704–7. The figures on gold flows for the United Kingdom were compiled from Beach (1935), pp. 46ff. These are for England alone, excluding Scotland and Ireland, but there is little doubt that they cover the great bulk of flows into and out of the United Kingdom. Gold flows for the United States are given in US Bureau of the Census (1960), ser. U6.
Line 2 = Line 3 − Line 1.
Line 3. Source as in Line 1.
Line 4. US real gross national product is from Simon Kuznets' worksheets, reported in Lipsey (1963), p. 423; for years before 1889, the Kuznets figure Lipsey used was inferred from Lipsey's ratio of GNP to farm income and his estimate of farm income (pp. 423–4). UK real gross *domestic* product is from Feinstein (1971), appendix table 6, col. 4. Line 5. For the US the figure is from Lipsey (1963), p. 423. For the UK the figure is from Feinstein, appendix table 61, col. 7.
Line 6. The US interest rate is Macauley's unadjusted index number of yields of American railway bonds (US Bureau of the Census, 1960, ser. X332). The UK rate is the yield of consolidated government bonds (consols) in Mitchell (1962), p. 455.

section) in the behaviour of prices and given the relative fall in American interest rates.

So much is apparent from the arithmetic of the British and American experience. To go further one needs a behavioural model explaining the annual balance of payments in terms of the monetary theory. The model is simplicity itself. It begins with a demand function for money, the only behavioural function in the model, asserting that the annual rate of change in the demand for money balances depends on the rates of change of the price level and of real income and on the absolute change in interest rates (asterisks signify rates of change):

$$M_d^* = P^* + f(y^*, \Delta i)$$

And it ends with a domestic money supply function (literally, an identity using the observed money multiplier, as explained in the footnote of table 4.2) and the statement that the money not supplied domestically was supplied through the balance of payments. It is evident that the monetary theory is simply a comparative statics theory of money's supply and demand, in which the balance of payments satisfies demands for money not satisfied by domestic sources.

By virtue of the unity of world markets and the assumed exogeneity of the growth of real income to the supply of money (which is itself a consequence of market unity and the availability of an elastic supply of money abroad), there is no simultaneous equation bias in estimating the demand for money by ordinary least squares. It is convenient to estimate the demand in real terms. The result for the United States 1884–1913 of regressing the rate of change of real balances on the rate of change in real income and the absolute change in the interest rate is (t-statistics in parentheses):

$$(M/P)^* = 0.030 + 0.61y^* - 0.10\Delta i \qquad R^2 = 0.59$$
$$(4.5) \quad (4.9) \quad (2.6) \qquad D.-W. = 2.02$$

And for the United Kingdom:[16]

$$(M/P)^* = 0.014 + 0.32y^* - 0.005\Delta i \qquad R^2 = 0.27$$
$$(2.4) \quad (2.2) \quad (1.2) \qquad D.-W. = 1.89$$

These appear to be reasonable demand equations, although the income elasticity in the equation for the United Kingdom is low, perhaps an artifact of errors in the series for income, which, given the low variability of British income, would reduce the fitted regression coefficient. Another explanation might be the substantial ownership of British money by foreigners, which would reduce the relevance of movements in British income to the 'British' money supply. Still, both demand equations accord reasonably well with other work on the demand for money.

The acid test of the model, of course, is its performance in predicting the balance of payments as a residual from the predicted demand for money and the actual domestically determined supply. Its performance is startlingly good. The good fit of the American demand equation offsets the relative unimportance of gold flows to the American supply, while the relative importance of gold flows to the British supply offsets the poor fit of the British demand

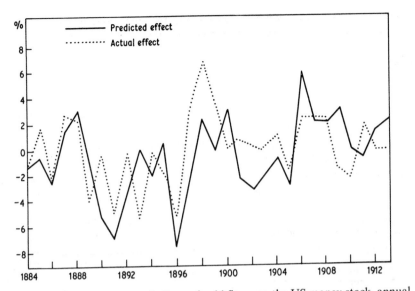

Figure 4.1 Predicted and actual effects of gold flows on the US money stock, annual rates of change, 1884–1913

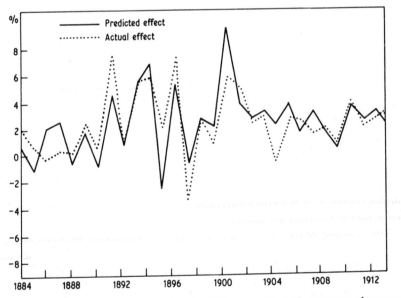

Figure 4.2 Predicted and actual effects of gold flows on the UK money stock, annual rates of change, 1884–1913

equation. Figures 4.1 and 4.2 exhibit the results, comparing the actual effect of gold flows on the American and British money supplies with the predicted effect. The actual effect is calculated annually by applying the observed ratio of money to reserves (including gold) to the actual flow of gold, the predicted effect by subtracting the domestic sources of money from the demand for money predicted by the regressions. In other words, the predicted effect is the excess demand for money predicted by the regressions in conjunction with the actual changes in the money supply due to domestic sources. One could just as well make the comparison of predicted with actual flows of gold, translating the predicted excess demand for money in each country into an equivalent demand for gold imports. The result would be the same, namely, a close correspondence between the predictions of the theory and the observed behaviour of the British and American stock of money and balance of payments.

No doubt the tests could be refined and more evidence could be examined. We believe, however, that we have established at least a prima-facie case for viewing the world of the nineteenth-century gold standard as a world of unified markets, in which flows of gold represented the routine satisfaction of demands for money. We do not claim to have rejected decisively the view of the gold standard that depends on poor arbitrage between national markets or the view that predicts an inverse rather than a positive correlation between gold inflows and income or any of the other variants of the orthodox theories. Indeed, it is perfectly possible that these variants are partly true, perhaps true in the very short run, or under special circumstances, such as mass unemployment – the monetary theory is, in the sense described earlier, an equilibrium theory, which could be consistent with any number of theories about how the British and American economies behaved out of equilibrium. But a balance-of-payments surplus or deficit is not in itself, as has often been assumed, evidence that the economy in question is in fact out of equilibrium. The monetary theory's central message is that a growing, open economy, buffeted by external variations in prices and interest rates, will have a varying demand for money, which would only fortuitously be supplied exactly from domestic sources. A country's balance of payments, in other words, could be positive or negative over the course of a year even if all asset and commodity markets in the country were continuously in equilibrium, for the flow of money into the country during the year could exactly meet the year's change in the demand for money. The source of the simplicity of the monetary theory of the gold standard is clear: the monetary theory is an equilibrium model, whereas the alternative theories are to a greater or lesser extent dynamic, dis-equilibrium models. We believe (as must be evident by now) that the simpler model yields a persuasive interpretation of how the gold standard worked, 1880–1913.

Jotes

1 An earlier and longer version of this essay (available on request) was presented to the Workshop in Economic History at the University of Chicago and to the Cliometrics Conference at the University of Wisconsin. We wish to thank the participants in these meetings for their comments. The friendly scepticism of Moses Abramovitz, C.K. Harley, Hugh Rockoff, Jeffrey Williamson and our colleagues at the University of Chicago, among them Stanley Fischer, Robert J. Gordon, A.C. Harberger, Harry G. Johnson, Arthur Laffer and H. Gregg Lewis, contributed to a sharpening of the argument.

2 Many of these have been published in the Princeton Studies in International Finance. For example, Bloomfield (1963) and Lindert (1969). Bloomfield (1959) is seminal to this literature.

3 Keynes (1930), II, pp. 306–7.

4 World official reserves at the end of 1913 of $7100 million (16 per cent of which was foreign exchange, a good part of it sterling) are estimated by Lindert (1969), pp. 10–12.

5 In 1964 Robert Triffin undertook to act as midwife, but as he concedes, the infant is still in poor health (see Triffin, 1964, appendix I).

6 Needless to say, these are crude estimates: to continue the metaphor above, the historical study of world income is barely into its adolescence. The estimate of $362 billion for 1913 world income in 1955 prices begins with Alfred Maizels' compilation of figures on gross *domestic* product at factor cost for twenty-one countries, given in Maizels (1965), appendix E, p. 531. Czech and Hungarian income was estimated from Austrian income (post-1919 boundaries) on the basis of Colin Clark's ratios among the three (Clark, 1951, p. 155). Russian income was estimated by extrapolating Simon Kuznets' estimate for 1958 back to 1913 on the basis of his figure for the decennial rate of growth, 1913–58 (Kuznets, 1966, pp. 65 and 360), yielding a figure of $207 per capita in 1958 prices, which appears to be a reasonable order of magnitude. The Russian per capita figure was then applied to the population of Bulgaria, Greece, Poland, Romania and Spain, completing the coverage of Europe (boundary changes during the decade of war, 1910 to 1920, were especially important for these countries, except Spain; estimates of the relevant populations are given in Palmer (1957), p. 193). Maizels gives estimates of national income for Canada, Australia, New Zealand, South Africa, Argentina and Japan in 1913. Income per head in 1955 dollars was taken to be $50 in Africa except South Africa, $100 in Latin America except Argentina, $50 in India, and $60 in Asia except India and Japan, all on the basis of Maizels' estimates for 1929 and an assumption of little growth. Population figures for these groups of countries around 1910 were taken from Glass and Grebenik (1965), p. 58, with adjustments for the countries included in Maizels' estimates, from his population figures (1965, p. 540).

7 The sample is described in the appendix of the longer paper, available from the authors on request.

8 From 1800–2 to 1889–91 the ratio of the Berlin to the British price of wheat increased 30 per cent and remained at the higher ratio thereafter.

9 This and all subsequent regressions were subjected to the Cochrane–Orcutt iterative technique, removing in all cases understatement of the standard errors of the coefficients resulting from any autocorrelation of the residuals.

10 We have received a good deal of enlightenment on this point from H. Gregg Lewis of

the University of Chicago and Hugh Rockoff of Rutgers University. The issue is a follows. Suppose, to simplify at the outset, that one chooses the same set of weight $(w_1, w_2, \ldots w_N)$ to form the two indexes of prices (I_A and I_B) in the two countries (A and B). What is the relationship between the weighted average of the individua correlations,

$$w_1(\text{corr } P_1^A, P_1^B) + w_2(\text{corr } P_2^A, P_2^B) + \cdots + w_N(\text{corr } P_N^A, P_N^B),$$

and the correlation of the weighted averages, corr (I_A, I_B) (where $I_A = w_1 P_1^A + w_2 P_2^A + \cdots + w_N P_N^A$)? For the case of two prices we have written out bot correlations in terms of the relevant covariances (expressing the prices i standardized form, thereby eliminating variances of the individual prices an making the corresponding covariances identical to correlation coefficients), with n very illuminating results. If no restrictions are placed on the covariances we ca generate counterexamples to the proposition that the two are equal. But we suspec that we are neglecting true restrictions among the covariances (one set implyin values for another set) and, further, that the case of large N would give more usefu results.

11   For the calculation for the UK in 1913, see McCloskey unpublished MS), ch. p. 18 (MS available on request).
12   Angell (1926), p. 381. Later Angell conceded in part the point made below, althoug he believed (p. 392) that 'it cannot be adequate to explain the comparatively quic adjustments [of domestic to international prices] that actually take place'.
13   Ohlin (1967), p. 104, his italics, question mark added. Contrast Viner (1924), p. 21('The prices of services and what may be termed "domestic commodities" commodities which are too perishable or too bulky to enter regularly an substantially into foreign trade, are wholly or largely independent of *direc* relationship with foreign prices. World price-factors influence them only throug] their influence on the prices of international commodities, with which the prices (domestic commodities, as part of a common price-system, must retain a somewha flexible relationship' (his italics). Although this is an improvement on the earlie formulation by Cairnes (quoted by Viner on the next page) that 'with regard t these, there is nothing to prevent the widest divergence in their gold prices' it fal short of a full analysis of what is meant by 'direct' and 'somewhat flexible', a analysis provided by Ohlin. In long-run equilibrium the distinction between direc and indirect is beside the point and the relationship of domestic to internationa prices is not even somewhat flexible. Viner's work, incidentally, is one of a series c books on the balance of payments published in the Harvard Economic Studies i the 1920s and 1930s under the influence, direct or indirect, of Taussig: William (1920); Viner (1924); Angell (1926); Ohlin (1933); White (1933); and Beach (1935 Students of the history of economic thought will find it significant that of thes Ohlin, who acknowledges explicitly his debt to the Stockholm School (among then Cassel, Heckscher and Wicksell, all of whom emphasized the intimate relationshi between domestic and international prices), broke most sharply with Taussig o this issue.
14   The notion of an 'Atlantic economy', incidentally, receives support from thes figures: the average correlation of French with other retail price indexes, a crud measure of the appropriateness of including a country in the Atlantic economy, i 0.36, while the same statistic for the United States is 0.37; on this reading, it woul be as appropriate to exclude France from the economy of Western Europe as t exclude the United States.
15   We have passed by, for example, the issue of how unified were the markets for assets

The correlation between the annual changes in the British and American long-term interest rates 1882 to 1913 included in the equations estimated in the next section was 0.36, and could no doubt be improved by a closer attention to gathering homogeneous data than we have thought necessary for now. Michael Edelstein (1982, p. 339) reports a correlation coefficient of 0.77 between annual changes in the levels of yields on first-class American railway bonds offered in London and New York from 1871 to 1913, a period including years before the refixing of the sterling–dollar exchange rate in 1879. The discount rates of central banks may be taken as a rough measure of the short-term interest rate. The recent revisionist literature on the gold standard has emphasized the close correlations between these rates in different countries. Triffin (1964, p. 9), for example, quotes Bloomfield (1959, p. 35) approvingly, to the effect that 'the annual averages of the discount rates of twelve [European] central banks reveal the … interesting fact that, in their larger movements at least, the discount rates of virtually all the banks tended to rise and fall together'. Bloomfield and Triffin attribute the parallelism to a corresponding parallelism in the business cycles of the nations involved, but the finding can also be interpreted as evidence of direct or indirect arbitrage in the international capital market. Lance E. Davis's finding that the internal American capital market was poorly arbitraged in this period, suggests that for America at least arbitrage was little better within than between countries (Davis, 1971). The widely believed assertion that domestic British industry was starved of funds in favour of British investment in Argentine railways and Indian government bonds can be given a similar interpretation.

6 The evidence is described in the footnote to table 4.2. The interest rate on three-month bankers' bills (Mitchell, 1962, p. 460) performed better than the consol rate, and was used here.

References

Angell, J.W. (1926), *The Theory of International Prices*, Cambridge, Mass., Harvard University Press.

Beach, W.E. (1935), *British International Gold Movements and Banking Policy, 1881–1913*, Harvard Economic Studies, Cambridge, Mass., Harvard University Press.

Bloomfield, Arthur I. (1959) *Monetary Policy under the International Gold Standard, 1880–1914*, New York, Federal Reserve Bank of New York.

——(1963), *Short-term Capital Movements under the Pre-1914 Gold Standard*, Princeton Studies in International Finance, no. 11, Princeton, Princeton University Press.

Clark, Colin (1951), *The Conditions of Economic Progress*, 2nd edn, London, Macmillan.

Davis, Lance E. (1971), 'Capital mobility and American economic growth', in R.W. Fogel and S.L. Engerman, *The Reinterpretation of American Economic History*, New York, Harper & Row, 285–300.

Edelstein, Michael (1982), *Overseas Investment in the Age of High Imperialism*, New York, Columbia University Press.

Feinstein, C.H. (1971), *National Income, Expenditure and Output of the United Kingdom, 1855–1965*, Cambridge, Cambridge University Press.

Friedman, Milton and Anna J. Schwartz (1963), *A Monetary History of the United States, 1867–1960*, Princeton, Princeton University Press.

Glass, D.V. and E. Grebenik (1965), 'World population, 1800–1950', in H.J. Habakku and M. Postan, *Cambridge Economic History of Europe*, Cambridge, Cambridg University Press, vol. VI, pt 1.

Keynes, J. M. (1930), *A Treatise on Money*, London, Macmillian.

Kuznets, Simon (1966), *Modern Economic Growth*, New Haven, Yale University Pres

Lindert, Peter H. (1969), *Key Currencies and Gold, 1900–1913*, Princeton Studies i International Finance, no. 24, Princeton, Princeton University Press.

Lipsey, R.E. (1963), *Price and Quantity Trends in the Foreign Trade of the Unite States*, New York, National Bureau of Economic Research.

McCloskey, D.N., 'Markets abroad and British economic growth, 1820–1913 unpublished MS.

Maizels, Alfred (1965), *Industrial Growth and World Trade*, Cambridge, Cambridg University Press.

Mitchell, B.R. (1962), *Abstract of British Historical Statistics*, Cambridge, Cambridg University Press.

Ohlin, Bertil (1967), *Interregional and International Trade*, rev. edn (1st edn, 1933 Cambridge, Mass. Harvard University Press.

Palmer, R.R. (1957), *Atlas of World History*, Chicago, Rand McNally.

Sheppard, D.K. (1969), 'Asset preferences and the money supply in the Unite Kingdom 1880–1962', University of Birmingham Discussion Papers, ser. A, no. 11 (November),

Triffin, Robert (1964), *The Evolution of the International Monetary System: Historica Reappraisal and Future Perspectives*, Princeton Studies in International Financ no. 12, Princeton, Princeton University Press.

US Bureau of the Census (1960), *Historical Statistics of the United States, ser. U(Washington, D.C., US Government Printing Office*.

Viner, Jacob (1924), *Canada's Balance of International Indebtedness 1900–191 Cambridge, Mass., Harvard University Press*.

White, Harry D. (1933), *The French International Accounts, 1880–1913*, Harvar Economic Studies, Cambridge, Mass., Harvard University Press.

Williams, J.H. (1920), *Argentine International Trade under Inconvertible Paper Money 1880–1900*, Harvard Economic Studies, Cambridge, Mass., Harvard Universit Press.

5

Money and the price level under the gold standard[1]

Robert J. Barro*

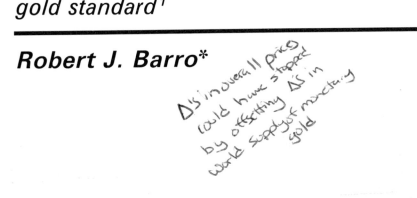

This paper deals with the determination of the price level under the gold standard. Since the 'central bank' supports the nominal price of the reserve commodity gold under this system, the determination of the absolute price level amounts to the determination of the relative price of the reserve commodity. In this sense the absolute price level becomes a determinate quantity that is amenable to usual supply and demand analyses, as applied to such things as gold production and non-monetary uses of gold. Although changes in the ratio of 'money' to its commodity backing or shifts in velocity can influence the price level, the system possesses an important nominal anchor in the fixed price of the reserve commodity.

By way of contrast the absolute price level is determinate under a fiat (government-issue) currency system only up to the determination of the quantity of the fiat currency. Analysis of the price level involves, as its major element, a theory of government behaviour with respect to the quantity of money. In particular, there is no obvious nominal anchor that prescribes some likely limits to changes in the absolute price level.

The above discussion suggests that an important aspect of the gold standard or similar standards in relation to a fiat system is the (partial) separation of price level determination from governmental policy. This separation can be only partial since, at the level of the choice of a monetary regime, it is clear that the determination of money and prices cannot be divorced from the political process. The possibility for alterations in the underlying regime is exhibited by the gradual erosion of the international gold standard since

*From *Economic Journal*, March 1979, pp. 13–27, 31–3, abridged.

1914, and especially since the 1930s. The present analysis does not deal with this sort of change in the underlying 'monetary constitution' (see Buchanan, 1962), but is rather confined to the workings of the system under a fixed monetary structure.

The gold standard

Determination of the price level and the money stock

The framework of analysis is a closed economy that can represent either a single country or the world economy under fixed exchange rates. The stock of money, denoted by M and denominated in a nominal unit such as dollars, represents a liability of the central bank(s). It can be assumed that money takes the physical form of a paper claim, rather than directly embodying gold or some other physical commodity. However, the bank is assumed to stand ready to buy or sell any amount of gold offered or demanded in exchange for money at the fixed (dollar) price, P_g.[2] If G_m represents the stock of gold held by the bank, then the supply of money would equal $P_g G_m$ under a strict commodity standard where the paper claims represent literal warehouse certificates, and would exceed this amount under a partial commodity standard. I assume that the total money supply is

$$M^s = (1/\lambda)P_g G_m,$$ (1)

where the parameter λ, which satisfies $0 \leqslant \lambda \leqslant 1$, measures the gold 'backing' of the monetary issue.[3]

The demand for circulating medium, M^d, is assumed to depend on the 'general price level of commodities', P, on real income, y,[4] and on the opportunity cost rate for holding money rather than alternative assets. In the present set-up I assume that the principal alternative store of value is a commodity stock (or capital with a fixed real rate of return), so that the opportunity cost rate for holding money is measured by the expected rate of inflation, $\pi \equiv (\dot{P}/P)$,[5] where a dot denotes a time derivative. Formally, money demand is represented by

$$M^d = k(\pi)Py,$$ (2)
$$(-)$$

where the minus sign denotes a negative derivative which signifies that expected inflation and desired money holding are inversely related. The indicated unit income elasticity of money demand is convenient but not essential for the main analysis. The k-function can be thought of as an expression for the reciprocal of velocity.

The equation of money supply and demand from equations (1) and (2) implies the price level condition,

$$P = \frac{P_g G_m}{\lambda k(\pi) y}. \tag{3}$$

In the subsequent analysis a principal issue is the implication of fixity in P_g – as guaranteed under the gold standard – for the short- and long-run behaviour of the general price level, P. Since equation (3) holds at all times, variations of P around P_g reflect movements in the right-hand-side variables, as represented in the combination, $G_m/(\lambda k y)$. For most of the analysis the variables, k, λ, and y are treated as exogenous, although subject to disturbances. For purposes of exposition I have also carried out the main analysis in a setting that omits sustained growth in output, y. However, I have indicated the necessary modifications to incorporate growth. At the present stage the focus is on endogenous movements of the monetary gold stock, G_m.

As stressed by Fisher (1922, pp. 99 ff),[6] the two key determinants of the monetary gold stock in a dynamic context are gold production and the extent to which gold is held for non-monetary purposes. Let g represent the rate at which new gold is produced. I assume that the current production function for a representative member of the gold-mining industry can be expressed by the (real) cost function, $c(g)$, which describes the cost in commodity units for producing gold at rate g. Production is assumed to involve positive and increasing marginal cost – that is, c', $c'' > 0$.[7] The nominal cost for producing gold at rate g is $Pc(g)$, while the nominal revenue is $P_g g$ (with a common price for gold in monetary and non-monetary uses). Revenue-maximizing behaviour on the part of gold producers, each of whom regards P_g and P as exogenous, entails

$$c'(g) = P_g/P, \tag{4}$$

which implies a supply function for new gold of the form,

$$g^s = g^s(P/P_g). \tag{5}$$
$$\underset{(-)}{}$$

Let G_n denote the stock of gold that is held for non-monetary (industrial, ornamental, etc.) uses. Gold held for these purposes is assumed to depreciate in an economic sense at the constant rate δ. (Gold held by the central bank is assumed not to depreciate.) Since the main analysis abstracts from real income growth, δG_n will turn out to measure the flow demand for gold in a steady state. More generally, this flow demand would also include the growth in G_m and G_n that is associated with sustained growth in y.

Non-monetary uses of gold would be deterred by a higher current relative price, P_g/P, but would be encouraged by expectations of higher future values of P_g/P. With P_g constant, expected future values of P_g/P vary inversely with π. Accordingly, I assume that the 'target' stock of privately held gold is determined by a function of the form

$$\underset{(+)\ \ (-)}{f(P/P_g, \pi)y,}$$

which assumes, for convenience, a unit income elasticity. The underlying assumption that P_g is fixed seems to rule out the principal rationale for 'speculative' gold hoards, so that the f-function should be thought of as pertaining to 'real' uses of gold (for industry, ornamentation, etc.), rather than to a portfolio demand, *per se*. In this context it also seems natural to rule out rapid (that is, discrete) shifts in the non-monetary gold stock. Accordingly, I specify the non-monetary demand for gold in the form of a flow function,

$$g_n^d = \alpha[\underset{(+)\ \ (-)}{f(P/P_g, \pi)y} - G_n] + \delta \underset{(+)\ \ (-)}{f(P/P_g, \pi)y}. \tag{6}$$

Equation (6) assumes a desired gradual adjustment of G_n toward its target position in accordance with the adjustment parameter, $\alpha > 0$. In addition, g_n^d incorporates the 'normal' replacement flow, $\delta f(\ldots)y$, that would be required to maintain the target value of G_n.[8] Note that the form of equation (6) implies that G_n has a negative effect on g_n^d. The form also implies $g_n^d = \delta f(\ldots)y = \delta G_n$ when G_n is equal to its target value. The net change in G_n at any point in time is given by

$$\dot{G}_n = g_n^d - \delta G_n = (\alpha + \delta)[\underset{(+)\ \ (-)}{f(P/P_g, \pi)y} - G_n]. \tag{7}$$

Finally, with the monetary authority standing ready to buy or sell any amount of gold at price P_g, the change in the monetary gold stock is given by

$$\dot{G}_m = g^s - g_n^d = \underset{(-)}{g^s(P/P_g)} - \alpha[\underset{(+)\ \ (-)}{f(P/P_g, \pi)y} - G_n] - \delta \underset{(+)\ \ (-)}{f(P/P_g, \pi)y}. \tag{8}$$

Consider the situation where y, λ, P_g, and the forms of the k- and f-functions are fixed. The steady state of the system described by equations (3), (7) and (8) corresponds to

$$\dot{P} = \dot{G}_m = \dot{G}_n = 0.$$

It can also be supposed that π, the expected value of $\dot{P}/P$, is equal to the actual value, zero, in the steady state. In order to simplify the analysis I assume at the outset that π is fixed at zero even when P is changing over time. The steady-state values of P, G_m, and G_n, which will be denoted by asterisks, can be determined from equations (3), (7) and (8). Equations (8) and (7), together with $\dot{G}_m = \dot{G}_n = 0$, imply

$$\underset{(-)}{g^s(P^*/P_g)} = \delta f(\underset{(+)}{P^*/P_g}, \underset{(-)}{\pi^*})y. \tag{9}$$

This condition (together with $\pi^* = 0$) determines the steady-state value, P^*/P_g – and, hence, P^* – from the equality between gold production and the replacement demand for non-monetary gold.[9] In a model where y was continually increasing, the steady-state flow demand for gold would have additional components that reflected the growing demand for gold stocks in monetary and non-monetary uses.

Equation (7) implies in a steady state that

$$G_n^* = f(\underset{(+)}{P^*/P_g}, \underset{(-)}{\pi^*})y, \tag{10}$$

which determines the value of G_n^* once P^* is set from equation (9). Finally, the money-supply-equals-money-demand condition, equation (3), implies

$$G_m^* = \lambda k(\pi^*)yP^*/P_g, \tag{11}$$

which determines the steady-state value G_m^* (and, therefore, the money stock $M^* = (1/\lambda)P_g G_m^*$), once P^* is determined.

Consider a situation in which the outstanding gold stocks, G_m, and G_n, are currently fixed at levels that need not correspond to a steady state. Given the values of y, π, and P_g, the value of G_m determines the current value of P from equation (3). With y, π, etc., constant, the movements of G_n and G_m (and hence, of P) are determined from equations (7) and (8).

Figures 5.1(a,b) depict the steady-state values, P^*, G_m^* and G_n^*, and also describe the dynamics of P, G_m and G_n. The line in figure 5.1(a), based on equation (3), relates the value of P to the value of G_m. In figure 5.1(b) the locus denoted by $\dot{G}_m = 0$ indicates combinations of G_n and G_m that yield $\dot{G}_m = 0$ in equation (8), taking into account the relation of P to G_m from equation (3). An increase in G_m raises P, which lowers g^s and raises g_n^s. Hence, $\dot{G}_m$ falls when G_m rises. Since an increase in G_n reduces g_n^d, which implies an increase in $\dot{G}_m$, the $\dot{G}_m = 0$ locus is positively sloped. Similarly, equation (7) implies that the $\dot{G}_n = 0$ locus is positively sloped. It can also be verified from equations (3), (7) and (8) that the $\dot{G}_n = 0$ locus has a steeper slope than the $\dot{G}_m = 0$ locus, so that the usual stability conditions are satisfied

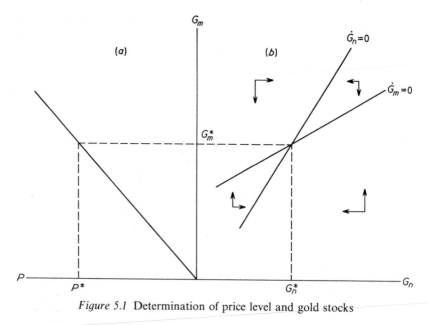

Figure 5.1 Determination of price level and gold stocks

in this model (at least in the present case where π is fixed throughout at its steady-state value of zero).

The following sections analyse the effects of various disturbances in the 'short- and long-run'. The focus is on the determination of P – notably, on the extent to which the gold standard insulates the price level from a variety of shocks.

Properties of the model

Technical progress in gold production (gold discoveries)

Consider a technical advance, discovery,[10] etc., that reduces the marginal cost of producing gold, $c'(g)$, for a given value of g. Since the supply function, g^s, shifts upward, equation (8) implies that $\dot{G}_m$ is higher for given values of P and G_n. Since there is no shift in the relationship between P and G_m from equation (3),[11] the figure 5.2(a) curve does not move, but the $\dot{G}_m = 0$ locus shifts upward in figure 5.2(b). (A higher value of G_m is now required, for a given value of G_n, to attain $\dot{G}_m = 0$.) The $\dot{G}_n = 0$ locus does not change, in accordance with equation (7).

Figure 5.2(b) shows that G_m begins to rise in response to the disturbance. There is no immediate response in P or in $\dot{G}_n$. As G_m rises over time – as

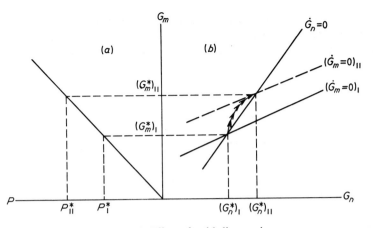

Figure 5.2 Effect of gold discoveries

shown by the arrows in figure 5.2(b) – there is a corresponding increase in P, which leads to an increase in G_n and to a retardation in the growth of G_m. The new steady state is characterized by higher values of G_m^*, G_n^* and P^*, the increases in G_m^* and P^* being equiproportional. It also follows from equations (4), (5) and (9) that (for a given shift in marginal production cost, $c'(g)$) the proportional increase in P^* will be larger the larger the price elasticity of the supply function, g^s, and the smaller the magnitude of the price elasticity of the non-monetary gold demand function, f.

This analysis accords with Mill's[12] in predicting, first, a delayed and gradual rise of the price level in response to an increase in gold production, and, second, a coincident movement of P and G_m (and, hence, of M). However, these conclusions depend on the fixity of inflationary expectations, π, or on the constancy of velocity. If gold discoveries are perceived and if such discoveries are known to produce later increases in the price level, then π would increase at the time of the discovery. The induced fall in money demand, $k(\pi)$, implies, from equation (3), that P would rise for a given value of G_m.[13] (A full analysis of the impact of a shift in k is carried out on p. 92.) In particular, there would be an initial jump in the price level before any movement occurred in G_m or the money stock. Hence, the workings of price expectations would eliminate part of the lagged response of P to gold discoveries and would produce a pattern where movements in P led movements in G_m and M.[14]

A natural assumption is that π corresponds to the time path of inflation that is generated by the model (rational expectations). However, I have not carried out this analysis within the present framework. One difficulty is that the various disturbances being considered here and below – to $c(g)$, y, λ, etc. – are presumably stochastic, which would have to be modelled explicitly in order to generate π in a rigorous manner. The information possessed by individuals about gold discoveries, etc., would also have to be specified. In any event the present mode of analysis may be adequate to ascertain the major types of responses to the indicated disturbances.

For evaluating the gold standard as a device for stabilizing the general price level, the main implication of the present exercise is that volatility in conditions of gold production (associated with gold discoveries and changes in mining technique) would lead to volatility in the general price level.

Without working through the details it can be noted that shifts in non-monetary gold demand – that is, movements in the f-function – have basically similar implications (although in the opposite direction) for the determination of the price level under the gold standard.[15]

Changes in real income

Consider a one-time increase in real income, y, while holding fixed the technology of gold production. This example would reflect the secular pattern in the economy if gold-mining were subject to less 'technical advance' or to greater diseconomies-of-scale than the typical industry. The analysis deals initially with a one-time income change, although the effects of sustained income growth are also noted.

Equation (3) implies that P declines in inverse proportion to y for a given value of G_m (with π held fixed), so that the curve shown in figure 5.3(a) shifts rightward. It follows from equation (7) that $\dot{G}_n$ increases for given values of G_m and G_n if and only if the magnitude of the price elasticity of the non-monetary gold target demand function, f, is less than one. Figure 5.3(b) depicts the case in which the elasticity equals one, so that there is no shift in the $\dot{G}_n = 0$ locus. In this situation equation (8) indicates that $\dot{G}_m$ rises for given values of G_m and G_n, because of the rise in g^s.

Equation (9) implies that the increase in y leads, in the steady state, to a fall in P^*, as shown in figure 5.3(a). The induced increase in g^s implies that G_n^*, which equals g^s/δ in a steady state, is increased. This property is exhibited in figure 5.3(b). The net movement in G_m^*, as determined from equation (11), is generally ambiguous, although G_m^*, must rise for the case depicted in figure 5.3.[16]

The most important response to a discrete rise in y is the immediate discrete fall in P. There is also, at least eventually, a period in which gold is accumulated in non-monetary form. The movement in G_m and the implied further movement in P are ambiguous. It is, however, unambiguous that the steady-state real stock of monetary gold – $P_g G_m^*/P^*$ – increases with y.

The basic conclusion is that output growth[17] – which dominates over 'technical advances' in gold production – would imply secular decline in the price level. This result is often cited as a failing of the gold standard, although

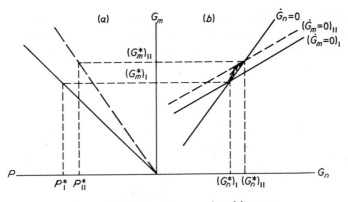

Figure 5.3 Effect of increased real income

there would seem to be no objection to this sort of systematic – and hence, anticipated – deflation on business cycle grounds. The next sections consider the 'remedies' for secular deflation of paper gold creation and of changes in the nominal price of gold.

'Paper gold'

It is frequently argued that the deflationist tendency of the gold standard can be countered by supplementing the world's gold stock with some form of paper gold. For example, the plans suggested by Keynes (1943), Triffin (1960, part II), and Mundell (1971, pp. 135–6) can be viewed in this context. Recent forms of monetary supplement include international reserve holdings in the form of US dollars and special drawing rights at the International Monetary Fund. In the present model the creation of paper gold can be modelled by a decrease in λ. Note that I retain the assumption that the central bank acts to maintain the (single) gold price, P_g.

Consider a one-time decrease in λ, which can be viewed as an increase in the money stock while holding fixed the initial amount of gold backing. Equation (3) indicates that P would rise for a given value of G_m, as represented by the leftward shift of the curve in figure 5.4(a). It follows from equation (7) that $\dot{G}_n$ would rise for given values of G_m and G_n. Hence, the $\dot{G}_n = 0$ locus shifts rightward in figure 5.4(b). Equation (8) implies that $\dot{G}_m$ would decline for given values of G_m and G_n, as indicated by the downward shift of the $\dot{G}_m = 0$ locus in figure 5.4(b).

The exact position of the new steady state in figure 5.4 can be ascertained from equations (9)–(11). Equation (9) implies that P^* is invariant with λ. It follows from equation (10) that G_n^* is also unchanged. The downward movement in G_m^*, as shown in equation (11), is therefore proportional to

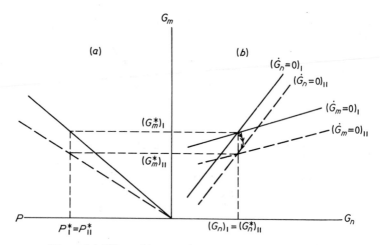

Figure 5.4 Effect of increased paper gold or rise in velocity

the fall in λ, so that the steady-state money stock, $M^* = (1/\lambda)P_g G_m^*$, remains fixed.

Initially, with G_m (and π) held fixed, the effect of the increase in M is to increase P in proportion. This price change induces a rise over time in G_n and leads also to a drop in gold production. G_m falls over time on both counts, with P declining from its initially higher position in proportion to the decrease in G_m. Eventually, a point is reached where G_n is sufficiently high and P is sufficiently reduced so that G_n begins to fall. In the new steady state G_n and P have returned to their initial positions and the only net effect is the decline in G_m. Hence, the ultimate impact of increased paper money issue is to drive out part of the monetary gold stock without affecting the price level. In this sense – and as long as the value of P_g is actually maintained – paper gold does not counter the deflationary tendency of the gold standard. However, volatility of paper note issue (that is, of the ratio of money to its gold backing) would lead to short-run volatility of the general price level.[18]

It is worth noting that steady-state real balances, $M^*/P^* = P_g G_m^*/\lambda P^* = ky$, are invariant with λ, but the real value of the gold backing, $P_g G_m^*/P^*$, is positively related to λ.[19] Hence, the resource cost associated with the maintenance of the gold standard is, on this count, an increasing function of λ. Correspondingly, the monetary authority's steady-state 'seigniorage' (in the sense of the *stock* of revenue from note issue)[20] can be written as $ky - P_g G_m^*/P^*$, which is negatively related to λ. However, the maximum (stock) amount of steady-state seigniorage – approached as $\lambda \to 0$ and $G_m^* \to 0$ – is M^*/P^*, which is fixed (for given values of y and π) at ky. In the steady state an excess of the lump-sum proceeds from note issue over ky is inconsistent with maintenance of the gold price, P_g. Attempts to secure additional revenue by issuing more paper currency would lead to more and more notes being presented to the central bank for conversion into gold at price P_g, which could lead to an increase in the gold price. (The next section deals with the effect of changes in P_g.) In this sense the paper gold route could eventually counter deflation by leading to the abandonment of the gold standard.[21] Mundell's (1971), pp. 133–5, discussion of the international economy during the decade after 1958 parallels this situation. The United States can be viewed as the world's central banker during this period.

The above analysis must be altered somewhat in the presence of sustained output growth. For present purposes the important consideration is that the steady-state flow demand for gold, which appears on the right side of equation (9), would include a term to account for the growth over time in G_m.[22] A decrease in λ would reduce the flow of gold for this purpose and would therefore tend to raise P at any point in time. Although this channel implies that a lower value of λ would be associated with a higher level of the time path of P, there would still be no effect of λ on the steady-state inflation rate (see note 17). Therefore it remains a valid conclusion that the (once-and for-all)[23] choice of the proportional allocation of currency backing between gold and paper does not alter the connection between the gold standard and secular deflation. This connection seems inescapable with P_g held fixed if the gold-mining industry is perpetually less subject to 'technical advance' than the rest of the economy.

Changes in the price of gold

Consider a one-time increase in P_g in a non-growth context. It follows from equation (3) that, for given values of G_m, λ,[24] etc., P would increase equiproportionately. Further, equations (9)–(11) imply that this short-run solution, in which P/P_g, G_m and G_n are all unchanged, is also the new steady state.

For the case of sustained increases in P_g, the new element is that the associated increase in P would be anticipated, as reflected in a rise in π. This increase would reduce the real demand for money (k – see the analysis of this shift in the next section),[35] but would not alter the principal conclusion from above that the growth rate of P_g would be incorporated one-to-one in the steady-state growth rate of P. Notably, the growth rate of P_g could be engineered so as to offset the deflationary tendency of the gold standard.[26] Further (as suggested in the stable money proposal of Fisher, 1920, ch. IV), the value of P_g could be adjusted continuously so as to prevent even short-run fluctuations in P.

A difficulty with this 'solution' is that it converts the problem of price level determination from an automatic mechanism under the gold standard (with P_g fixed) to a political choice of the time path of P_g. If this choice process is 'reliable', then the gold standard could have been dispensed with all along and replaced by a paper standard (at the saving of the resource cost for maintaining monetary gold stocks). Under a paper standard it would 'only' be necessary to ensure a 'reasonable' growth rate of the quantity of fiat money.

Shifts in velocity

Consider a one-time decrease in real money demand, $k(\pi)$. In the context of a fractional-reserve banking system where M represents high-powered money, this shift could reflect an increase in the demand for deposits relative to currency. Equations (3), (7) and (8) indicate that this shock can be described exactly as in figure 5.4, which was constructed for the case of a decrease in λ. The immediate effects of the drop in money demand are a discrete increase in P, a tendency for G_m to fall over time, and a tendency for G_n to rise over time. As G_n rises and P falls along with G_m, the rising trend of G_n is diminished and eventually reversed. The new steady state involves a restoration of the initial values of P^* and G_n^*, with the only net effect being a decline in G_m^*. Real balances, $M/P^* = ky$, and the real value of monetary gold, $P_g G_m^*/P^*$, are both reduced in the new steady state. One implication of this exercise is that the endogenous movement of monetary gold stocks under the gold standard operates to buffer the price level against velocity shifts.[27]

As in the paper gold case, the analysis requires some modification in the presence of sustained output growth. A one-time reduction in k lowers the steady-state flow of gold that is required to maintain growth in G_m. On this count, the disturbance would produce an upward shift in the price level path. However, the steady-state inflation rate would be invariant with k (see note 17).

Some international analysis

The model can be readily extended to a multiple country setting in which the gold standard prevails. Suppose that country i ($i = 1, .., N$) is characterized by parameter values P_{g_i}, λ_i, k_i, y_i. The (fixed) exchange rate between country i and, say, country 1 is then P_{g_i}/P_{g_1}.[28] Arbitrage implies that the relative price of gold and (tradable) commodities would be the same in each country, so that P_i/P_{g_i} can be assumed to equal a common value, denoted by P/P_g. The equality between money demand and supply in each country at all points in time requires, from equations (1) and (2),

$$G_{m_i} = \lambda_i k_i y_i (P/P_g) \quad (i = 1, \ldots, N). \tag{12}$$

For a given current value of the world's monetary gold stock, G_m, equation (12) can be satisfied for all N countries by determining the allocation of G_m across countries[29] ($N - 1$ independent conditions) and by determining the value of P/P_g – that is, by determining the 'world price level'. The latter condition can be seen by summing over equation (12) and rearranging terms to get

$$\frac{P}{P_g} = \frac{G_m}{\sum_i (\lambda_i k_i y_i)}. \tag{13}$$

In the long run P/P_g is determined by the equality between steady-state flow supply and demand for gold, as in equation (9). The world's monetary gold stock adjusts in the long run to satisfy equation (13) at this value of P/P_g. Conditions for determining G_n in each country are analogous to those discussed in the one-country model.

In terms of volatility of general price levels, equation (13) indicates that the relevant influence is the variance of the world's 'excess demand' for gold,

$$\left(\frac{1}{G_m}\right)\sum_i (\lambda_i k_i y_i).$$

Notably, if there is some independence across countries in movements of λ_i, k_i and y_i, then (because of a law-of-large-numbers effect) the variance of the general price level in each gold standard country would tend to decline as the number of countries adhering to the standard increased.[30] In this sense the attractiveness of the set-up to a new country tends to rise with the number of countries that have already adopted the standard. However, it is possible that the inclusion into the gold standard regime of a country with an especially volatile real demand, $\lambda_i k_i y_i$, would raise the variance of P/P_g. A mixing of countries with negative covariances of $\lambda_i k_i y_i$ would also tend to reduce the price level variance, although the empirical relevance of this point is not apparent.

I discuss below some examples of international disturbances that can be treated within the present framework.

(a) Devaluation

Consider a one-time devaluation in country j, which can be represented by an increase in P_{g_j}. If λ_j remains fixed (implying that paper money in country j rises equiproportionately with the increased nominal value of that country's monetary gold holdings), then it is immediate from equations (12) and (13) that the only impact of the devaluation would be an equiproportional increase in P_j. In particular, it follows from equation (13) and the fixity of P_{g_i} for all the other countries that there is no spillover effect of the devaluation to prices abroad.

On the other hand, if λ_j is allowed to rise with the devaluation (which is, perhaps, the point of the devaluation), then it follows from equation (13) – for a given value of G_m – that P/P_g would decline. That is, P_i would fall in all countries $i \neq j$ that were maintaining the nominal price of gold (or were maintaining a fixed exchange rate with a country that was pegging the gold price). Further, P_j would rise less than equiproportionately with P_{g_j} in the devaluing country.[31] The explanation of these effects, indicated in equation (12), is that the fraction of the world's monetary gold stock held in country j rises with the increase in λ_j.[32] The smaller remaining stock can satisfy the demand in other countries only with a decrease in P/P_g.

As in the one-country case analysed before, the long-run solution would also include the adjustment of G_m from gold production, etc. In the no-growth situation the steady-state effect of the devaluation on P/P_g would be nil, although some long-run effect (to the level of the P/P_g path but not to the world inflation rate) would remain in a growth context.

(b) Increased adoption of the gold standard

If an additional country, labelled $N + 1$, adopts the gold standard, then

$$\sum_i (\lambda_i k_i y_i)$$

in equation (13) would rise with the inclusion of the term, $\lambda_{N+1} k_{N+1} y_{N+1}$. There would be a corresponding decline in P/P_g while G_m is held fixed.[33] Since $G_{m,N+1}$ will now be absorbed by country $N + 1$ in accordance with equation (12), the remaining countries can be satisfied with the reduced amount of monetary gold only if P/P_g falls. As an example of this effect, the acquisition of large amounts of gold by the United States during the Resumption Period from 1875 to 1879 and somewhat thereafter (and, similarly, by Germany after 1871) should have exerted a depressing effect on prices in gold standard countries, such as England. Further, a country's (credible) announcement of a future plan to adopt the gold standard (as by the United States in 1875) would have an immediate downward effect on prices in gold standard countries – that is, even before the new country increased its gold holdings. The mechanism is a decline in the expected inflation rate, π, in the gold standard countries, which raises the demand for money (as well as the demand for non-monetary gold) and correspondingly lowers the price level.

The analysis can be extended in the usual way to consider the long-run effects when G_m is allowed to vary. In particular, for the no-growth case in which all countries are identical, the steady-state value of G_m would be proportional to the number of countries on the gold standard (see note 30).

(c) Multiple commodity standards

It is, of course, possible for different groups of countries to adhere to different commodity standards – for example, there could be a gold standard group and a silver standard group (or a group of countries on a fiat standard, possibly tied together via fixed exchange rates). It should be noted that this multiple-standard set-up differs from bimetallism. One observation on a multiple-standard world is that the exchange rate between, say, the gold and silver blocs would be determined by the relative price of gold and silver (which can be assumed to be the same within either bloc). Some empirical evidence that supports this proposition is presented in Sayers (1931) in a study of the Indian/English exchange rate during 1919–20, and in Fisher (1935), pp. 4–5 and chart 5, and Friedman and Schwartz (1963), pp. 361–2 and 489–90, in analyses of the Chinese exchange rate and price level from 1929 to 1935.

An interesting application of the analysis, which amounts to an extension of optimum currency area theory (Mundell, 1968, ch. 12), would be to a determination of the optimal groupings of countries and the optimal number of groups. (I am abstracting here from means-of-payments considerations involved with a particular country's use of a particular commodity for transactions, and I am also not considering the transactions benefits derived from adherence to a fixed-exchange-rate regime.) From the perspective of price level variance it seems that (1) a country that has an especially low variance of demand – that is, of $\lambda_i k_i y_i$ – may find it advantageous to be isolated from the rest of the world; (2) with 'free entry' to an existing commodity standard it seems infeasible to exclude from a group a 'contaminating' country that has an especially high variance of demand; and (3) there could be incentive for an assortment among groups that exploits any negative covariances of demands. The empirical relevance of these propositions is not apparent. [...]

Some concluding remarks

In relation to a fiat currency regime, the key element of a commodity standard is its potential for automaticity and consequent absence of political control over the quantity of money and the absolute price level. Essentially, the adoption of a commodity standard by any country would require a constitutional-type (political) decision that rules out the determination of the quantity of money over time through a series of political decisions. (See Buchanan, 1962.) It is not clear, *a priori*, that this sort of constitutional provision is more likely to obtain than, for example, a provision to expand the quantity of fiat money at a constant rate. In this context the choice among different monetary constitutions – such as the gold standard, a commodity-reserve standard, or a fiat standard with fixed rules for setting the quantity of money (possibly in relation to stabilizing a specified price index) – may be less important than the decision to adopt *some* monetary constitution. On the other hand, the gold standard actually prevailed for a substantial period (even if from an 'historical accident', rather than a constitutional choice process), whereas the world has yet to see a fiat currency system that has obvious 'stability' properties.

Notes

1 This research was supported by the National Science Foundation. I have benefited from comments by Russ Boyer, Stanley Engerman, Herschel Grossman, Peter Howitt, David Laidler, Don McCloskey, Mark Rush, Nasser Saidi, Larry Sjaastad, Alan Stockman and two referees.
2 This set-up for a convertible currency is the one described by Ricardo (1821), p. 241.
3 If money is defined to include commercial bank deposits, then the ratio of deposits to currency would influence the value of λ under a fractional-reserve banking system. Alternatively, if M is defined as high-powered money, then shifts in the deposit–currency ratio would influence the demand for 'money', as represented by the k-function below.
4 Real income would include the value added in the gold industry net of depreciation on gold stocks. Similarly, P would include P_g with an appropriate weight.
5 Substitution between money and gold holdings implies that $E(\dot{P}_g/P_g)$ would enter as an additional negative argument of the money demand function. Since P_g is assumed constant, the inclusion of this term would not alter the subsequent analysis.
6 See also Thornton (1802), p. 266, Mill (1848), ch. IX, Friedman (1951), pp. 207 ff., and Whitaker (1976), section I. Niehans (1978), in an interesting recent contribution, also discusses some of the topics that I consider in my analysis.
7 The exhaustible-resource property of gold could be captured by entering the accumulated stock of previously mined gold as a positive argument in the cost function. When the possibility of new discoveries and technical changes in mining are admitted, it is not clear that exhaustibility is an important characteristic over a relevant horizon. In any case the pertinent issue for subsequent analysis is the rate of 'technical advance' in gold production relative to that in other industries – see pp. 86–8.
8 The alternative specification that substitutes δG_n for $\delta f(...) y$ in equation (6) would seem appropriate if adjustment costs applied to the net change in G_n, which equals $g_n^d - \delta G_n$, rather than to alterations in the gross flow, g_n^d. The alternative assumes that changes in the gross flow that are associated with changes in the actual

depreciation, δG_n, do not involve any adjustment costs. Hence, the alternative has the odd property that a rise in G_n, for a given value of $f(...)$, could raise the value of g_n^d. Although my preference is for the form of equation (6), the substitution of the alternative form would affect only a minor part of the dynamic analysis. (The form of the $\dot{G}_m$ expression, below, would be altered.)

9 If the stock of previously mined gold were entered as a negative argument of the supply function (see note 7), then P would not be constant in a steady state. Because of the depreciation of non-monetary gold stocks, P would have to fall continually in a steady state in order to provide the replacement flow of gold.

10 This analysis abstracts from the possibly different intertemporal implications of changes in technique versus discoveries of new gold sources. (See notes 7 and 9.)

11 Unless the contrary is noted, this and subsequent analyses neglect changes in y or π. Real income would change in the present case because of the technical advance in gold production. I have neglected this income effect because it is likely to be of second-order significance. See p. 87 for a discussion of expected inflation effects.

12 'Alterations...in the cost of production of the precious metals do not act upon the value of money except just in proportion as they increase or diminish its quantity...' (Mill, 1848, p. 29).

13 There would also be a downward shift in the target stock of non-monetary gold, which would retard the acquisition of G_n.

14 This behaviour also appears in the perfect-foresight model developed by Brock (1975).

15 An upward shift in the f-function leads to decreases in P^* and G_m^* (which are in the same proportion), and to an increase in G_n^*. Again, if π is held fixed, the dynamic movement of P would lag behind the disturbance and would be coincident with the movement in G_m.

16 Generally, G_m^* rises if and only if the sum of the absolute price elasticities of g^s and f exceeds one.

17 If growth in output is sustained over time, a new element is that the corresponding steady decline in the price level would be anticipated in the steady state – that is, π^* would be negative. The forms of equations (6) and (7) would also have to be modified to incorporate the regular effect of changes in y and P on the flow demand for non-monetary gold. With growing real income and constant values for λ and k (and the assumed unit income elasticities for stock demands), it is possible to find a steady state in which the ratio of G_m to G_n remains constant only if the (steady-state value of the) price elasticity of the f-function is equal to minus one. In this case it can be shown that the steady-state inflation rate is $-\rho/(\eta_f + \eta_s) = -\rho/(1 + \eta_s)$, where $\rho = (1/y)dy/dt$, η_f is the magnitude of the price elasticity of the f-function, and η_s is the elasticity of g^s. Note that this inflation rate is invariant with shifts in the k- or f-functions or with changes in λ. See Mundell (1971), chs 8 and 13, for some other aspects of the case of sustained output growth.

18 Since P falls steadily after its initial discrete rise, π would tend to become negative. This decline in π would dampen the initial upward movement in P. More generally, the automatic response in π would seem to reduce the short-run price level variance associated with a given variance of λ.

19 In this sense a partial commodity standard can 'economize' on gold relative to a strict commodity standard. See Friedman (1951), pp. 215–16.

20 In the model where y and P_g are constant, the flow of revenue from new note issue is zero in the steady state.

21 Even before the standard was officially abandoned, paper gold issue could increase the price level by raising doubts about the maintenance of the price of gold. A rise in

the expected future price of gold would reduce the demand for money and (depending on the reaction of π) also tend to raise the demand for non-monetary gold. The price level would rise with the decline in money demand, k, as shown in equation (3). Over time (with the actual value of P_g held fixed), there would be a tendency for G_n to rise and for G_m and M to decline (so that P would tend to return to its original value unless the actual value of P_g were altered).

22 The term is $(\rho + \pi)\lambda k(\pi)P/P_g$, where ρ is the proportionate growth rate of y.
23 A steady decrease in λ would have a positive effect on the movement of P over time. However, this connection is subject to 'diminishing returns'. That is, as λ declines the flow demand for gold for monetary purposes becomes less important relative to the flow for non-monetary uses. If λ decreases at a constant rate, G_m/G_n would approach zero, and the steady-state value of π would still be the one given in note 17.
24 Fixity of λ implies that there is sufficient new currency issue to maintain the ratio of M to $P_g G_m$. If λ rises (which would occur, for example, if M were held fixed when P_g increased), the above analysis could be used to analyse the additional effects.
25 Anticipated growth in P_g may also shift the demand for non-monetary gold – see note 21.
26 An exact offset would require setting $\dot{P}_g/P_g = \rho/(1 + \eta_s)$, where ρ is the growth rate of output and η_s is the price elasticity of g^s. See note 17.
27 As in the case of a decrease in λ, a fall in π at the outset would improve this buffering action.
28 Under a fixed-exchange-rate regime it is necessary for only one country to peg the price of gold directly.
29 I am allowing instantaneous stock transfers of monetary gold (in exchange for commodities) across countries, although non-monetary gold still moves only in a smooth manner. The basic analysis would not seem to be altered if discrete shifts in G_{m_i} were ruled out (in which case equation (2) might be replaced by a flow demand for money function) or if discrete shifts in G_{n_i} were permitted.
30 This analysis assumes that G_m is proportional to the number of countries on the gold standard. See p. 94.
31 This response is closer to equiproportional and the spillover effects to other countries are weaker the smaller the weight of country j in the world's overall demand for monetary gold – that is, the lower the value of $\lambda_j k_j y_j / \sum_i (\lambda_i k_i y_i)$.
32 A 'period' of balance-of-payments surpluses would be required for country j to obtain the additional gold.
33 I am assuming no change in world demand for non-monetary gold.

References

Brock, W. (1975), 'A simple perfect foresight monetary model', *Journal of Monetary Economics*, I (April), 133–50.
Buchanan, J.M. (1962), 'Predictability: the criterion of monetary constitutions', in Leland B. Yeager (ed.) *In Search of a Monetary Constitution*, Cambridge, Mass., Harvard University Press.
Cagan, P. (1956), 'The monetary dynamics of hyperinflation', in M. Friedman (ed.), *Studies in the Quantity Theory of Money*, Chicago, University of Chicago Press.
Chen, C. (1972), 'Bimetallism: theory and controversy in perspective', *History of Political Economy*, 4 (Spring), 89–112.

Fisher, Irving (1920), *Stabilizing the Dollar*, New York, Macmillan.
——(1922), *The Purchasing Power of Money*, 2nd edn, reprinted by Augustus Kelley, New York, 1971.
——(1935), 'Are booms and depressions transmitted internationally through monetary standards?', *Bulletin of the International Statistical Institute*, 28, 1–29.
Friedman, M. (1951), 'Commodity-reserve currency,' *Journal of Political Economy*, 59 (June), 203–32. Reprinted in his *Essays in Positive Economics*, Chicago, University of Chicago Press, 1953.
Friedman, M. and Anna J. Schwartz (1963), *A Monetary History of the United States, 1867–1960*, Princeton, Princeton University Press.
Goldman, S.M. (1972), 'Hyperinflation and the rate of growth in the money supply', *Journal of Economic Theory*, 5 (October), 250–7.
Graham, Benjamin (1937), *Storage and Stability*, New York, McGraw-Hill.
——(1944), *World Commodities and World Currency*, New York, McGraw-Hill.
Graham, Frank D. (1942), *Social Goals and Economic Institutions*, Princeton, Princeton University Press.
Hepburn, A.B. (1903), *History of Coinage and Currency in the United States*, London, Macmillan.
Jevons, W. Stanley (1884), *Investigations in Currency and Finance*, reprinted by Augustus Kelley, New York, 1964.
Judd, J.H. (1965), *United States Pattern, Experimental and Trial Pieces*, 3rd edn, Racine, Wis., Whitman.
Keynes, J.M. *et al.* (1943), 'Proposals by British experts for an international clearing union' (April), reprinted in *Proceedings and Documents of the United Nations Monetary and Financial Conference*, 2, Washington, D.C., US Government Printing Office, 1948.
Laughlin, J.L. (1896), *History of Bimetallism in the United States*, 4th edn, New York, D. Appleton.
Luke, J.C. (1975), 'Inflation-free pricing rules for a generalized commodity-reserve currency', *Journal of Political Economy*, 83 (August), 779–90.
Marshall, A. (1887), 'Remedies for fluctuations of general prices', reprinted in A.C. Pigou (ed.) *Memorials of Alfred Marshall*, London, Macmillan, 1925.
——(1923), *Money, Credit and Commerce*, London, Macmillan.
Mill, J.S. (1848), *Principles of Political Economy*, 2, Boston, Little, Brown.
Mundell, R.A. (1968), *International Economics*, New York, Macmillan.
——(1971), *Monetary Theory*, Pacific Palisades, Goodyear.
Niehans, J. (1978), 'Commodity Money', in J. Niehans, *The Theory of Money*, Baltimore, Johns Hopkins University Press, 140–65.
Ricardo, D. (1821), *The Principles of Political Economy and Taxation*, 3rd edn. Reprinted by J.M. Dent, London, 1911.
Sargent, T.J. and N. Wallace (1973), 'The stability of models of money and growth with perfect foresight', *Econometrica*, 41 (November), 1043–8.
Sayers, R.S. (1931), 'The Indian exchange problem 1919–20', *Economica*, 11 (November), 450–62.
Thornton, H. (1802), *An Enquiry into the Nature and Effects of the Paper Credit of Great Britain*, reprinted by Allen & Unwin, London, 1937.
Triffin, R. (1960), *Gold and the Dollar Crisis*, New Haven, Yale University Press.
Weber, W.E. (1976), 'Price level variability and commodity reserve standards', unpublished MS.
Whitaker, J.K. (1976), 'An essay on the pure theory of commodity money', unpublished MS.

Part II

The gold standard in history

Introduction

The operation of the classical gold standard in the period 1880–1913 diverged markedly from the predictions of economists' theoretical models. W.M. Scammell, in the first selection in Part II, presents a comprehensive account of the classical gold standard's operation which emphasizes precisely those features which do not conform to standard models. Robert Triffin's article moves beyond Scammell's by focusing on potential asymmetries in the gold standard's operation, arguing that the system operated to the benefit of Europe but was a burden to the countries of the periphery. The third selection, by A.G. Ford, draws together the perspectives adopted by Scammell and Triffin. It contrasts the gold standard's operation at the centre, namely in Britain, with its effects in the periphery, where Argentina is taken as a case study.

6

The working of the gold standard

W.M. Scammell*

The period 1870 to 1914 was the high summer of the international gold standard. Neither invented nor consciously planned, it had grown steadily during the eighteenth and early nineteenth centuries as countries, from a choice of different metallic standards, silver, gold or bimetallic, had adopted gold as their monetary base.[1] In 1871, the German Empire made gold its standard and Switzerland and Belgium followed in 1878. Thereafter gold was the basis of international payments among the leading countries until the Great War transformed the international economy which the standard had served. Its subsequent history in the interwar period is of a series of short and disastrous experiments aimed at its rehabilitation as an international system of payments and adjustment. This paper examines some aspects of the gold standard during its heyday. After preliminary discussion we will consider: (a) what were the techniques by which the Bank of England operated the system for Britain during the period; (b) to what extent the practical gold standard of this period differed from the classical model of gold standard adjustment which is so familiar, and (c) why it was that the gold standard of the nineteenth century endured so long and with such apparent stability.

*

Since the various national experiments in the re-establishment of the gold standard in the 1920s involved important qualitative differences from the gold

* *Yorkshire Bulletin of Economic and Social Research*, May 1965, pp. 32–45.

standard which existed before 1914 and since much latter-day discussion of the gold standard is coloured by its operation in the break-down period, it is necessary to set down briefly the elements of the earlier system. Three features are noteworthy.

Firstly, the nineteenth-century gold standard was a gold *coinage* standard,[2] in which gold coins circulated domestically and were interchangeable with notes at the central bank, which held a gold reserve to maintain and safeguard interchangeability. Whenever this reserve was threatened by an undue demand for gold to replace notes (e.g. to make foreign payments) or whenever the reserve was increased by gold sold to the central bank in return for notes (e.g. gold received from abroad) then certain monetary techniques were available to redress the undesired movement.

Secondly, within the gold standard of the later nineteenth century, sterling operated as an international currency on equal[3] terms with gold. Sterling was for many countries the normal means of settling trading indebtedness and gold was transferred only as a balancing item, as, for example, when a country's commercial banks were called upon to make more payments to foreigners than were compensated by receipts. In such a situation any tendency for banks to quote higher rates for foreign currencies would be checked by the purchase of gold from the central bank and its shipment abroad.[4] Apart from this trading use, sterling was used equally with gold as a means of settling international balances between countries, i.e. for compensatory monetary movements. Overseas banks in many countries held working balances of sterling, either in the form of London acceptances, loans to the London discount market or London bank deposits, and were prepared to use these balances for residual clearing. Moreover, in some countries, central banks held part or all of their main reserve in sterling, preferring sterling to gold, partly for the interest which the sterling assets yielded and partly because the bulk of their trade lay with the United Kingdom and sterling balances were a trading convenience. Thus the picture of gold standard operation in the period before 1914, is one of a close interchangeability of gold and sterling which gave to the Bank of England not only the role of regulator of the British monetary system but, in great part, that of regulator of the gold standard and the international payments system.

Thirdly, it is interesting to compare the gold standard of 1870–1914, based on gold and influenced predominantly by the relation of gold and sterling, with the gold exchange standards of the post-1918 period. In the former the system was, in essence, a gold exchange standard but one in which gold and only one other currency, itself based on gold, served as international money. This system was only capable of enduring as long as the international currency operating with gold was unimpeachably strong, was backed by financial institutions of strength and probity and as long as its convertibility into gold at any time was assured. In the post-1918 period not only was sterling weaker as a currency and incapable of resuming its prewar role but other gold-based currencies, of varying strength, operated with it as reserve currencies in a gold exchange system whose structure, thus based, was inherently weak. It can be seen from this that the gold standard of the late nineteenth century was both simpler and stronger than the reconstruction of it which was attempted in the 1920s. Two other features lacking in the later version worked to its advantage. The first was that, as an international payments system, the nineteenth-century gold standard functioned in an epoch of unparalleled commercial and industrial expansion and that the inherently deflationary tendencies, so strongly to be revealed in the dismal 1930s, did not manifest themselves. Secondly, the nineteenth century saw the steady growth of an international financial fraternity, which expressed itself through international banking and the co-operation of the great central banks of the leading countries. This gave to the system a loosely knit, flexible, institutional framework through which to function. Such central bank co-operation was very real, involving all the participant countries in some surrender of national sovereignty – a surrender partly to the objective gold standard rules of the game and partly to the discretionary authority of the London money market and the Bank of England, who virtually managed the gold supply. Although it is customary to regard the nineteenth-century gold standard as an automatic system without formal organization or specified modes of operation, it is, in the writer's view, arguable that the gold standard was in fact quasi-organizational, being operated by a team of central bankers co-operating under the leadership of the Bank of England on behalf of the world business community. During the nineteenth century, and as long as an international monetary system was a working reality, surrender of national monetary sovereignty was, for a variety of reasons, tolerable. When, in the interwar period, the international economy splintered into a congeries of national monetary systems, each pursuing its own monetary policy and prepared to flout the rules of the gold standard game, central bank co-operation as a force was at an end. The restored gold standard of the 1930s had no institutional framework and was diversely operated, mainly by national governments and politicians, for national ends:[5] the old gold standard had been operated by monetary technicians, according to widely accepted technical criteria.

Before turning to more detailed aspects of gold standard operation it is necessary to remind ourselves that essentially the gold standard was a system of international balance-of-payments adjustment, that the technical criteria of management recognized this and that it must primarily be judged by the extent to which it was capable of adjusting short-term deficits or surpluses in the external balances of individual countries and of doing this with minimum interference with their domestic monetary stability, employment condition and rate of economic growth.

Although never consciously planned as such, the gold standard was the manifestation of the classical approach to the problem of balance-of-payments adjustment as it had been developed by economists from David Hume to John Stuart Mill. In this view the movement of goods in international trade is assumed to be the result of relative price-levels as explained in the theory of comparative costs. The upward or downward movement of an individual country's price level changes the volume and direction in which goods flow and therefore, since the classicists initially assumed away the existence of international capital movements, alters the balance of payments of the countries concerned. It follows that a disequilibrium, being the result of a change in relative price levels, can be adjusted by a subsequent opposite change. One might then describe a country's external equilibrium as a unique position reflecting its own cost/price relationship relative to that of other countries in the world system. In the determination of national price levels the Quantity Theory of Money, which since the time of Hume had dominated ideas on general price-level determination, was basic. For equilibrium to obtain, the world monetary supply must be distributed between nations in the same ratio as their national products, such a monetary distribution ensuring price ratios appropriate to general equilibrium. The gold standard ensured such a distribution, for through it international and national prices could be equalized. With such a system in operation differences between foreign receipts and payments for any country would be counterbalanced by such gold flows as would, by enlarging or depleting the monetary stock, produce appropriate price changes to alter demand for the imports and exports of the countries concerned and thus correct imbalance. In brief, the theory of adjustment which underlay the gold standard was one of the equalization of prices internationally, gold movements preserving the distribution of the world's monetary supply in a way appropriate to this.

Underlying this view of the adjustment process were several important assumptions. For example, the chain of reasoning required that, with an inflow of gold into a country's central bank, the strategic reserve ratios would rise making credit expansion both possible and desirable and that, with this, prices would rise so as to curtail foreign demand for the country's exports and stimulate domestic demand for imports whose prices would have fallen relatively to those of home-produced goods. Thus the view of the banking mechanism and its response to gold reserve changes was mechanistic, begging all the questions of the technique of monetary management involved. Apart from whether banking mechanisms were capable of producing the desired price changes there were also wider questions of the impact of these changes on the economy as a whole. For example, it was assumed that the processes of inflating and deflating the system in response to gold inflows and outflows were without friction, that the whole effect would be upon the price level and that there would be no adverse effects upon output and employment. Finally, it was assumed that the changes in price wrought by the gold movements would bring about switches of demand for imports and exports sufficient to redress the original trade imbalance, i.e. that demands for imports and exports were price-elastic. All these were big assumptions, not all of which were satisfied even in the classic period of the gold standard and certainly were not in the period of its breakdown.

In the last years of the nineteenth century the model of national price changes induced by gold flows in and out of central banks was supplemented by the argument that, for short-term external imbalance, changes in interest rates would produce an adjustment effect. Thus when, for example, the Bank of England lost gold as a result of a British payments deficit a rise in Bank Rate would serve to draw short-term funds to London and give immediate relief to the imbalance. A rise in Bank Rate was, in any event, the first step in the process of price deflation and indeed in many cases might be the only step necessary. By 1914 there was universal confidence that central banks by their interest-rate policies could go far to control world movements of gold. Full-scale engineered deflations and expansions of an economy were not likely to be necessary.

Conceptually, and later in practice, this model involved, for any individual country within the system, a conflict between its external stability, i.e. the stability of its balance of payments and its domestic stability, i.e. a steady price level, full employment and some measure of economic growth. If the balance of payments was regarded as paramount and was to be continually adjusted by induced price changes then, at best, the price level was a more mercurial variable than it might otherwise be; while at worst the price changes would be accompanied by changes in output and employment which were seriously destabilizing. Only if wages and prime costs were infinitely flexible would gold standard adjustment be a tolerable process for a participant country. During the period of the gold standard's history with which we are concerned this conflict of the domestic and the external interest was not vital. Wages were then a much more flexible cost and much of the onus of adjustment fell on Britain who in this period of expansion was capable of making what were no more than 'rolling' adjustments to her monetary position without embarrassment. But in the postwar period when the gold standard had been restored in the major countries and demanded of them a purposive deflation in a deflationary world, it was this factor more than any other which made it unworkable.

We are now in a position to end these preliminary remarks by setting down briefly the essential conditions or 'rules of the game' for operation of a gold standard. They are:

(i) a gold value must be fixed for the currency of every country within the system;

(ii) there must be free movement of gold as between countries within the system;

(iii) the monetary system of all member countries must be such that the domestic money supply is linked more or less automatically to movements of gold in and out of the country.

If these three rules are satisfied then the balance of payments or adjustment function of the standard will be satisfied. But if this is to be accompanied by domestic balance a fourth rule is necessary. This is,

(iv) that within each country there must be a high degree of wage flexibility.[6]

We shall return to these conditions at later stages of this article.

*

Any examination of Bank of England technique under the gold standard between 1870 and 1914 must be concerned (a) with the development of machinery for making Bank Rate effective, and (b) with alternative weapons to Bank Rate, namely the various 'gold devices' which were used by the Bank in its operations in the gold market. It is apparent that there were three fairly distinct stages of development.

From 1870–1880 the techniques used were rudimentary, reliance being placed upon the ordinary processes of expansion and contraction of the monetary base with frequent changes of the discount rate.[7] Technical operations in the sense of a purposive monetary policy were few and, in accordance with the precepts of the Bank Charter Act 1844, the gold standard functioned with simplicity. When the balance of payments became adverse gold was lost to other countries and the domestic monetary supply contracted. In the short term interest rates rose and, after a time-lag, prices fell and equilibrium was restored. In the case of a surplus the process was reversed. In practice the process was more complicated than this in that, by the loss or gain of gold, the whole credit base was affected and with this the *modus operandi* of discount-rate changes became important. But the Bank of England's influence on interest rates was, at this stage, slight and largely ineffective. It rested purely on the fact that the Bank was ordinarily one of the largest buyers of bills in the market. This meant that the Bank of England discount rate was, in certain circumstances, usually near to market rate but, as the discount market grew in size the relative importance of the Bank of England in fixing the rate diminished. Only if the Bank of England could become a monopoly buyer in the market could it make its own rate effective.[8] There were halting steps during this period towards the purposive use of interest rates by the Bank but their effective use had to wait upon certain developments in the institutional framework of the monetary system, particularly upon recognition of the Bank of England as lender of last resort and the subjection of the market rate of interest to Bank Rate.

In the years 1880–90 and while these institutional developments were taking place we find the Bank of England resorting to certain practices in the gold market which to some extent took the place of Bank Rate changes and were regarded by it as a means of minimizing the effects on the domestic economy of such changes.

Finally, from about 1890 to the beginning of the Great War we find a swift development of the power of the Bank of England, the working-out of a Bank Rate policy and the abandonment of the gold devices – in short a definite movement towards a more confident and purposive monetary management.

In considering the development of Bank Rate techniques it is well to remember that changes in Bank Rate depend fundamentally on (a) deciding the direction and size of the change and (b) making it effective. The first condition is one which will be conditioned by the circumstances obtaining at the time and depends on the skill and experience of the monetary authority. The second depends on financial institutions but the primary requirement is that the central bank should be able to induce a shortage of funds in the money market and then itself make money available at the chosen rate, which is thus made effective. Since borrowers can only obtain money at this rate they alter their own lending rates accordingly. The arrangement which ultimately evolved in England was the well-known one under which, by open market operations, the Bank of England created a shortage of short-term credit and drove the discount houses to borrow from it at whatever rate it chose to enforce. This system did not develop until late in the period we are discussing and it is necessary to look at its development since Bank Rate played such an important part in gold standard theory.

After a period of drift in central bank evolution in the third quarter of the century the tempo of change quickened after 1870 and in the years which followed the main features of the new system emerged: recognition of the Bank of England as leader of the banking system with special reserve responsibilities; recognition of the special role played by the Bank of England's discount rate; growth and concentration of the discount market; formation of a market in short-term paper augmented (after 1877) by Treasury bills; and, perhaps tardiest of all, recognition by the Bank of England of its own special tasks and responsibilities.

So far as the use of Bank Rate to influence the foreign exchanges was concerned the Bank's policy before 1870 was wellnigh nonexistent. The London discount market was not yet susceptible to foreign influences and the 'internationalization' of the market still lay in the future. Wide rate differences often existed between London and West European capitals without much effect and, with New York three weeks away in communication, Bank Rate differences with that city were of little importance. Even in the 1860s, while it was recognized that any large crisis or panic abroad would ultimately affect London, it was felt that, in the short term, rate disparities would have little effect on short money movements. By 1870 however, international financial intelligence was improving, there was a growing use by foreigners of the London capital market, and from then onwards international influences grew swiftly. But before 1870 the views of the Bank on its operations in the market were purely domestic; it insisted that Bank Rate in its movements should follow and not lead the ordinary market rate and that, while Bank Rate should conform more or less closely to market rate, the Bank ought never to initiate rate changes.[9] The 1860s had been a period in which there was marked lack of co-operation between the Bank of England and the discount companies. The shadow and controversy of the crisis of 1857 still lay across the city and money market borrowing from the Bank, even during the 'shuttings',[10] fell considerably. With the decline in the number of bills the Bank of England had felt obliged to keep its own discount rate as close to the market rate as possible so that changes were frequent, while for long periods Bank Rate was ineffective. Moreover, when large foreign balances were in London the market rate and its shadowy follower, Bank Rate, were low just at a time when a rise in Bank Rate to protect the reserve might be necessary. Bagehot and others frequently criticized the Bank in the early 1870s for this state of affairs and for failing to anticipate pressure on the reserve. In 1873 Bank Rate was changed twenty-four times in order to keep near to the market rate. Between 1865 and 1874 Bank Rate changes averaged twelve per year. Between 1845 and 1859 the average had been four per year.

In 1870 it was clear that the main aim of Bank Rate policy should be to exercise a positive influence on the interest-rate structure. There were, in effect, two short-term discount rates in London: Bank Rate, controlled by the Bank of England but ineffectually following market rate, which was far more important since it was the rate at which foreign bills could be discounted in London. The Bank as custodian of the reserve could not control market rate. Clearly responsibility for the reserve and control of the main short-term rate should both reside in the monetary authority.

In late 1871 for the first time Bank Rate (at 5 per cent) was temporarily above market rate (at $3\frac{1}{2}$ per cent) and despite criticism[11] it was soon clear that the rule of conformity of Bank Rate to market rate had been abandoned. Henceforward the differential between the two rates became steadily wider. In 1874 Bank Rate was raised to deal with a potential foreign demand for gold at a time when adherence to the rule of following market rate would have meant a reduction. Moreover, there were signs that not only was the Bank pursuing a new policy in changing the Rate but also that it appreciated the need to make the Rate effective.

The struggle for the effectiveness of Bank Rate was to be a long one and was to occupy the next two decades. Not until 1890 was the Bank able to deal with the problem of what Bonamy Price in July 1877 referred to as 'two money markets in London, two rates of interest'. Under a rule of 1858 the Bank of

England would only lend to the market during the shuttings so that any development of a 'market in the Bank' was impossible. But during the 1870s the increasing volume of Treasury business began to have its effect on the market, extending stringency over longer periods than the shuttings and often placing the Bank in unaccustomed command of the market. In 1878 the Bank announced that it would be prepared to lend to the market, at or near Bank Rate, not only in times of crisis and at the shuttings, but at any time. It would not discount bills but would be prepared to make advances for very short periods to discount houses and bill brokers. Bank Rate became for a time not a discount rate but a loan rate for short help-loans to the discount houses. Thus, with growing effect, the Bank relaxed the 1858 rule giving help to the market virtually at its discretion.[12] But this was insufficient to give control and by the early 1890s the Bank was under criticism for its failure to protect the gold reserve whose movements still responded not to Bank Rate but to the market rate. The seriousness of the problem varied with the volume of bills coming to the market and with the flow of available funds but, in general, Bank Rate still moved ineffectually in the wake of the market rate. This was a crucial period for London's leadership of the gold standard for such leadership depended upon the Bank of England being able to control interest rates in London which it patently could not do. The Baring crisis in 1890 heightened criticism of the Bank of England's lack of power to maintain the gold reserve and the Bank began to take steps to increase its power over the market. In that year the Bank at last formally annulled the 1858 rule and readmitted the discount houses to rediscount facilities, thus recognizing not only the need to fix an effective Bank Rate but that, for that purpose, the Bank had to be in the market and not aloof from it.

In July 1890 it began to discount for its regular customers at a rate below market rate. Later in July it told the bill brokers it would discount fifteen day bills for them at Bank Rate. In 1894 the stipulated currency for bills was increased to thirty days, in 1897 to three months and in 1910 to four months. These increases gradually strengthened the Bank's hold over the market.

But there was another approach to the problem of how the Bank might try to make the market rate comply with its own rate. Market rate fundamentally depended on the flow of funds available. It was clear that if the Bank could increase or decrease the available funds it could lower or raise the market rate. It could reduce the funds in the market by reducing its own liabilities to the banking system or alternatively by bringing about a switch of its liabilities to non-bank depositors. In fact it used both these methods, combining them in a variety of devices which, apart from open market operations in consols, involved borrowing in the market, borrowing from the clearing banks and borrowing from its own depositors. Apart from these methods we have isolated instances of 'moral suasion' which have a faintly modern air. The years 1890 to 1914 thus form a period in which the market and the Bank taught one another the theory of centralized money-market control by the use of these devices and the Bank gained, by convention, a fair degree of control over the market when the foreign balance required it. Yet it was only in the last years of the nineteenth century that bank rate became a swiftly variable and effective means of adjusting the interest-rate structure and of influencing capital movements and the balance of payments. Certainly during the 1890s Bank Rate changes in themselves were regarded as only one possible weapon for influencing the external balance.

Other countries, notably France, made less use of discount-rate changes than did the Bank of England but they were less liberal in their gold import and export policies and were prepared to impose restrictions on gold movements, charge premiums on gold and use other arbitrary devices to protect their gold reserve. If these were to be countered by the Bank of England through Bank Rate changes alone they would often have required large and domestically destabilizing increases of the Rate. To avoid these the Bank of England came in the late 1880s to use methods in its gold dealings which were designed to counter those of foreign central banks yet which lay within its own statutory obligations. These obligations were (i) to exchange sovereigns for notes, and (ii) to purchase bar gold with notes at the price of £3.17s.9d. per standard ounce. These conditions served to determine the narrow range of variation in the exchange rate outside of which gold would be imported or exported, i.e. the so-called gold points. There were, however, two quasi-legal ways in which the Bank could exert pressure on the exchanges; firstly, by paying more than £3.17s.9d. per ounce for bar gold, which it was quite free to do; and secondly, by varying the prices at which it would purchase certain foreign gold coins. Yet a further covert attraction to draw gold to itself was to provide interest-free advances to gold importers to recompense them for the time that gold was in transit. Some of these so-called 'gold devices' came into partial use by the Bank from the middle 1880s. Not until 1890, however, did the Bank use the device of increasing its buying price for bar gold.[13] This met with such success that throughout 1891, a year in which the Bank had considerable difficulty in controlling the discount market, the Bank manipulated its prices, both for gold bars and coin, in such a way as to supplement its Bank Rate policy. In 1892 the gold devices were used as an alternative to Bank Rate which was allowed to stand ineffective at 3 per cent. During the mid-1890s, a period of cheap money, the Bank had no need to seek to attract gold but the gold devices were used again during the years 1896–1910 at any time when the Bank wished to conserve or attract gold. As Sayers says 'a gold policy became in some degree a substitute for a bank rate policy' and a means whereby the Bank might 'protect its gold stock when it found itself unable to control the discount market except at great cost'.[14]

The Bank's justification of these gold devices was (a) that other central banks resorted to more extreme and arbitrary methods to conserve their gold and these could not go uncountered, and (b) that if these were to be met purely by Bank Rate variations, changes of Rate would require to be of such magnitude as would seriously curtail British business activity. This defence implied a limited use of the devices but we find in the later 1890s the gold devices being used in cases where moderate and easily effected changes of Bank Rate might have sufficed. The Bank, it seems, had come to regard the gold devices as not only a reinforcement to Bank Rate but as a means often to be preferred. It appears from the cases between 1896 and 1910 that in making the choice between Bank Rate or the gold devices a case had to be made for a Bank Rate change. If such a change were at all questionable on other grounds then the gold devices were used. From 1910 to 1914 were difficult years for the Bank and after 1907 the gold devices appear to have fallen into progressive disuse in favour of the straight Bank Rate method. This seems to have been at least partly due to increasing confidence on the part of the Bank, demonstrated by a very successful use of Bank Rate in November 1907, that it could use Bank Rate with great effectiveness and that the method had support.

When we look at the technical operations of the Bank of England in our period so far as they were aimed (and that was almost always their dominant aim) at preservation of the convertibility of the pound it is difficult to reduce them to order and to set down what seem to be the general principles of operation. The Bank's control over the discount market and the banking system was developing. Its methods were in constant transition. Offsetting action is often hard to recognize. Operations can be listed but we can only conjecture why many of them took place. Conditions promptly and energetically met in one instance seem to have been ignored or taken lightly in another. We must assume that, at the time, the Bank and the best informed opinion surrounding it were capable of assessing the situation in a way which we cannot do at this remove. We can only distil out of this steady stream of activities some generalizations which appear to be consistent.

(i) The Bank regarded the maintenance of the convertibility of sterling to gold as paramount and any sustained gold movement always led to action sooner or later.

(ii) In spite of this, and in contrast to the conventional model of the gold standard, the action taken was by no means automatic and implied a high degree of discretion on the part of the authorities. This discretion was exercised not only in the matter of choice of how the Bank reacted to a gold flow but also of timing in that the Bank by its anticipation often forestalled a gold movement or even allowed one to go unchallenged if it judged it likely to be transient. Nevertheless, it is no exaggeration to say that the dilemma of choice between domestic and external stability was ever in the forefront of Bank thinking from about 1880 onwards and that the Bank sought to soften this dilemma by the selection and timing of its actions.

(iii) The weapons used to deal with gold flows during the years 1870 to 1914 were two: to alter Bank Rate, with all that that implied for domestic trade and business; or to operate on the free gold market in London. In general the early use of Bank Rate was tentative and a Bank Rate policy had to wait until the Bank of England had learned the art of making its own rate quickly effective. This did not come until the last years of the period. In the early part of the period much use was made of a number of devices by which the Bank of England intervened in the gold market.

(iv) The effectiveness of Bank of England operations during the period may be questioned. The best that can be said is that there was a steady improvement from about 1900 as the Bank gained power and recognition as a central bank, but before that time it was seriously handicapped by its uncertain control of Bank Rate and by its hesitancy and lack of a concerted and continuous policy.[15] Sayers draws attention to the Bank's failure to deal with seasonal drains of gold each autumn as a serious 'blot on its record'.[16]

*

In comparing the classical model of gold standard adjustment to the practical operation of the standard in the later nineteenth century it quickly becomes apparent that model and reality do not always accord. Even admitting that any economic model is but an approximate picture of the variables it seeks to explain there are here certain differences which are fundamental enough to make us believe that the classical model of the gold standard seriously clouds the picture of what took place in nineteenth-century international adjustment.

First, it is fairly clear from empirical evidence that gold movements between countries were in many cases actuated by forces other than a difference in their price levels and that, of these forces, the most important was differences between countries in the level of interest rates. That relative interest rates did influence gold movements was of course known, and indeed became a built-in part of gold standard theory, but whether they acted in concert with relative price movements or were a separate force in themselves, or what, if separate, were their comparative powers as impellers of a gold flow was not, and indeed still is not, known. There are problems of timing here. For example, when a country experienced a boom and its price level rose did it experience a gold inflow after the boom (a) because its interest rate had risen with the boom, (b) because, as a booming country, it attracted capital, or (c) because the interest rate had broken the boom and was causing the home price level to fall relative to other countries? The prime mover here is difficult to locate. On the whole the power of (b) seems to be the most likely force and the empirical evidence would bear this out. By the end of the nineteenth century, however, the Bank of England was acting as if it regarded interest rate changes as the main force compelling gold movements but whether it looked upon such changes as being sufficient in themselves or as providing a short-term adjustment effect on the balance of payments, which if not sufficient in itself would in due time be fortified by the price change which the change in interest rates would induce, is not clear. It seems, on the whole, probable that the Bank considered that to meet most gold flows a change in Bank Rate was sufficient, without considering as part of the adjustment process, the inflationary or deflationary trend which such a change might initiate.

Second is the fact that in the classic period of the gold standard the main central banks did not in fact observe the rules of the game with that mechanistic precision often ascribed to them. The Bank of England by no means allowed a mechanistic relation between gold movements and the domestic monetary system to obtain but, as we have seen, exercised a discretionary authority as to the particular monetary weapons to be used in given circumstances. In particular, the use of discount-rate changes was often avoided in favour of some other device if it were deemed that at that time an interest-rate change would have an adverse effect on the domestic credit situation. The clash of domestic and external stability was fully realized even at this early stage but was minimized by this discretionary choice and timing of monetary action. Where the exercise of discretion was limited, however, was that the working processes of a centralized banking system were as yet imperfectly understood and that in a situation where monetary weapons were still developing the scope for choice in their use was small. In such circumstances an element of automaticity is perhaps inevitable and an advantage, but this automaticity was not complete and tended to diminish as the period progressed. Central banking was developing and 'the essence of central banking is discretionary control of the monetary system'.[17]

The third and perhaps most important difference between the gold standard model of adjustment and the actual adjustment of the nineteenth-century system is that, as we now realize, forces far more powerful than the relative price changes of the Ricardian model are built in to balance-of-payments changes. The new emphasis on income changes which stemmed from Keynesian economics in the late 1930s has transformed the approach to adjustment theory which is now seen as a complex relation between the balances of payments of individual countries and their national incomes and also of the price effects which balance-of-payments changes may create. It is usual nowadays to think of balance-of-payments adjustment in income terms[18] but price changes must still be regarded as a causal factor and any adequate model of the adjustment process must take cognizance of both price and income changes. What is important to note here is that the adjustment attributed to price changes and gold flows in the nineteenth century was swift and smooth, not because of the power of price changes to effect adjustment, but because income changes were always acting in the same direction to reinforce the price changes. When a balance of payments went into deficit the income of the deficit country fell and with the fall in income a fall in imports improved the merchandise trade balance. Several early exponents of the classical theory of adjustment noted the speed and ease with which adjustment took place and suspected that some force other than price changes was at work. Moreover, the potency of income adjustment can be judged from the fact that, on certain occasions, balance-of-payments adjustment has taken place in spite of simultaneous neutralizing action by the central bank to offset the effects of gold flows.[19]

Finally, the great emphasis placed on price and cost movements as means of balance-of-payments correction has tended to obscure the significant part played by long-term capital movements. In fact long-term capital movements in certain cases offset large and enduring deficits or surpluses so that there was no call for correction of the trade balance, except in a historically long run. The developing countries of the time – USA, Canada, Australia, etc. – were able to maintain long-standing deficits on current account financed by corresponding capital imports from Western Europe.

*

It remains to explain briefly why the international adjustments of the gold standard in the late nineteenth century were relatively smooth compared to the frustrated adjustments of the gold standard of the interwar period. It is a tribute to the efficacy of the nineteenth-century system that it worked with such smoothness during a period when the world total of international liquidity, provided by central bank gold reserves was a smaller percentage relative to total world trade than at any time since. We are today much concerned with the so-called 'international liquidity problem' when total gold and foreign exchange reserves run at over 50 per cent of world imports. In 1913 the comparable figure was 20 per cent. What was there in the nineteenth-century gold standard which protected it from chronic imbalance and enabled it to function with such a low level of liquidity?

The first reason for success is undoubtedly that the basic conditions for the working of the classical model were much more nearly realized in the late nineteenth century than later. Apart from the legalistic conditions of gold standard operation, which in themselves assure the adjustment function, the fourth condition of flexibility[20] was achieved to a greater extent in this period than before or since. There was widespread reliance on the price system and in finished goods, raw materials and factor prices there was scope for smooth adjustment unobstructed by the many institutional impediments which precluded such flexibility in later years. Moreover, and particularly after the Cobden Treaty of 1860, international trade was comparatively free. When, in the last years of the century, Germany and the USA raised tariff walls it seemed to have little effect on the smoothness of international adjustment.

Secondly, in an era of swift industrial expansion, adjustment of the gold standard type could be achieved without deflationary effects. With little surplus capacity in the industrial countries and investment opportunities abundant, the switches of demand involved could be accomplished easily and smoothly. In so far as adjustment required movements in relative prices these could be achieved without squeezing of profit margins and deleterious effects upon employment and, in so far as adjustment was brought about by movements in relative national income, these were achieved in great part by disparities in rates of growth rather than by positive inflations and negative deflations.

Thirdly, in so far as gold was linked closely to sterling as the main international currency, it was essential that sterling should not be scarce. It was a currency to be used and not to be hoarded. The trading position of Britain in this period was exactly suited to her role as world banker and manager of the leading currency. Because of its large and growing revenue from invisible trade Britain was able to develop a large import surplus and the sterling disbursed abroad by British importers was available to finance trade in many parts of the world. The newer industrial countries such as Germany, as they too became net importers, were able to pay for their excess imports by exporting to Britain or to markets of their own choice rather than by competing with Britain for the sale of manufactures in the countries from which she too imported. Sterling was able to become a world currency in which payments were made either through offsetting entries in the books of international bankers, or through investment in commercial bills of exchange. Moreover, the structure of the British balance of payments protected the international economy from the development of sterling shortage during the successive stages of the business cycle. Britain's inelastic demand for imports and the elastic nature of the demand for her exports ensured that in times of depression Britain ran a deficit on her balance of payments. Thus, if during a slump British capital export declined, the deficit on current account compensated for this; while in times of boom the situation was reversed.

Fourthly, the strain of imbalance between countries, when it occurred, was often cushioned from international reserves by the international credit system which in the environment of the time allowed for longer trade credit (than in the unsettled conditions of the interwar years) and allowed international liquidity to be supplemented in the same way as domestic liquidity is boosted by longer trade credit within a country.

Fifthly, there was built in to the classical adjustment mechanism the unrecognized force which, with a balance-of-payments deficit, income changes impart to the trade balance and which when added to the forces already recognized in the gold standard model, created under the conditions then obtaining a formidable stabilizing effect. Thus when the balance of payments of a country was not in equilibrium variations in relative national incomes strengthened the price effects to achieve adjustment by a strong counter thrust on the balance of merchandise trade.

Finally, it must be said that in the policies of central banks in responding to the stimuli of gold flows there was a far greater element of discretion than is generally supposed. The Bank of England, while regarding protection of its gold reserve as paramount, nevertheless exercised considerable discretion in the choice and timing of its actions and was ever mindful of its need to achieve external stability with at least the minimum interference with the level of domestic business activity.

There can be no doubt that the international gold standard as it evolved in the nineteenth century provided the growing industrial world with the most efficient system of adjustment for balances of payments which it was ever to have, either by accident or conscious planning. No wonder that in 1918 the monetary wishes of the world were 'to get back to normal', normality implying above all the use of gold-based currencies. But it implied much more, above all the conditions we have set down. These were not to be reproduced in the gold standard of the twenties and thirties. The new conditions called for new systems of adjustment the nature of which we are still exploring.

Notes

1 The gold standard was a predominantly English development. After an uneasy period of bimetallism with silver between 1663 and 1798, in which year the coinage of silver was suspended, the Coinage Act of 1816 definitely established the gold standard, with the pound as the unit of account and a fixed value for gold in terms of sterling. After 1850 the French franc became a gold unit so that the two great financial markets of London and Paris were from then gold based. The German currency reform of 1871, which established the mark as a gold-based unit, virtually completed the gold standard in Western Europe. In the United States monometallism based on gold did not come until the Gold Standard Act of 1900.

2 This is in contrast to the gold *bullion* standard of the postwar period under which gold was no longer freely coined and did not serve as an internal currency. Under the later system only gold bullion was freely importable and exportable and a fixed price between this and the notes which circulated domestically secured a fixed exchange rate with the currencies of all countries operating a similar system.

3 Controversy might hang on the word 'equal'. Tew (1948) goes so far as to hint that sterling was the stronger of the two and that gold derived its value as a monetary asset from its convertibility into sterling. Certainly, as Tew points out, the record of sterling as an international currency after the collapse of the gold standard shows its great power to stand alone as such.

4 This shipment would in practice be undertaken by bullion merchants as an arbitrage transaction.
5 There were exceptions to this. One thinks, for example, of the influence on monetary affairs of the friendship of Montagu Norman of the Bank of England and Benjamin Strong of the Federal Reserve. The point remains, however, that such exceptions are few and that concerted monetary co-operation between central bankers had, after 1918, completely broken down.
6 Readers seeking a fuller and more sophisticated theory of the gold standard than is given in this brief summary should consult Meade (1951), vol. I, ch. 14 for an excellent account of the basic gold standard conditions.
7 Between 1871 and 1880 changes in Bank Rate averaged more than ten a year.
8 The practice of changing its discount rate weekly and in multiples of $\frac{1}{2}$ per cent also hindered the Bank and meant that the market could respond to demand more quickly and quote finer rates.
9 This rule was supposed to demonstrate the Bank's wish to abstain from competition in the market.
10 That is, the periods just before the dividend dates on government stock, at which time the market had traditional right of recourse to the Bank of England.
11 Bagehot, *Lombard Street*, pp. 321–2.
12 It often exercised this discretion powerfully. For example, in 1883, mindful of the effects and dangers of discount market overtrading before 1858, it revived the 1858 rule temporarily.
13 This was in January 1890 when Bank Rate had been raised to 6 per cent without much effect in bringing in gold. In February the Bank raised its buying price for bars to £3.17s.9½d.per ounce and, impressed by the resultant gold inflow, covertly raised the gold price again by removing from importers of large bars the obligation to bear the cost of smelting.
14 Sayers (1936), pp. 71–101.
15 Sayers asserts that this was due to the system whereby governors of the Bank served for two years and were then succeeded by their deputies. Bank operations tended, therefore, to reflect the ability and forcefulness of the Governor for the time being (Sayers, 1936, p. 136).
16 ibid., p. 135.
17 Sayers (1957), p. 1.
18 For a statement of the income theory of balance-of-payments adjustment see Scammell (1957), pp. 39–49.
19 See Paish (1936).
20 See above.

References

Meade, James (1951), *The Theory of International Economic Policy*, London, Oxford University Press.
Paish, F. (1936), 'Banking policy and the balance of international payments', *Economica* (November).
Sayers, R.S. (1936), *Bank of England Operations 1890–1914*, London, P.S. King.
——(1957), *Central Banking After Bagehot*, Oxford, Clarendon Press.
Scammell, W.M. (1957), *International Monetary Policy*, London, Macmillan.
Tew, Brian (1948), 'Sterling as an international currency', *Economic Record* (June).

7

The myth and realities of the so-called gold standard

Robert Triffin*

The monetary traditions and institutions of the nineteenth century provided a remarkably efficient mechanism of mutual adjustment of national monetary and credit policies to one another, essential to the long-term maintenance of exchange-rate stability between national currencies.

The reasons for this success, and for the breakdown of the system after World War I, are very imperfectly reflected in most of our textbooks. Most of all, however, over-concentration on the mechanism of *intercountry* adjustments fails to bring out the broader forces influencing the *overall pace* of monetary expansion on which individual countries were forced to align themselves.

The mechanism of adjustment among countries

Textbook abstract

Starting from an initial position of balance-of-payments equilibrium, the emergence of a fundamental deficit is generally described in terms of divergent movements of exports – downward – and imports – upward – in the deficit

*Our International Monetary System: Yesterday, Today and Tomorrow, New York, Random House, 1968, ch. 1. Also appears in The Evolution of the International Monetary System: Historical Reappraisal and Future Perspectives, Princeton, Princeton University Press, 1964, pp. 2–20.

countries, with opposite, and equally divergent, movements in the surplus countries.

The money flows associated with the international settlement of such imbalances if not offset by domestic 'neutralization' policies, should then tend to prompt downward price readjustments in the deficit countries, and upward readjustments in the surplus countries. This would restore a competitive price and cost pattern among them, and bring their balances of payments back into equilibrium.

These 'automatic' adjustment forces were strengthened and speeded up by central banks through the so-called 'rules of the game'. Discount-rate policy and open-market interventions would raise interest rates and tighten credit in the deficit countries, while lowering interest rates and expanding credit in the surplus countries. This would both cushion balance-of-payments and monetary transfers in the short term, by stimulating compensatory capital movements from the surplus to the deficit countries and accelerate the desirable downward readjustment of prices and costs in the latter countries and their upward readjustment in the first.

The 'rules of the game' were widely violated after World War I. The surplus countries adopted 'neutralization' policies which increasingly concentrated upon the deficit countries the burdens of adjustment previously distributed between surplus and deficit countries alike. At the same time, the development of stronger resistance to downward price and wage adaptations – particularly as a result of the growing strength of the trade unions – blocked the price-adjustment mechanism in the deficit countries, transfering its impact to fluctuations in economic activity and employment. The resulting social and political strains gradually became unbearable, particularly during the world depression of the 1930s, and induced governments to abandon the harsh gold standard disciplines in favour of fluctuating exchange rates and/or trade and exchange restrictions.

Historical abstract

The highly simplified digest of the theory of international adjustment under the actual gold standard certainly meets the first test of an economic theory, i.e. the test of logical consistency. Does it meet equally well the second test by which a theory should be judged, i.e. its conformity to the major facts calling for explanation?

It undoubtedly fits *some* of the facts. Comparative price – or exchange-rate – movements obviously play a role in the fluctuations of balances of payments on current account, and are themselves influenced by the tightening or expansion of money flows arising both from international settlements and from domestic policies or lack of policies.

Other facts, however, must also be taken into account if we are to develop a general and politically meaningful theory of balance-of-payments adjustments.

1 First of all, the most cursory look at international trade statistics reveals an enormous degree of parallelism – rather than divergent movements – between export and import fluctuations *for any one country*, and in the general trend of foreign-trade movements *for the various trading countries*. Over the eighty years from 1880 to 1960, all significant increases or decreases in the exports of Western Europe were marked by *parallel* increases, or decreases, *for the eleven major trading countries of the world* in 91 per cent of the cases, and by *simultaneous* increases, or decreases, of *exports and imports for each country*, taken separately, in 88 per cent of the cases. These proportions fall to 77 and 73 per cent, respectively, for fluctuations of one year only, but rise to 95 and 92 per cent for fluctuations of more than a year's duration, and to 98 and 100 per cent for movements extending over more than four years.[1]

2 Equally impressive is the overall parallelism – rather than divergence – of price movements, expressed in the same unit of measurement, between the various trading countries maintaining a minimum degree of freedom of trade and exchange in their international transactions. In spite of wide differences and fluctuations in the composition of each country's exports, the indexes of export unit values – measured in current dollars – for the same eleven countries over the period 1870–1960 moved in the same direction in 89 per cent of the observed fluctuations, and in the opposite direction in only 11 per cent of the cases.[2]

This solidarity of national price movements – when measured in a common unit of account – is not incompatible, of course, with sharp divergences in national price levels, offset by opposite divergences in exchange-rate fluctuations. One does find indeed that any large variations in the evolution of national prices are invariably offset, more or less rapidly, by exchange-rate fluctuations, and vice versa. Such variations were, however, eschewed – except in wartime – by most industrial countries in the nineteenth century, but were relatively frequent in the countries of the so-called 'periphery', and particularly in Latin America.

3 Downward wage adjustments rarely reached any sizeable amplitude, even in the nineteenth century, among the countries which maintained exchange-rate stability, and it may be doubted whether they would have proved much more acceptable at that time, economically, politically and socially, than they are today. Wherever substantial inflation had been allowed to develop, international cost competitiveness was nearly invariably restored through devaluation rather than through downward price and wage adjustments.

Standard statistical series for the United States, the United Kingdom, France and Germany show only four or five instances of actual declines in any broad-based indexes of money wages during the fifty years preceding World War I. Such declines were, moreover, usually confined to one or a few percentage points only. They were far exceeded, in post-gold-standard days, by the much sharper wage drops of the 1920–2 recession – 37 per cent in the United Kingdom – and of the first years of the great depression – 22 per cent in the United States and Germany.[3]

4 The 'neutralization' policies stigmatized by Ragnar Nurkse as another major cause – along with increasing price and wage rigidity – of the downfall of the gold standard (Nurkse, 1944, pp. 66–8) were by no means a postwar innovation. Using exactly the same techniques of measurement as Nurkse, Arthur I. Bloomfield found that 'central banks in general played the rules of the game just as badly before 1914 as they did thereafter!'[4] It might be noted in passing, however, that Nurkse's method defines as neutralization the cases where fluctuations in a central bank's domestic portfolio offset only a fraction – no matter how small – of the changes in its international assets. In many cases, however, there remained a *positive* correlation between the latter and changes in the central bank's sight liabilities. The impact of the latter changes upon the country's money supply would most often be magnified, in turn, several times by the operation of the private banking system under customary cash and liquidity requirements. Nurkse's 'neutralization' policies, therefore, could still permit a *multiple* impact of international gold – or foreign-exchange – movements upon money supply, as contrasted with the mere one-to-one impact which would have resulted under the pure gold coin system of monetary circulation assumed in the most abstract formulations of gold standard theory (Triffin, 1947, pp. 52–3).

5 The impact of discount rates on *cushioning* capital movements and on *corrective* changes in cost competitiveness was also far less general and uniform than is usually assumed.

The first seems indeed to have been particularly effective for the well-developed money and capital markets of the major creditor countries and financial centres, and most of all in the case of the United Kingdom. Discount and interest-rate changes could accelerate, or slow down, the normal, or average, pace of capital exports, and had to be resorted to frequently by the Bank of England to defend its very slender gold reserves. The much higher reserve levels of the Bank of France enabled it, on the other hand, to cushion temporary deficits out of its own reserves, with much rarer recourses to discount-rate changes. Most of all, however, capital-importing countries were far less able to influence in the same way the pace of their capital imports, these being primarily determined by the ease or stringency prevailing in the major financial centres.

The impact of Britain's international surpluses and deficits on British bank reserves was cushioned, moreover, by the ample use of sterling balances as cash reserves by overseas banks, particularly throughout the British Empire. Surpluses and deficits between Britain and its Empire – and even, to some extent, with other countries – merely led to a reshuffling of British bank deposits, rather than to an overall expansion or contraction in their amount and to correlative gold inflows or outflows.

Finally, the enormous role played by the London discount market in the financing of the food and raw-materials exports of the less developed countries probably imparted to the Bank of England's discount-rate policy an influence on British terms of trade – and balance of payments – which has escaped the attention of economic theorists. Increases in discount rates did – as is usually pointed out – tend to reduce British prices and costs, improving the competitiveness of British exports in world markets and of home-made import-substitute goods on the domestic market. What is forgotten, however, is that the tightening of the London discount market also affected, most directly and overwhelmingly, the ease with which inventories of staple foods and raw materials could be financed, thus forcing also a quicker liquidation and attendant price declines in Britain's chief import goods. Such declines could be expected to be far larger than those in the less sensitive and volatile prices of British industrial exports. Thus, the favourable impact of discount-rate increases on British competitiveness (lowering British prices in relation to foreign prices in competing industrial nations) would be reinforced in its balance-of-payments effects by a simultaneous improvement of Britain's terms of trade (i.e. by decreases in the prices of foreign suppliers of complementary goods to Britain, larger than the decreases in British export prices to them). (See Triffin (1947, pp. 60–3), and Kenen (1960, pp. 59–62).)

6 The importance of international capital movements, and of their fluctuations, is often obscured by the disproportionate emphasis often placed on comparative price and cost fluctuations as the major factor in balance-of-payments disequilibria and their correction. Attention is thereby centred on the current-account items of the balance of payments, and tends to suggest that most disturbances arose in this area and had to be corrected promptly by the restoration of equilibrium between receipts and expenditures on current – or even merely merchandise – account.

In fact, however, international capital movements often did cushion – and even stimulate – vast and enduring deficits, or surpluses, on current account without calling for any correction whatsoever, except in an extremely long run indeed. Developing countries, such as the United States, Canada, Argentina and Australia, could maintain, over an average of years, large and persistent deficits on current account, financed by correspondingly large, persistent and growing capital imports from the more advanced countries of Western

Europe. Rough estimates, compiled by the United Nations (1949, p. 2), place at about $40.5 billion, on the eve of World War I, the gross long-term foreign investments of the principal creditor countries of Western Europe, and at $3.5 billion those of the United States. Of this $44 billion total, $12 billion had been invested in Europe itself, $6.8 billion in the United States – which was still a net debtor country at the time – $8.5 billion in Latin America, $6.0 billion in Asia, $4.7 billion in Africa, $3.7 billion in Canada, and $2.3 billion in Australia and New Zealand.

The lion's share of these investments was that of the United Kingdom ($18 billion), followed by France ($9 billion) and Germany ($5.8 billion). The United Kingdom had indeed been running persistent and growing surpluses on current account for more than a century, without any tendency whatsoever towards equilibrium. On the contrary, these surpluses rose continually from about $35 million a year, on the average, over the years 1816–55 to more than $870 million a year in the last years before World War I (1906–13). Nobody could ever dream of explaining this favourable balance – and its fluctuations – in terms of the cost-competitiveness adjustment mechanism depicted in the textbooks, since it arose primarily from Britain's earnings on its swelling foreign-investment portfolio, and coincided with large and increasing *deficits* on merchandise account – close to $670 million a year over the period 1906–13 – offset themselves, for the most part, by net receipts on services and remittances account.

These current-account surpluses were nearly fully absorbed by Britain's investments abroad, which rose over the same period from an average of less than $30 million a year in 1816–55 to more than $850 million a year in 1906–13, and indeed more than a billion dollars a year in the last three prewar years, i.e. about a third of the British export level at the time, and 10 per cent of net national income (Imlah, 1958, pp. 70–5).

Foreign investments on such a scale undoubtedly accelerated economic development and helped at times relieve balance-of-payments pressures in the recipient countries. In the case of the United States, for instance, net capital inflows from Europe – primarily Britain – financed large and growing deficits on current account throughout most of the nineteenth century. They reached a peak of close to $300 million in 1888, tapering off afterwards, and shifting to net capital exports around the turn of the century, as the United States finally turned from chronic deficits to equally chronic surpluses on current account (US Bureau of the Census, 1960, pp. 562–6).

7 The cyclical pattern of international capital movements, however, had a very different impact upon the capital-exporting and the capital-importing countries.

A mere slowdown of capital exports could help relieve, in the first countries, any pressures on central-bank – and private-bank – reserves arising from unfavourable developments in other balance-of-payments transactions. In the British case, for instance, capital exports dropped year after year, from their 1872 peak of roughly $480 million to $60 million in 1877, recovered again to $480 million in 1890, and declined once more in the following years to $110 million in 1898, rising nearly uninterruptedly afterwards to $250 million in 1904, and booming to $400 million in 1905, $570 million in 1906, to reach finally close to $1100 million in 1913 (Imlah, 1958, pp. 73–5).

The borrowing countries, on the other hand, were far less able to control the rate of their capital imports which tended, on the whole, to swell in boom times and dry up in hard times, contributing further to the economic instability associated with their frequent dependence on one or a few items of raw material or foodstuff exports, themselves subject to wide quantity and/or price fluctuations. All in all, therefore, the balance of payments of the countries of the so-called 'periphery' would be assisted, over the long run by the large capital imports available to them from the financial markets of industrial Europe, but these countries would pay for this dependence through perverse fluctuations in the availability of such capital and in their terms of trade over the cycle. The exchange-rate instability of most underdeveloped countries – other than those of colonial or semi-colonial areas tightly linked to their metropolitan country's currency and banking system – finds here one of its many explanations.[5]

8 Another important qualification of the traditional theory of balance-of-payments adjustments relates to the international timing of reserve movements and discount-rate changes. The textbook explanation suggests that rate increases were undertaken by the deficit countries in order to relieve a drain of their reserves to the surplus countries. As noted by Bloomfield, however:

the annual averages of the discount rates of twelve central banks [England, Germany, France, Sweden, Finland, Norway, Denmark, Belgium, Switzerland, the Netherlands, Russia, and Austria-Hungary] reveal the... interesting fact that, in their larger movements at least, the discount rates of virtually all the banks tended to rise and fall together.... To some degree, and certainly for many of the banks, this broad similarity reflected competitive or 'defensive' discount rate changes.... But a more important explanation lies in the fact that discount rates in most... of the individual countries tended... to show a positive correlation, though generally not a very marked one, with domestic business cycle fluctuations. Since, as is well known, major cyclical fluctuations tended to be broadly synchronous in all countries, discount rate movements thus generally tended to exhibit a broad parallelism over the course of the world cycle – although there were, of course, many dissimilarities with respect to short-term movements in the various countries. (Bloomfield, 1959, pp. 35–7)

This importance of parallel movements, associated with the international business cycle – as against divergent movements between surplus and deficit countries – brings us back to the first two points made on pp. 123–4, and to the comparative neglect of this parallelism in textbook discussions centred nearly exclusively on intercountry balance-of-payments adjustments.

Reinterpretation and conclusions

1 The nineteenth-century monetary mechanism succeeded, to a unique degree, in preserving exchange-rate stability – and freedom from quantitative trade and exchange restrictions – over a large part of the world.

2 This success, however, was limited to the more advanced countries which formed the core of the system, and to those closely linked to them by political, as well as economic and financial ties. The exchange rates of other currencies – particularly in Latin America – fluctuated widely, and depreciated enormously, over the period. This contrast between the 'core' countries and those of the 'periphery' can be largely explained by the cyclical pattern of capital movements and terms of trade, which contributed to stability in the first group, and to instability in the second.

3 The adjustment process did not depend on any tendency towards equilibrium of the national balances of payments on current account. Vast and growing capital movements cushioned over many years, up to a century or more, correspondingly large and increasing surpluses – and deficits – on current account.

4 The preservation of exchange-rate stability depended, however, on the impact of international monetary settlements – of the combined current and capital accounts – upon domestic monetary and credit developments. Large or protracted deficits or surpluses had to be corrected, residually, by a slowdown or acceleration of bank-credit expansion sufficient to bring about – through income and/or price and cost adaptations, and their impact on export and imports – a tenable equilibrium in overall transactions, and a cessation of persistent drains in the deficit countries' stock of international money (i.e. gold and silver initially, and increasingly gold alone as all major countries shifted from the silver or bimetallic standard to the gold standard).

5 This residual harmonization of national monetary and credit policies, depended far less on *ex post* corrective action, requiring an extreme flexibility, downward as well as upward, of national price and wage levels, than on the *ex ante* avoidance of substantial disparities in cost competitiveness in the monetary policies which would allow them to develop.

As long as stable exchange rates were maintained, national *export* prices

:mained strongly bound together among all competing countries, by the
ιere existence of an international market not broken down by any large or
.equent changes in trade or exchange restrictions. Under these conditions,
ational price and wage levels also remained closely linked together inter-
ationally, even in the face of divergent rates of monetary and credit
xpansion, as import and export competition constituted a powerful brake on
ιe emergence of any large disparity between internal and external price and
ɔst levels.

Inflationary pressures could not be contained within the domestic market,
ut spilled out *directly*, to a considerable extent, into balance-of-payments
eficits rather than into uncontrolled rises of internal prices, costs, and wage
·vels.[6] These deficits led, in turn, to corresponding monetary transfers from
ιe domestic banking system to foreign banks, weakening the cash position of
omestic banks and their ability to pursue expansionary credit policies leading
ɔ persistent deficits for the economy and persistent cash drains for the banks.
3anks in the surplus countries would be simultaneously subject to opposite
ressures, which would also contribute to the harmonization of credit policies
round levels conducive to the re-equilibration of the overall balance of
ayments.)

Central banks could, of course, slow down this adjustment process by
ɔplenishing through their discount or open-market operations the cash
ɔserves of the commercial banks. As long as exchange controls or devaluation
ɣere effectively ruled out from their horizon, however, they would themselves
ɩe responsive to similar pressures, arising from the decline in the ratio of their
wn reserves to liabilities. While their liabilites were internal, and thus easy to
xpand, their reserves were – and still are today – limited to international
ssets over which they had no direct control.

6 These pressures for international harmonization of the pace of monetary
ind credit expansion were indeed very similar in character to those which
ontinue today to limit divergent rates of expansion among private banks
ɣithin each national monetary area.

They were further reinforced, as far as central banks were concerned, by the
ιct that a substantial portion of the domestic monetary circulation itself was
ɩ the form of commodity money – gold and silver – wholly or partly
nternational in character, rather than in credit money. Expansionary credit
ɔolicies were thus accompanied by an outflow of gold and silver assets from
ɩe coffers of central banks into internal circulation and commercial banks'
eserves, as well as to foreign countries. This movement of specie into internal
:irculation was all the more pronounced, as the lowest denomination of paper
·urrency was usually much too high – often equivalent to several times the
ɛvel of monthly wages – to be usable in household and wage payments.
ɔentral bank credit expansion was therefore limited not only by *foreign*

deficits and gold losses, but also by *internal* gold and silver losses, very much a commercial banks' credit and deposit expansion may be limited today by th drain on their paper currency reserves. While the latter can be replenished b central-bank credit, central banks themselves did not have access to any gol or silver 'lender of last resort'.

The overall pace of advance of commercial banks' credit and deposit-mone creation in a national economy was and remains subject today to the policie of the central bank. Similarly, the *overall* pace of credit creation by the centra banks *as a group* was limited, in the nineteenth century's internationa economy, by their ability to increase *simultaneously* their internationa reserves.

7 This latter observation brings once more into the limelight a mos important question left unanswered by the theory of balance-of-payment adjustment among countries: granted the need for mutual harmonization c national monetary policies among the gold standard countries, what were th factors determining the *international pace* on which such alignments did take place? The question is all the more significant in view of the size an parallelism of major fluctuations in national price, export, and import level over the period 1815–1914 as a whole.

The international pace of adjustment

A gentle reminder of the apostles of gold money

1 The gold standard is often credited with having reconciled, to a unprecedented degree, price stability with a high rate of economic growth ove the nineteenth century. Contemporary advocates of a return to gold rarel miss the opportunity of quoting, in this respect, Gustav Cassel's observatio that 'the general level of prices in 1910 was practically the same as in 1850'. This stability is then attributed to the safeguards erected against inflation b the small size of new gold production and monetary gold increases in relatio to existing stocks, and, more generally and optimistically, to the respons elasticity of new gold production to any substantial decreases or increases i the price level: price declines or increases would be kept in check by thei impact on gold-mining costs and profitability, and the resulting stimulation o slowdown of new gold production and monetary expansion.

2 As pointed out by Cassel himself, however, price fluctuations were by n means inconsiderable in the nineteenth century. Increases and decreases of 3(to 50 per cent, or more, accompanied the famous Kondratieff cycle (Kondratieff, 1926), and have been attributed by many writers – includin

assel – to fluctuations in gold production, following new mining or refining iscoveries.

The evidence of long-term stability – or rather reversibility – of prices seen a the return of the 1910 index to its 1850 level is, to say the least, extremely nisleading. Such an arbitrary choice of dates would allow us, for instance, to emonstrate equally well the 'stability' of the price level over the period from 913 to the early 1930s, since the precipitous fall of prices during the Great Depression brought back both the US and the UK price indexes down to pproximately their 1913 level in 1931–2!

The starting point of Cassel's comparison – 1850 – is taken close to the very ottom of a long depression during which prices had fallen by 50 per cent or nore, while the end year – 1910 – comes at the end of a fifteen-year upward rend during which the index used by Cassel had risen by more than 30 per ent.

Making the same comparison from peak to peak, or from trough to trough, ve would find a rather pronounced downward long-run trend of wholesale

Table 7.1 Wholesale price indexes, 1814–1913

	US	UK	Germany	France	Italy
ndexes					
(1913 = 100)					
814	178	178	129	132[1]	
849	80	90	71	96	
872	133	125	111	124	
896	67	76	71	71	74
913	100	100	100	100	100
Changes (in %)					
814–1849	− 55	− 49	− 45	− 27[2]	
849–1872	+ 66	+ 39	+ 56	+ 31	
872–1896	− 50	− 39	− 36	− 43	
896–1913	+ 49	+ 32	+ 41	+ 41	+ 35
814–1913	− 44	− 44	− 22	− 24[2]	

Sources:
a) *For the United States:*
    (a) Warren and Pearson index until 1890
    (b) BLS index since 1890
b) *For the United Kingdom:*
    (a) Gayer, Rostow and Schwartz index until 1849
    (b) Rousseaux index from 1844 to 1871
    (c) Board of Trade index since 1871
c) *For Germany, France and Italy:* France (1952), pp. 513–15.

Notes:
1 1820
2 since 1820

prices in all major countries (table 7.1). Prices declined, for instance, by 25 per cent in the United States from 1814 to 1872, and by 25 per cent again from 187 to 1913, adding up to a cumulative 44 per cent decline over the century, from 1814 to 1913. In the United Kingdom, price declines of 30 per cent from 181 to 1872, and 20 per cent from 1872 to 1913 also add up cumulatively to a similar 44 per cent decline for the century as a whole.

3　The influence of fluctuations in gold production upon these broad price trends seems far more plausible than the supposed inverse relationship from commodity prices to gold production. The significance of any such relationship as may have existed was certainly dwarfed by the gold avalanche unleashed by the discovery of new gold fields and the improvement of mining and refining techniques, both after 1848 and after 1888. On both occasions current production just about doubled, over twenty-four or twenty-five years, the gold stock accumulated over the previous three-and-a-half or four centuries. The yearly rate of growth in the estimated *monetary* gold stocks – after deduction for hoarding, industrial and artistic uses – rose abruptly from 0.7 per cent in the first half of the nineteenth century to 4.3 per cent over the years 1849–72, declined precipitously to only 1.3 per cent in 1873–88, and rose again to 3.2 per cent in 1889–1913.

4　The neat mechanistic explanation derived by some authors from this broad parallelism between gold production and long-run trends in commodity prices fails, however, to give a full account of the complex factors involved in the process of nineteenth-century economic growth. The Kondratieff long waves were certainly influenced also to a major degree by the clustering and spread of technological discoveries and innovations in production, transportation, etc., by the vast migrations from old to new settlement areas, and – last but not least – by the preparation, waging and aftermath of wars. These powerful influences, brilliantly analysed by Schumpeter (1934, 1939) among others, obviously cannot be reduced to any mechanistic monetary explanation. It would be equally absurd, on the other hand, to deny that monetary and banking developments also had a role – even if primarily permissive rather than initiating – on the acceleration or retardation of price trends and production growth. Schumpeter himself insisted abundantly on the role of bank credit in the process of capitalistic development.

One might well wonder, indeed, whether the unprecedented stability of the major currencies in terms of gold – and exchange rates – in the nineteenth century was not due to the spectacular growth of bank money or 'credit money' – in the form of paper currency and bank deposits – rather than to the residual, and fast declining, role of gold and silver 'commodity money'. Certainly, full dependence of the monetary system on gold and silver, in pre nineteenth-century days, to the exclusion or near-exclusion of credit or paper money, did not prevent wide inflationary excesses – through debasement of the coinage – and wide fluctuations in exchange rates. The pound sterling lost three-fourths of its gold value and the French franc more than nine-tenths, from the middle of the thirteenth century to the end of the eighteenth century.

5 It is rather ludicrous to reflect that the vast literature devoted to the so-called nineteenth-century gold standard is practically devoid of any quantitative estimates of the enormous changes that modified, out of all recognition, the actual structure of the volume of money, or means of payments, as between gold, silver, currency notes, and bank deposits, between the end of the Napoleonic Wars and the outbreak of World War I.

Yet, according to the League of Nations estimates, paper currency and bank deposits already accounted in 1913 for nearly nine-tenths of overall monetary circulation in the world, and gold for little more than one-tenth. Comprehensive estimates for earlier periods are practically nonexistent and can only be pieced together from disparate sources, the reliability of which is most difficult to assess. Yet, some broad facts and orders of magnitude can hardly be in doubt. Bank currency and demand deposits probably constituted less than a third of total money supply at the beginning of the nineteenth century, but close to nine-tenths by 1913. Silver exceeded gold in actual circulation by about two or three to one until well into the second half of the century, but dropped considerably behind in the latter part of the period, the previous proportion being just about reversed by 1913. Increases in credit money – paper currency and demand deposits – accounted, in the major and more developed countries, for two-thirds or more of total monetary expansion after the middle of the century, and more than 90 per cent from 1873 to 1913.

These facts can hardly be reconciled with the supposed *automaticity* still ascribed by many writers – particularly in Europe – to the so-called nineteenth-century gold standard. The reconciliation of high rates of economic growth with exchange-rate and gold-price stability was made possible indeed by the rapid growth and proper management of bank money, and could hardly have been achieved under the purely, or predominantly, metallic systems of money creation characteristic of the *previous* centuries. Finally, the term 'gold standard' could hardly be applied to the period as a whole, in view of the overwhelming dominance of silver during its first decades, and of bank money during the latter ones. All in all, the nineteenth century could be far more accurately described as the century of an emerging and growing credit-money standard, and of the euthanasia of gold and silver moneys, rather than as the century of the gold standard.

Monetary expansion and international reserves before World War I

A more precise assessment of the nature of the nineteenth-century international monetary mechanism and of its relation to production and price fluctuations must await the development of better monetary and reserve statistics than are now available, not only for the world as a whole, but even for the major countries which formed the basic core of the so-called gold standard.

The task should not prove impossible, if two limitations are accepted from the start. The first relates to the dearth of meaningful and reasonably reliable statistics for many countries. This should not prove too damaging for an appraisal of the international monetary mechanism in the few major countries which formed in the nineteenth century – and still form today – the core of the system. I have assembled some rough estimates of this sort, running back to

Table 7.2 Comparative evolution of money and reserve structure, 1885 and 1913

End of	Three countries[1] 1885	1913	Eleven countries[2] 1885	1913	World 1885	1913
(in billions of US dollars)						
1 Money supply	**6.3**	**19.8**	**8.4**	**26.3**	**14.2**	**33.1**
a Gold	1.4	2.0	1.8	2.7	2.4	3.2
b Silver	0.7	0.6	1.0	1.2	3.0	2.3
c Credit money	4.1	17.2	5.6	22.4	8.8	27.6
i Currency[3]	*1.6*	*3.8*	*2.3*	*5.9*	*3.8*	*8.1*
ii Demand deposits	*2.6*	*13.3*	*3.3*	*16.5*	*5.0*	*19.6*
2 Monetary reserves	**1.0**	**2.7**	**1.5**	**4.0**	**2.0**	**5.3**
a Gold	0.6	2.1	0.9	3.2	1.3	4.1
b Silver	0.4	0.6	0.6	0.8	0.7	1.2
3 Total gold and silver	**3.1**	**5.4**	**4.3**	**7.9**	**7.4**	**10.8**
a Gold	2.0	4.1	2.7	5.9	3.7	7.3
b Silver	1.1	1.2	1.6	2.0	3.7	3.5
(in % of money supply)						
1 Money supply	**100**	**100**	**100**	**100**	**100**	**100**
a Gold	23	10	21	10	17	10
b Silver	11	3	12	5	21	7
c Credit money	66	87	67	85	62	83
i Currency[3]	*25*	*19*	*27*	*22*	*27*	*25*
ii Demand deposits	*41*	*67*	*39*	*63*	*35*	*59*
2 Monetary reserves	**16**	**14**	**18**	**15**	**14**	**16**
a Gold	9	11	11	12	9	12
b Silver	7	3	7	3	5	4
3 Total gold and silver	**49**	**27**	**51**	**30**	**52**	**33**
a Gold	32	21	32	22	26	22
b Silver	17	6	19	8	26	11

Notes:
1 United States, United Kingdom and France
2 United States, United Kingdom, France, Germany, Italy, Netherlands, Belgium, Sweden, Switzerland, Canada and Japan
3 Including subsidiary (non-silver) coinage, except in last column

1885, for eleven such countries (the present so-called Group of Ten, or Paris Club, plus Switzerland). They accounted in 1885 and 1913 for 60 to 80 per cent of the world money supply and monetary reserves. Earlier estimates – back to 1815 – are for three countries only (the United States, the United Kingdom, and France) but accounted for about half the world money and reserves in 1885 and 1913, and for about two-thirds to three-fourths of the eleven core countries.[8] Table 7.2 gives further indications in this respect, revealing an encouraging parallelism between the estimates in the three groups.

The second limitation lies in the incompleteness and lack of full comparability of available data even for the major countries. Yet, this could hardly be more damaging than similar – and often far worse – limitations on the validity of other nineteenth-century estimates, in the field of national accounting for instance. They certainly remain, moreover, very minor in relation to the broad orders of magnitude involved in the enormous shifts in the monetary structure. [...] In any case, imperfect as they are bound to be, such estimates are essential to an understanding of the nineteenth-century international monetary mechanism, and far better than the implicit and totally unwarranted assumptions that underlie most of past and current theorizing about the so-called gold standard.

With these qualifications in mind, the following observations can be derived from these tables:

1 Although the 1816–48 estimates are particularly venturesome, there can be no doubt about the very slow growth of monetary gold stocks – just about nil, if we can trust the estimates – and of total money supply – about 1.4 per cent a year – over this period. Monetary expansion was sustained, not by gold accretions, but by an approximate doubling of silver stocks, accounting for about two-thirds of the total increase in the money supply, and for the remaining third by the incipient increase in internal credit monetization.[9]

2 The gold avalanche of the next twenty-four years produced an average increase of 6.2 per cent yearly in the total stock of monetary gold. This rate of growth declined sharply, to about 1.4 per cent a year, from 1873 to 1892, but recovered to about 3.7 per cent in the last twenty years preceding the outbreak of World War I.

These enormous fluctuations in gold-stock increases were significantly smoothed down by concurrent adaptations in the functioning of the monetary and banking system. The yearly rate of growth of money supply declined only from 4.2 per cent in 1849–72 to 3.3 per cent in 1873–92, and recovered to 4.3 per cent, on the average, in the period 1893–1913.

This smoothing down was due, to a minor extent, to the partial offsetting of gold fluctuations by opposite fluctuations in the monetary silver stocks. These contracted substantially in the two periods of fastest gold expansion, but more than doubled during the leaner gold years from 1873 through 1892. Far more

Table 7.3 Composition of money and reserve increases, 1816–1913: United States, United Kingdom and France

	1816–1913	1816–48	1849–72	1873–92	1893–1913
(in millions of US dollars)					
1 Money Increases	**18,791**	**581**	**2,688**	**3,863**	**11,659**
a Gold	1,673	−55	913	81	734
b Silver	287	379	−167	132	−57
c Credit money	16,831	257	1,942	3,650	10,982
i Currency and coin	*3,551*	*44*	*1,044*	*461*	*2,002*
ii Demand deposits	*13,280*	*213*	*898*	*3,189*	*8,980*
2 Reserve increases	**2,675**	**81**	**215**	**1,046**	**1,333**
a Gold	2,097	62	218	379	1,438
b Silver	578	19	−3	667	−105
3 Total gold and silver increases	**4,635**	**405**	**961**	**1,259**	**2,010**
a Gold	3,770	7	1,131	460	2,172
b Silver	865	398	−170	799	−162
4 Internal Credit Monetization (1 − 3 = 1c − 2)	**14,156**	**176**	**1,727**	**2,604**	**9,649**
(in % of money increases)					
1 Money increases	**100**	**100**	**100**	**100**	**100**
a Gold	9	−9	34	2	6
b Silver	2	65	−6	3	—
c Credit money	90	44	72	95	94
i Currency and coin	*19*	*8*	*39*	*12*	*17*
ii Demand deposits	*71*	*37*	*33*	*83*	*77*
2 Reserve increases	**14**	**14**	**8**	**27**	**11**
a Gold	11	11	8	10	12
b Silver	3	3	—	17	−1
3 Total gold and silver increases	**25**	**70**	**36**	**33**	**17**
a Gold	20	1	42	12	18
b Silver	5	69	−6	21	−1
4 Internal credit Monetization	**75**	**30**	**64**	**67**	**83**
(% absorption of new gold into)					
1 Reserves	56	886	19	82	66
2 Circulation	44	−786	81	18	34

significant is the dwarfing of gold and silver stock changes by the spectacular growth of credit money, which fed more than 70 per cent of total money increases over the years 1849–72, to about 34 per cent (see table 7.3).

3 Credit money – i.e. paper currency and bank deposits – did not, however,

normally circulate beyond the national borders of the issuing country and banking institutions. Exchange-rate stability thus depended on their ready convertibility – directly by the issuing banks, or ultimately through a national central bank – into the foreign currencies required, or into metallic currencies or bullion of international acceptability. Silver bullion lost its previous role in this respect around 1872, and silver coin settlements remained acceptable only among the countries of the Latin Monetary Union. Silver, however, was no longer 'full-bodied' money, as the commercial value of silver coins fell well below their nominal value.[10] Gold thus emerged increasingly as the primary guarantor of international exchange stability even for the countries which remained on a so-called 'limping' bimetallic standard.

Three factors explain the maintenance of stable exchange rates in the face of growing issues of *national* credit moneys, side by side with fast declining proportions of *international* gold and silver moneys.

The first is the *de facto* harmonization of the national rates of monetary and credit expansion among the gold standard countries. This harmonization itself, however, depended, as pointed out on pp. 124–5, on the reaction of the issuing banks to the fluctuations in their reserve ratio arising from cyclical movements in internal circulation, as well as from external settlements of balance-of-payments disequilibria.

The *overall* pace of expansion, in turn, could not but be strongly influenced by the ability of the national banking systems to accumulate sufficient gold reserves to guarantee the convertibility of their national credit money issues into the gold through which foreign currencies could be acquired at stable exchange rates. The maintenance of relatively fast rates of monetary expansion after 1848 was thus conditioned by two further factors which the tables bring clearly into light.

The first was the spectacular spurt in gold production that followed the discovery of new gold fields and improved mining and refining techniques, and was of course predominantly accidental in character.

The second lay in the resiliency and adaptability of monetary and banking institutions, and the enormous economy of the precious metals which resulted from their increasing transfers from actual circulation in the public to the reserve coffers of commercial banks and of national central banks – or Treasury in the case of the United States.[11] The proportion of monetary gold and silver stocks absorbed in centralized monetary reserves rose from about 10 per cent in 1848 to 16 per cent in 1872, 41 per cent in 1892, and 51 per cent in 1913.[12] Even more significant is the relative proportion of new gold accretions absorbed by central reserves, on the one hand, and by the public and banks on the other. During the first gold avalanche of 1849–72, 81 per cent of the new gold was dispersed among the public and banks, only 19 per cent being accumulated in reserves. These proportions were nearly exactly reversed in the leaner gold years from 1873 through 1892, 82 per cent of the new gold feeding the increase of central reserves, with a multiple impact on overall money creation. When gold production rose again at a faster pace in the period 1893–1913, the proportion absorbed by central reserves declined to 66 per cent, while that of private holdings rose from 18 to 34 per cent (see table 7.3).

These spectacular changes in the structure of money and reserves thus contributed powerfully both to the maintenance of relatively fast rates of monetary expansion, and to a considerable smoothing out of money supply fluctuations in relation to fluctuations in the available gold stocks.

4 There was nothing inherently stable, however, in a process of monetary creation so heavily dependent on the accidents:
 (a) of gold and silver discoveries and production rates;
 (b) of uncoordinated – and largely irrational – national decisions regarding the adoption, retention or abandonment of silver, gold or bimetallism as the basic monetary standard; and
 (c) of compensatory adaptations in banking structure, the scope of which would inevitably taper off over time, especially when central banks could no longer replenish their own reserves from the dwindling – relatively, if not yet absolutely – amounts of gold still in circulation.

In any case, the slow evolution which had adjusted gradually the international monetary system of the nineteenth century to the economic requirements of peacetime economic growth, but had also changed it out of all recognition between 1815 and 1913, was brutally disrupted by the outbreak of World War I. The ensuing collapse of the system ushered in half a century of international monetary chaos, characterized by widespread exchange-rate instability and/or trade and exchange controls, with only brief interludes of nostalgic and vain attempts to fit upon the twentieth-century economy the monetary wardrobe of the nineteenth-century world.

Notes

1 The above percentages are derived from 287 observations of national increases or decreases for eleven countries (the United States, the United Kingdom, France, Germany, Italy, Belgium, the Netherlands, Switzerland, Sweden, Austria and Canada), in the course of seventeen upward or downward movements of more than 1 per cent in Western European exports, in the period 1880–1960. The estimates used in these calculations are those of Maddison (1962), pp. 179–81.
2 Based on estimates from Maddison (1962), pp. 189–90.
3 See, for instance, US Bureau of the Census (1960), pp. 90–2; Mitchell (1962), pp. 343–5; and France (1939), pp. 443–4.
4 Bloomfield (1959), p. 50. The evidence of neutralization, measured by Nurkse's formula, was present in 60 per cent of total observations, in the period 1880–1913, coinciding exactly with Nurkse's results for the 1922–38 period.

5 Another, closely connected with the main topic of this study, lies in the retention of a silver standard long after the effective abandonment of silver or bimetallic standards in Europe and the United States.

6 This is still true today, in the absence of major changes in exchange rates and/or trade and exchange restrictions. See Triffin and Grubel (1962), pp. 486–91.

7 See Cassel (1930), p. 72. The calculation is based on the Sauerbeck–Statist index of wholesale prices, and carried back to 1800 on the basis of Jevons's index. See also Kitchin (1930), pp. 79–85.

8 World totals, however, are somewhat incomplete and particularly unreliable.

9 The latter being measured, indifferently, by the excess of money supply increases over the increase of monetary gold and silver stocks, or by the excess of credit-money increases over the increase of monetary reserves.

10 The valuation of silver at nominal par in the tables thus *understates* the importance of credit money, since silver coinage included in effect a substantial credit money component. Its acceptance at par among the countries of the Latin Union demonstrates the feasibility of international credit-money settlements, even under the very imperfect arrangements negotiated to this effect among the countries of the Latin Union.

11 The reserve estimates of the tables refer to the centralized holdings of central banks and treasuries only. The gold and silver components of money supply estimates include, therefore, gold and silver held by other issuing banks and commercial banks, thus overstating once more the metallic component of money supply in the modern sense of the word – coin, currency and demand deposits in the hands of the public – and understating the proportion of credit money in circulation outside banks.

12 The proportion of gold alone temporarily dropped from 31 per cent in 1848 to 20 per cent in 1872, rising later to 35 per cent in 1892, and 51 per cent in 1913. The 1848–72 decline, however, was more than compensated by the increased absorption into centralized reserves of silver which could still be regarded at that time as a valid reserve component. After 1872, the movements of gold alone are more significant than those of gold and silver combined.

References

Bloomfield, Arthur I. (1959), *Monetary Policy under the International Gold Standard: 1880–1914*, New York, Federal Reserve Bank of New York.

Cassel, G. (1930), 'The supply of gold', in *Interim Report of the Gold Delegation of the Financial Committee*, Geneva, League of Nations.

France (1939), (1952), *Annuaire Statistique for 1938, 1951*, Paris, Institut National de la Statistique et Etudes Economiques.

Imlah, A.H. (1958), *Economic Elements in the Pax Britannica*, Cambridge, Mass., Harvard University Press.

Kenen, Peter B. (1960), *British Monetary Policy and the Balance of Payments*, Cambridge, Mass., Harvard University Press.

Kitchin, J. (1930), 'The supply of gold compared with the prices of commodities', in *Interim Report of the Gold Delegation of the Financial Committee*, Geneva, League of Nations.

Kondratieff, N.D. (1926), 'The long waves in economic life', *Review of Economic Statistics*, November 1935 (abridged in English by W. Stolper).

Maddison, A. (1962), 'Growth and fluctuations in the world economy', *Banca Nazionale del Lavoro Quarterly Review* (June).

Mitchell, B.R. (1962), *Abstract of British Historical Statistics*, Cambridge, Cambridge University Press.

Nurkse, Ragnar (1944), *International Currency Experience*, Geneva, League of Nations.

Schumpeter, Joseph A. (1934), *The Theory of Economic Development*, New York, McGraw-Hill.

——(1939), *Business Cycles*, Cambridge, Mass., Harvard University Press.

Triffin, R. (1947), 'National central banking and the international economy', *International Monetary Policies*, Washington, D.C., Federal Reserve System.

——and H. Grubel (1962), 'The adjustment mechanism to differential rates of monetary expansion among the countries of the European Economic Community', *Review of Economics and Statistics* (November).

United Nations (1949), *International Capital Movements during the Inter-war Period*, New York, United Nations.

US Bureau of the Census (1960), *Historical Statistics of the United States*, Washington, D.C., US Government Printing Office.

8

Notes on the working of the gold standard before 1914

A.G. Ford*

The pre-1914 gold standard may be seen as a sterling standard largely, with London as its pivot, which had gradually developed in the nineteenth century. Despite the use of a common international currency, some striking features of this standard and its operation were the differences in the economic behaviour of the countries who were members of this 'club'.

Much of the theoretical and practical discussion of the gold standard has centred on the repercussions of gold movements and of the consequential banking measures on international capital movements, incomes, and prices in the countries concerned. Less attention has been paid to the following two questions: (a) why did the exchanges move to either of the gold points and gold move? (b) what equilibrating forces might be set in motion by the factors causing the gold movement? It will be argued that it is of crucial importance to ask these questions in order to understand the actual operation of the gold standard, for the same factors (e.g. a fall in export values or a fall in receipts from foreign borrowing) causing the export of gold or the loss of foreign balances may automatically set in motion income movements which reduce the initial discrepancy between foreign-currency receipts and payments. Two cases will be considered: (a) Great Britain, and (b) Argentina, an economy which had a chequered history of adherence (and otherwise) to the gold standard before 1914. Contrasts will emerge between the operation of the gold standard for the central country and for a 'periphery' country, both of which were geared together by trade and capital flows. This approach will thus follow

*Oxford Economic Papers, February 1960, pp. 52–76.

up the suggestion of P. Barrett Whale, who, after emphasizing that the suggestions in his well-known article[1] were tentative, stated: 'They provide a hypothetical view of the working of the gold standard...; but it is admitted that my view requires a more exhaustive testing, with regard to both the cases in which the gold standard has worked successfully and those in which it has broken down, before it can claim acceptance.'[2]

*

This section will attempt to set up a general model of adjustment for gold standard conditions, although certain portions may well be absent or lack importance when actual conditions of particular economies are considered. The principal answers to the question 'Why did an excess of foreign currency payments over receipts occur in an economy and gold move out?' may be classified as follows:[3]

1 An increase in import purchases due to an increase in incomes generated by domestic forces (not by an increase in exports), or at the expense of savings with given incomes.

2 An increase in import purchases, more being spent from a given income on foreign goods and less on home goods – for example, because of changes in tastes, tariffs or prices.

3 A fall in the net proceeds of foreign borrowing transferred to the country and being used to finance domestic expenditure.

4 An increase in lending abroad at the expense of domestic purchases of consumption goods or at the expense of home investment.

5 A fall in export values, either because foreign markets were lost, world prices fell, or more exportables were purchased at home.

6 A transfer of bank deposits from one international monetary centre to another. This might well be an unrepeated 'stock' transaction, rather than a change in a continuing flow of payments, and the loss of gold would cease automatically in this case.

First, if gold is lost because of factors 2, 3, 4, 5, these disturbing factors will set in motion contractionary income movements in the country, which will be equilibrating in the sense that they will reduce the discrepancy between foreign-currency receipts and payments by reducing import purchases[4] (vice versa for an influx of gold). These equilibrating income movements, I suggest, deserve more attention when the actual operation of the gold standard is considered – they account for the speedy adjustment of imports noted in certain cases – and will be dubbed 'automatic' forces for the purposes of this paper. Secondly, if the loss of gold is allowed to affect the domestic supply of money (i.e. no Exchange Equalization Account), then the contraction of the quantity of money will bring rising interest rates[5] and a contraction in bank credit, both of which will tend to reduce incomes and import purchases. This forms a second 'automatic' equilibrating force.

Thirdly, these may very well be 'induced' measures undertaken to check the loss of gold – an increase in 'Bank Rate' and the measures taken to make it effective. These will also tend to reduce incomes and import purchases. Moreover, in countries where there is a substantial gold coin circulation, falling domestic activity and incomes will reduce the demand for this type of money so that there will be an 'internal reflux' of gold coins to swell the banking system's or the central bank's gold reserves.

In summary, then, the loss of gold is seen to be associated with equilibrating income movements in certain cases, or to bring about such movements, and falling incomes and activity may very well cause prices to fall and further promote adjustment.[6] Furthermore, the fact that domestic interest rates have risen and that the 'exchange risk' is zero, assuming perfect confidence in the stability of the mint par rate of exchange, will provide an additional speedy but temporary means of stopping the loss of gold through an induced influx of short-term international capital which is seeking maximum remuneration. This capital movement will provide a 'cushion', whilst other forces are bringing about a more fundamental readjustment.

All this analysis may be reworked for the cases of net imports of gold and associated expansionary income movements.

In order to decide what parts of this 'general' model are applicable to particular economies it is necessary to examine their financial, commercial, and political structures before 1914. It will be found that this will lay low any hopes of a general explanation such as that proffered by the old 'rules of the game' school, except that changes in incomes provide the basic longer-run equilibrating mechanism. Indeed, not all the countries participating in the gold standard followed these rules – many 'limped' – and devices to prevent gold exports varied from country to country. Again, actual adjustment processes varied: a creditor country found adjustment to a loss of gold easier than a debtor, for it was (and is) always easier to refrain from lending abroad or to recall funds from use abroad than to increase foreign borrowings to staunch the drain of gold. Indeed, differences in structure and nature of a country's economy are crucial, when attempting to assess why the gold standard worked so successfully for some countries and failed for others, and may be summarized briefly. (1) A creditor or a debtor country. (2) An industrial or a primary-producing country. In this case it is of vital importance to realize the differences in export price formation – on a cost basis, or determined in the world commodity markets. (3) Whether domestic investment activity or export receipts was the principal determinant of fluctuations in national income. (4) The size of the economy relative to the world markets. (5) The size of the marginal propensity to import, for on this would depend the speed, or otherwise, of balance-of-payments adjustments in response to income changes. (6) The financial organization of the country. Where was the banking system based? (7) The political framework and social system. Were any particular economic interests (e.g. exporters or landowners or rentiers) dominant politically? Was there any past history of depreciation? (8) Gold-mining or non-gold-mining countries.

This list does not pretend to be exhaustive, but it does emphasize the need for examining the positions of particular countries before making any wide theoretical generalizations.

*

In this period an efflux of gold from Britain was stopped first by short-term international capital movements, which had been induced by the Bank of England's actions, and secondly by longer-run equilibrating changes in imports, exports and long-term loans, which occurred as a result of the automatic and induced forces associated above with a loss of gold. The short-term capital movements responded speedily and provided a 'cushion' whilst the latter forces, which needed time to make their effect felt, gradually changed items in the balance of payments so that monetary pressure might be relaxed without the danger of a renewal of the gold loss. This adjustment mechanism will now be considered in more detail.

When confronted with a net export of gold (which it desired to stop) the Bank of England's main object was to lever up the London market rate of discount in order to bring about equilibrating international capital flows to London, and indeed quick action was necessary because of low gold holdings (these were unremunerative and disliked by profit-seeking British bankers) as compared with British international transactions. The main weapon used was an increase in Bank Rate, together with measures to make it 'effective' by reducing the available pool of short-term credit in London. However, on occasion devices other than Bank Rate were employed if the Bank of England did not want internal trade to be affected, but only international capital transactions.[7]

A rise in the market rate of discount had a speedy effect on the exchanges by bringing short-term funds into London, partly because of the complete confidence in the stability of the link between sterling and gold and partly because of institutional reasons peculiar to Britain at this period. For Britain was a short-term creditor – to the tune of £150–200 million in 1909 according to Hartley Withers's estimates – and higher Bank Rate, when effective, speedily induced the repatriation of British funds employed abroad to the (now) more lucrative home uses.[8] This unique technical position of London provides much of the explanation of the efficacy of Bank Rate in speedily staunching gold losses before 1914. Secondly, foreign-owned sterling balances were provided with an added inducement to stay, and fresh foreign money was attracted, more especially as the exchange risk was zero with sterling at the gold export point. Furthermore, the demand for foreign currency was curtailed as borrowing in London became more expensive and difficult, whether short-term loans, raised by discounting finance bills, or long-term issues on the Stock Exchange,[9] whilst some foreign bills were diverted to less expensive money markets for discounting. Thus high market rates of discount by affecting international capital movements served to float the exchanges off the gold export point and to staunch the efflux of gold.

It was indeed important that the main world gold market was located in the same country and controlled by the same financial organization that also regulated these international capital funds. Thus London could, by extending or restricting short-term credits, considerably enhance or restrict the ability of non-residents to buy and ship gold abroad. In other words, such operations enabled London to retain more of the new-mined gold passing through and, if these capital movements shifted the exchanges to the gold import point, to attract gold from other monetary centres. However, it was a feature of the gold standard before 1914 that this latter movement of gold was never 'automatic': for when the German and French exchanges were at their gold export points, on occasion no gold moved because foreign central banks dissuaded bankers by one means or another.[10] Ultimately, though, gold did move from Paris and Berlin, perhaps through fear of what might happen if Bank Rate had to go yet higher.

It should be pointed out that international capital movements of this nature did not form a permanent flow, but were equivalent to 'stock' transactions, being temporary and very likely to be reversed as soon as the interest differential disappeared. This mechanism, however, would eliminate gold losses which had arisen from excessive speculative short-term capital movements (too many 'finance' bills). The longer-run forces which provided a more basic cure for the loss of gold will now be considered and included here will be a discussion of the internal effects of the gold loss and higher interest rates. Much of what follows will be rather tentative in the sense that detailed empirical studies of particular crises would need to be made to come to any definite conclusions. Nevertheless, I believe that the underlying theoretical structure and approach would prove fruitful for such studies and would stand justified.[11]

Why, then, did the sterling exchanges sag to the gold export point? Let us consider the case where export values fell relatively to imports, other items in the balance of payments remaining constant, because of a decline in foreign buying. (It is assumed that there was a positive marginal propensity to save and that there were lags in the income process so that a fall in exports did not bring an equivalent fall in imports immediately and thus eliminate the gold loss.) Besides bringing a gold loss, the fall in exports caused incomes, activity and import purchases to fall, thereby alleviating the strain on the balance of payments, the more so if falling British demand for primary produce reduced their prices so that import payments fell on this count also. If this decline in British activity induced a fall in domestic investment, then incomes and imports were reduced still more.

Furthermore, the loss of gold reduced the supply of money, the more so if the gold exported had been paid for by cheque on a joint-stock bank and thus a contraction of bank deposits had been set in motion. Secondly, the increase in Bank Rate brought increases in domestic interest rates conventionally tied to it, as well as the rise in the London market rate of discount. Borrowing, besides being more expensive, became more difficult, so that domestic expenditure was checked and import purchases were reduced – provided that the monetary stringency lasted long enough. Furthermore, a sustained spell of stringency affected the ability to hold stocks of primary produce, so that stock liquidation or the lack of ability to buy brought falling primary product prices, thereby reducing import payments and reinforcing the effects on import prices noted above.

In so far as in such a crisis incomes and activity declined the internal reflux of sovereigns from domestic transactions use helped to swell the Bank of England's gold reserves. But without a decline in activity the reflux in response to interest-rate changes alone was slight.[12]

In this case export prices also tended to fall both because of falling activity in Britain and because of the falling prices of raw materials (e.g. raw cotton prices and their influence on textile prices). This would only help adjustment on those occasions when the foreign price elasticity of demand was greater than one. Lastly, if the prices of home goods fell relatively to imported goods there would be some expenditure – switching effects which helped to promote adjustment. However, these price effects, when they occurred, were of minor importance as compared with the automatic income effects. It will be noticed in this outline that we have neglected the repercussions of variations in British activity and import purchases on the rest of the world and the reaction on purchases of British exports. In any detailed case study it would be improper to neglect such reactions, but the intention of this section is to sketch out certain adjustment forces which have not received enough attention in the past.

If gold was lost because of an increase in import purchases, other balance-of-payments items remaining the same, two cases must be distinguished: (a) rising domestic activity and expenditure (because of a domestic investment boom) which brought rising imports; (b) a switch in expenditure from home-produced goods to imports, money incomes initially remaining the same.[13] In the first case the only 'automatic' effects were those resulting from the influence of the loss of gold on the quantity of money, whilst the 'induced' monetary effects also helped to promote balance-of-payments adjustment as noted above. In the second case incomes and activity automatically fell as expenditure was switched away from home goods, thereby reducing import purchases, to which force the monetary effects were added to promote adjustment.

Consider now the case where gold was exported (net) because an increase occurred in the flow of funds which overseas borrowers were seeking to transfer (in the form of sterling bills or gold) to finance domestic expenditure in their countries, and the exchanges sagged to the gold export point.[14] Now the spending of such funds in the borrowing countries raised their incomes and their purchases of imports, particularly of consumption goods. Since Britain was an important supplier of such goods, this increased activity abroad eventually increased the demand for British exports and provided an offsetting force to adjust the balance of payments after short-term capital movements had provided a temporary cushion.[15] To this general adjustment force may be added the automatic and induced monetary effects of the gold loss. Again, if gold was lost because more funds were transferred abroad from a given volume of overseas borrowing and less spent directly on British capital goods for export, then incomes and import purchases declined in Britain; likewise if more was lent to overseas countries at the expense of domestic spending.

It was very important for her operation of the gold standard pre-1914 that *ex ante* British foreign lending (i.e. overseas issues in London or undistributed profits retained abroad) generated increases in British exports relative to imports (either by increased sales of investment goods or by induced sales of consumption goods as overseas activity rose) and so facilitated its transfer without balance-of-payments disruption and prolonged gold loss.[16] Such a process would be facilitated if the pressure of overseas demand turned the terms of trade in Britain's favour by pushing up export prices.

Why, however, in these periods of active lending abroad did rising export values not bring roughly similar increases in imports through rising incomes, so that the tendency of exports to rise relatively to imports and so to bring an increased current account surplus would have been eliminated? First, a sustained increase in exports per period will only bring eventually, *ceteris paribus*, an equivalent increase in imports per period if the marginal propensity to save is zero – a condition certainly untrue for Britain at that time. Secondly, although home and foreign investment tended to move together in the short run, nevertheless the longer-run tendency was for increased foreign investment to take place at the expense of home investment. If the series for these are smoothed with nine-year moving averages, it is clear that the long-run waves of foreign investment have their peaks opposite the troughs in the waves of home investment, so that when foreign investment was relatively high, home investment was low, and vice versa. Thus the income-generating influence of increased export sales was offset by the decline in home investment – so far as these underlying trends are concerned. Again, British lenders, besides switching from home to foreign investment, might perhaps have been tempted to decrease the proportion of their incomes spent on consumption goods so that they could employ their increased savings to purchase the now attractive foreign securities being offered.[17] All these factors would militate against the rise in imports which otherwise might have been expected from rising export values.

It is possible thus to explain why these bursts of overseas investment by Britain were managed with so little disruption to the British balance of payments and her adherence to the gold standard. The necessary (increased) current-account surplus was created by inducing directly and indirectly increased export sales relative to import values, and thus the danger of increased foreign lending leading to a severe loss of gold averted. However, if British foreign lending had not influenced export values, as in the French case,[18] then less might have been heard about the smooth operation of the gold standard in this period.

In summary, then, apart from the transfer of short-term deposits and the 'domestic investment boom' cases the other factors causing balance-of-payments disequilibria and the loss of gold brought equilibrating tendencies through income movements either in Britain or in borrowing countries, whilst present in all cases were the automatic and induced monetary effects. The speedy staunching of gold losses from Britain is to be attributed partly to the peculiar institutional position of Britain which made for rapid changes in the movement of short-term funds and partly to the income forces (automatic in many cases) which were set in motion and brought about a more permanent balance-of-payments adjustment so that Bank Rate could then be relaxed. The automatic and induced monetary effects of the gold loss, to which earlier writers assigned much importance in explaining balance-of-payments re-adjustment in the longer run, are thus seen to be only *part* of the adjustment mechanism. (The above discussion has concentrated on the export of gold, but the arguments may be reworked for the import of gold.)

In conclusion of this section it should be pointed out that not all countries and territories 'took gold' when they had a balance-of-payments surplus with Britain. Those in which the 'Anglo' banks were of paramount importance increased their sterling holdings or 'London balances' in such cases – the embryo of the sterling area. Balance-of-payments adjustment was thus facilitated for Britain when it meant in some cases not the loss of gold, but the transfer of bank deposits in London from domestic to overseas ownership.

*

Argentina, of vast land area and with various climates and vegetations, and sparsely populated, advanced rapidly as a primary producer in the nineteenth century as transport barriers were removed. The federal constitution, adopted in 1862, resembled the American, but gave much more power to the President, whilst the dominant political group was the conservative landowning (and export-producing) oligarchy, whose rule was maintained until 1910 either by fraud or by force at the 'free' elections. The fact that power was seated here will enable us to understand certain economic actions of the national governments.

Export values expanded sevenfold within the period 1880–1913, and their composition changed sharply, the main exports in 1880 being wool, fleeces, and hides, whilst after 1890 grains (i.e. wheat, maize, linseed) rose in importance. The twentieth century saw the decline of sheep farming and the rapid rise of cattle ranching and export of frozen beef. It is important to note that Argentina was a relatively small *producer* of these products, whose prices were determined in centralized commodity markets, and thus she had little or no control over her export prices. Additionally, Argentina was heavily dependent on export sales for her well-being, since roughly half of her primary produce was exported. Imports, which expanded six times in value, were composed of food, drink, tobacco, manufactures of all kinds, fuel, machinery and rails, whilst their prices were largely determined by suppliers, since Argentina was a relatively small part of the world market for these products. Moreover, since Argentine production comprised exportable goods mainly and little import-competing industry existed, there was little substitution between home-produced and imported goods.

Foreign investment by European centres – especially London – together with immigration, from Italy and Spain particularly, had brought about this expansion with the railway as the basic factor which had permitted this 'export-biased' development to take place. Other important destinations of foreign funds were governmental borrowings, public utilities, land mortgage bonds, tramways and land companies. One important consequence of this borrowing must be noted – the foreign debt-service charges incurred had a large element fixed and payable in gold or sterling.

The domestic currency, the paper peso (a gold peso was an oddity), had a history of depreciation in the nineteenth century, whilst Argentine banking was anarchic, there being no central bank, although in later years after 1900 the Bank of the Nation tended to be dominant through sheer size. The commercial banks were sharply divided into international banks, based on other monetary centres, which specialized in foreign trade and remittance business, and domestic banks, which looked to local business. Argentina, however, hardly belonged to the English monetary area, as much of the banking system was purely local.

In summary, then, Argentina was an economy predominantly dependent on the production of exportables and the level of foreign-currency receipts for the determining of her income and well-being. Her export and import prices together with prices of domestically consumed exportables were determined externally, whilst there was low substitutability between imports and home-produced non-exportables, so that the scope for price changes to promote balance-of-payments adjustment was severely limited.[19] Furthermore, fluctuations in foreign-currency receipts provided the principal cause not only of fluctuations in income, but also of balance-of-payments disequilibria, so that in this setting the question 'Why did gold move?' is to be answered frequently by pointing to changes in export proceeds or in the flow of funds from abroad. Changes in either of these variables brought directly associated income movements and hence equilibrating changes in import purchases.

In 1881 monetary reforms were enacted in Argentina to remedy the previously chaotic condition of the currency; the main provisions were the definition of the new gold peso, the replacement of the existing paper currencies by a new national paper peso (at par with the gold peso) whose issue by approved banks was subject to regulation by the national government, and the convertibility of paper pesos into gold. In 1883 these were put into operation and Argentina had *formally* rejoined the gold standard. Yet the internal banking system, although sizeable, was rudimentary, whilst the foreign-based banks were not dominant nor did they hold the major part of the Argentine gold and foreign-exchange reserves. This situation may be contrasted with the institutional arrangements prevailing in New Zealand and Australia, for example, where overseas banks did provide considerable internal facilities and where London branches (or head offices) held the countries' foreign-exchange reserves in the form of sterling balances. Sanctions on excessive note issue were weak; indeed the country had a tradition of these being ignored or removed by governments in difficulties, as indeed it had a tradition of depreciated paper money, so that popular confidence in the stability of the paper peso–gold peso link was not high.

Furthermore, the dominant political interests, the export producers and landowners, were not adversely affected by a depreciating exchange; rather a depreciating exchange shifted the distribution of a given real income in their favour whilst an appreciating exchange moved it against them. For, with constant world prices, depreciation increased the paper peso prices of exportables *pari passu*, and hence producers' receipts in paper currency for a given output. Wage-rates (both urban and rural), however, were sluggish, showing no comparable increase, and the landowners' mortgage debts were for the most part fixed in terms of paper currency, so that the gap between their receipts and costs widened by more than the depreciation. On the other hand, an appreciating exchange rate with constant world prices cut the paper prices of exportable produce *pari passu*, shifted the income distribution in favour of wage-earners, for wages were 'sticky' in paper currency, and increased the real burden of a given paper peso debt for landowners. Lastly, less moral shame (such as prevailed widely in Britain) was felt at a depreciating exchange. Accordingly, it is not surprising to find in times of balance-of-payments deficit a bias in favour of a depreciating exchange rate, and in times of persistent surplus a distinct preference for a stable exchange rate rather than an appreciating rate. Indeed, these effects are of the utmost importance in explaining Argentina's lapse from the gold standard in 1885 and her decision to rejoin in 1900.

With this background it would be reasonable to expect that a small disturbance in the balance of payments, which an older member of the gold standard club could have withstood either from its own resources or by means of short-term foreign loans, might have more serious repercussions. Any sustained export of gold would provoke internal speculation, the populace becoming bulls of gold, and thus the note-issuing banks' gold reserves (in any case none too plentiful) would be subjected to a further drain as gold was absorbed into private hoards in the expectation of a breakdown of the system and the emergence of a gold premium.

Indeed, as early as January 1885 a gold premium had appeared despite the attempts of the issuing banks to preserve paper convertibility at par. In their attempts the Banco Nacional and the Bank of the Province of Buenos Aires had lost 77 million pesos worth of gold and foreign exchange, of which the major share, perhaps 50 million pesos, was absorbed *internally*, the rest internationally. The international drain in 1884 had arisen because the proceeds of foreign borrowing declined whilst imports and foreign debt-service charges had increased and exports barely expanded – these items giving rise to a deficit of 14 million pesos, as compared with a surplus of 7 million in 1883. Doubtless this drain encouraged some domestic speculative hoarding of gold, but this is not the whole story, for as early as June 1884 the Bank of the Province of Buenos Aires suspended specie payments. This would seem early for international forces to have made their impact; rather, one suspects, it was the victim of some autonomous domestic speculation, perhaps even a deliberate run on gold by special interests who stood to gain by the emergence of a gold premium. Domestic lack of confidence, justified by precedent, was the first cause of Argentina's withdrawal from the gold standard. The second was the lack of any institutional mechanism for coping with a balance-of-payments deficit by short-term capital movements and in the longer run by credit contraction.[20] This illustrates a previous theme: a creditor (lending) country can always – easily – bring relief to its balance of payments by lending less abroad; a debtor (borrowing) country will find it hard or even impossible to bring relief by borrowing more – the more so if it has a history of currency depreciation and is thus 'suspect' internationally. Yet to some extent similar economic conditions prevailed in other primary producing countries and exchange stability was preserved before 1914. More, indeed, depended on social, political, and moral attitudes to exchange stability, on the structure of society and the political system, and on tradition.

After 1885 exchange-rate stability was forgotten in Argentina until 1898–9, although income movements still provided the main balance-of-payments adjustment force.[21] The years 1896–9 saw a steady fall in the gold premium as

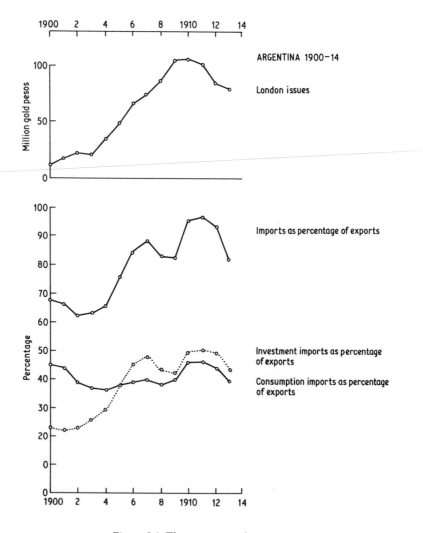

Figure 8.1 Three-year moving averages

export values rose, both on account of rising production and rising world primary product prices, so that the distribution of incomes moved against the export-producing and landed interests and in favour of those whose incomes were relatively stable in terms of paper currency, the fall in the gold premium being sufficient to outweigh the rising export prices. Accordingly, the former used their considerable political influence to prevent any further appreciation of the paper peso by enacting in 1899 a measure to stabilize the exchange of paper notes for gold at the rate of 44 gold pesos to 100 paper, or 227.27 paper to 100 gold. Furthermore, these interests claimed that stability would encourage trade and stimulate foreign investment in Argentina, which would become 'respectable' again with fixed exchange rates, in addition preventing too drastic a price–cost deflation which would have occurred otherwise, and which might have inhibited the growth of the economy. Nevertheless, their basic reason for rejoining the gold standard was to prevent any further adverse shift in the distribution of income.

This measure which was put into operation in 1900 provided that the note circulation could only increase if gold were deposited at an exchange bureau, or *Caja*, which in exchange would issue notes at the fixed legal ratio. Conversely, the bureau was legally bound to give out gold in exchange for paper currency. Since Argentina was not a gold producer, international gold movements formed the main determinant of the note issue (see table 8.1), and secondly of the level of bank deposits and bank credit, as banks' cash reserves varied. The institutional framework thus allowed gold exports, if obtained from the *Caja* or from banking reserves, to contract the quantity of money; gold imports, unless hoarded privately, to expand the money supply (except in so far as the Bank of the Nation tried to offset such forces temporarily). Thus far, then, all was in accordance with the 'rules of the game', but the considerable institutional and structural differences from Britain noted earlier still persisted.

After 1900 Argentina remained a member of the gold standard club until 1914, in these years experiencing considerable growth of production, population, railway length, exports and imports, within which context her successful gold standard adjustments must be studied. Export values, which expanded at an annual trend rate of 7.5 per cent (her export prices, it is important to note, rose at 3 per cent per annum), provided the main force promoting rising incomes and rising profitability of investment projects. After 1904 rising foreign investment and immigration were helpful not merely in bringing income increases as the funds were spent, but also in expanding the capacity of the economy to produce exportables. These movements are illustrated in table 8.1 where also the uneven response of total imports to these forces may be noted. However, if imports are split into consumption imports and investment imports (following the official subdivision), this may be explained by the resurgence of foreign borrowings. For, on the one hand, rising export

Table 8.1 Argentina 1900–14

	(1)	(2)	(3) London issues for Argentina	(4) Gold imports (net)	(5) Actual note issue	(6) Potential note issue	(7) (5) as % of (6)
	Exports	Imports					
	million gold pesos				million paper pesos		
1900	155	113	7	6.7	295	310	95
1901	168	114	25	0.1	295	310	95
1902	179	103	16	5.5	296	317	93
1903	221	131	26	24.5	380	379	100
1904	264	187	21	23.3	408	423	96
1905	323	205	61	31.7	498	480	104
1906	292	270	63	16.6	527	506	104
1907	296	286	72	20.4	532	545	98
1908	366	273	80	28.6	581	598	97
1909	397	303	109	65.7	685	740	92
1910	373	352	115	35.4	716	817	88
1911	325	367	84	9.8	723	838	87
1912	480	385	101	35.9	800	920	87
1913	484	421	60	3.6	823	938	88
1914	349	272	76	−13.3	803	966	83

Sources: (1) and (2), *Extracto Estadistico* (1916), p. 3; (3) Author's computations based on *The Economist* 'New Issues' sections; (4) *Extracto Estadistico*, (1916), p. 203; (5) and (6) ibid., p. 297.

Notes: £1 = 5 gold pesos.

Import values are somewhat unreliable, as they resulted from the valuation of volumes at Argentine official customs values, which were changed infrequently or suddenly with no close relation to variations in world prices of the goods in some cases. If Argentine imports from UK are compared with UK exports to Argentina, both series display similar fluctuations and are of comparable absolute magnitude. Export values are more reliable, except that frozen meat exports were valued at constant 'prices' 1900–14, so that official figures are a little too low in total, but by not more than 5 per cent. Despite these difficulties the official figures do give a good indication of what happened.

Potential note issue is the issue which would have resulted if all gold imports (less the quantity of gold absorbed by the Conversion Fund of the Bank of the Nation) had been deposited at the *Caja* in exchange for notes.

proceeds brought rising incomes and hence rising consumption good imports, together with extra imports of investment goods if extra domestic investment was induced; on the other hand, the increased foreign-investment funds were partly spent directly abroad on investment goods; whilst the remainder was transferred to Argentina to finance local spending, thus increasing incomes and imports of consumption goods. The influence of this increased foreign investment after 1904 is most noticeable in the behaviour of imports expressed as a percentage of exports as depicted in figure 8.1. This ratio fell until 1903 as debt-service charges and profits remitted were claiming an extra share of export proceeds; thereafter the ratio increased until 1911 under the influence of rising foreign investment, declining after 1911 as foreign borrowings fell. When the ratios of consumption imports and investment imports as a percentage of exports are considered, it is noticeable how sharply the latter was affected by rising foreign investment, whilst the former was mildly affected, for foreign funds transferred to Argentina then were of relatively minor importance as a generator of incomes as compared with export proceeds.

The expansion of foreign-currency receipts, despite the increases in payments on account of growing import purchases and foreign debt-service payments, brought a net influx of gold into the economy in all years except 1914, which was either deposited in the *Caja* (or Conversion Bureau) in exchange for notes or added to the banking system's reserves. International movements of gold thus enabled the note issue to expand at an annual trend rate of 8.8 per cent, whilst bank deposits rose both because of increases in cash reserves and because of declines in the cash/deposit ratios as the economy prospered. On the other hand, in the second half of 1913 and in 1914 when gold was exported on a considerable scale, the note circulation fell and likewise bank deposits, both because of falling cash reserves *and* because of rising cash/deposit ratios. Thus the monetary system served to intensify the influence of rising foreign-currency receipts on incomes by increased liquidity and credit, whilst it aggravated the influence of falling foreign-currency receipts, since liquidity and credit were curtailed.

The balance-of-payments adjustment mechanism for Argentina under gold standard conditions may be outlined as follows. Foreign-currency receipts, it is asserted, provided the principal cause both of fluctuations in domestic incomes and of changes in Argentina's balance-of-payments position, whilst foreign-currency payments were a dependent variable. Fluctuations in receipts were large enough to swamp any contrary 'autonomous' changes in domestic expenditure – indeed it is to be expected that domestically financed investment would be affected directly by earlier variations in foreign-currency receipts.[22] The fluctuations in export prices which were world-determined as noted earlier and must be treated as an independent variable, were quite unconnected with gold movements into or out of Argentina, as the dissimilar behaviour of grain export prices as compared with wool and meat prices clearly indicated (see table 8.2). Indeed, the scope here for gold movements to influence prices was severely restricted to the prices of home-produced non-exportables, land, and real estate, for import prices were fixed by the foreign sellers. Low elasticities of substitution (a) between imports and non-exportables and (b) between exportables and non-exportables rendered slight the influences of any relative price changes, which international gold movements had brought about via changes in domestic credit policy, on domestic purchases.[23] Nevertheless, these changes would help to promote adjustment, assuming given terms of trade.

Balance-of-payments adjustment to the main disequilibrating force

Table 8.2 Export and import price index numbers for Argentina 1900–14

	(1) Total exports	(2) Grain exports	(3) Pastoral exports	(4) Total imports	(5) Terms of trade (1) ÷ (4)
1900	100	100	100	100	100
1901	99	108	85	87	114
1902	107	114	97	86	123
1903	97	94	102	88	110
1904	103	103	103	88	117
1905	116	114	118	90	129
1906	121	114	132	96	126
1907	125	123	129	100	125
1908	120	133	101	92	131
1909	138	150	119	89	155
1910	142	148	133	87	146
1911	137	143	128	100	137
1912	137	142	130	108	127
1913	139	135	144	108	129
1914	142	136	152	n.a.	n.a.

Source: Ford (1955).

(variations in foreign-currency receipts) was achieved predominantly by corresponding changes in incomes and in imports (more especially consumption goods, since investment good purchases were linked to foreign borrowing) and in invisibles, e.g. dividends and remittances would be higher in years of high activity; of these, imported consumption goods were the principal pliable item. Finally, movements in incomes affected slightly the domestic consumption of exportable products and hence the supply of exports in an equilibrating fashion. Furthermore, this process was aided by the response of the banking system. For changes in imports lagged behind changes in foreign-currency receipts so that a rise in export values per month, for example, brought a balance-of-payments surplus and import of gold, which gradually declined per month as imports rose, disappearing if the marginal propensity to save was zero. Thus income changes were reinforced by the liquidity and credit changes resulting from the gold movements – indeed the note issue and circulation would move in a close direct relationship with the level of incomes.

For completeness, it is necessary to consider the responses of this system to changes in imports unconnected with foreign-currency receipt changes. Suppose imports increased on account of a shift in tastes, or a rise in domestic investment, whilst foreign-currency receipts remained steady, so that gold was exported and the money supply contracted. In both cases the liquidity check would operate to reduce spending and incomes, whilst in the former case, if more were spent from a given income on imports, less would be available to spend on home goods and thus incomes would be reduced further. Any such change in imports, then – apart from the assertion that it would be of small magnitude in the Argentine setting – contained its own adjustment mechanism to damp its influence down.

It is difficult to verify these mechanisms because of insufficient data (e.g. the lack of *full* estimates of capital influx) and because of the comparative unreliability of some available material (e.g. export and import valuations). Nevertheless, if first differences of annual figures of exports and London issues for Argentina are compared with actual gold movements (both international and internal), it will be found that:

1 International gold movements were associated with these first differences of the main constituents of foreign-currency receipts – the curves of the net import of gold and the first differences of exports, for example, show broadly similar movements.

2 The supply of gold from private hoards varied closely with export first differences – the net supply being greater when exports rose. (Net supply from private holdings = excess of absorption of *Caja* and banking system over net gold imports for any time period. A negative value indicates an increase in private gold holdings.)

3 The supply of gold from banking reserves (or alternatively the absorption of gold by banks) was not at all closely associated with export first differences, or in other words changes in banks' visible holdings were very much a residual, balancing the potential supply of gold for note issue and the actual demand for notes.

These movements are illustrated in figure 8.2, and in table 8.3 with correlation coefficients.

The potential supply of gold per time period available for changing the note issue thus depended largely on the behaviour of foreign-currency receipts and the confidence (or otherwise) which this generated in private holders of gold so that fluctuations in the *potential* note issue would be closely associated with fluctuations in foreign-currency receipts and national income. Furthermore, the predominant demand for notes in Argentina was for transactions purposes, so that the actual issue would also be closely linked to movements in national income. Accordingly, it would be reasonable to expect average note issue per year (average of figures for end-March, June, September, December) to be a reliable indicator of the behaviour of national income. If values for consumption imports and average note issue are compared for 1900–14, a correlation coefficient of $+0.95$ results, whilst the correlation coefficients for deviations from linear and exponential trends are $+0.79$ and $+0.83$ respectively. (With thirteen degrees of freedom the t-test indicates

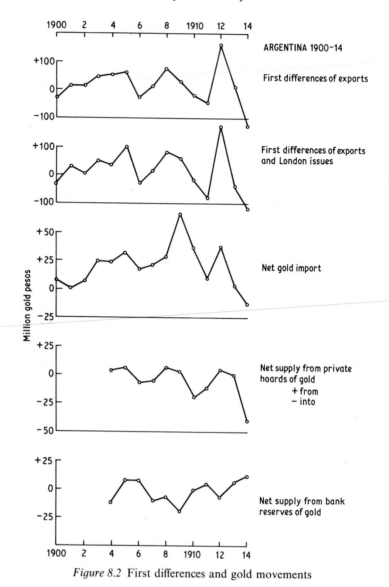

Figure 8.2 First differences and gold movements

that coefficients above + 0.76 are significant at the 0.1 per cent level.) Although these coefficients, it is suspected, would have been higher if Argentine official customs valuations had not varied so much in the years 1904–6, nevertheless the results do demonstrate the close connection between national income and consumption import purchases.

Table 8.3 Correlation coefficients

(a) Net gold imports and export first differences (15 observations)	+ 0.54
(b) Net gold imports and export *plus* London issues first differences (15 observations)	+ 0.61
(c) Net gold supply from private holdings and export first differences (11 observations)	+ 0.85
(d) Net gold supply from banking reserves and export first differences (11 observations)	− 0.53

Note: The *t*-test indicates that in cases (a) and (b) correlation coefficients above 0.59 are significant at the 1 per cent level and above 0.45 at the 5 per cent level; in cases (c) and (d) those above 0.68 at the 1 per cent level and above 0.52 at the 5 per cent level.

Argentina had rejoined the gold standard in 1900 largely to stop a shift in income distribution which was unpleasant to the politically dominant landed and export-producing groups, and had employed a system whereby international gold movements affected the note issue. The adjustment mechanism to changes in the balance of payments (reflected in gold movements) consisted of consequent income movements, which were reinforced by the monetary system, and of their effects on import purchases and remittances. In addition, in years when foreign investment was changing, direct purchases of investment goods abroad changed likewise. Short-term international capital movements, which were so responsive to Bank Rate and market rate of discount changes in the British case, were largely absent.

Why was this system successful in preserving exchange-rate stability until 1914, whilst the system of 1884 collapsed within a year? First, the system never met with the serious test of a sharp efflux of gold as foreign-currency receipts declined relatively to payments until the second half of 1913 and afterwards,[24] whilst it was in the interests of the export-producing and landed groups to see that the system worked. After 1902 there were no runs on gold reserves for private speculative reasons until early 1914. Indeed the *Caja* system, which contemporary commentators dubbed 'fair weather', met 'fair weather' conditions until late 1913. For foreign-currency receipts grew steadily as export values and foreign investment rose, and here must be emphasized the importance of rising export prices, which enhanced the value of the growing output of these products, cut the 'produce' value of fixed interest debt, and increased the attractiveness of Argentina to foreign investors. So rapid was the growth of the economy that any temporary setbacks to export values through poor harvests, or to foreign loans, meant a slackening in the rate of growth of incomes, consumption, and imports rather than any sustained downturn.

The difficulties which a primary producing country, heavily dependent on export sales for its prosperity, may experience in maintaining exchange stability, are well known, and in Argentina were aggravated by her international debtor status; a debtor has service charges, which for Argentina had a large core fixed in gold or sterling and formed a considerable item in her foreign-currency payments.[25] Further, in times of world depression or adversity there was a tendency for short-term funds to move back to creditor countries and away from debtors, irrespective of the latter's interest rates – a movement which affected Argentina especially keenly because of the lack of international confidence in the peso. Thus no short-term capital movements served to soften the export of gold, which had to be staunched speedily by income movements if exchange stability was to be preserved.

Again, Argentina illustrates the weakness for an 'export' economy where the quantity of money is determined by international gold and foreign-currency movements, in that booms and slumps generally arose because of changes in foreign-currency receipts which also brought imports or exports of gold as well so that the initial income movements were exaggerated by changes in liquidity. It was thus difficult to accumulate a sufficient gold reserve during a boom to cope with bad times – apart from the itching palm of some early Argentine governments for idle gold! Furthermore, the fact that in years of depression the initial contractive effects were intensified by monetary factors tended to alienate support for the gold standard system. This is quite different from the cases of some other countries where booms and slumps originated for domestic reasons and met with a fairly stable monetary supply so that rising or falling interest rates tended to mitigate these initial income movements. Here booms were associated with adverse balances of payments, slumps with favourable balances so that the monetary policy dictated by gold movements tended to lessen (not enhance) income fluctuations and the gold standard system was more acceptable than in the former case.

These economic difficulties which might have sufficed in themselves to render adherence to the gold standard impossible, were supplemented by political and social factors which in the last resort proved decisive. The domestic convertibility of notes for gold, which was the prime object for Britain and certain other economies and from which the international gold standard sprang, was not such a point of honour and morality. Other primary producers, such as Australia and New Zealand, maintained exchange-rate stability, which is explained by different administrative and political systems with different social structures, and by their banking systems being based on London. However, in Argentina, aided by the particular economic and political structure, the landed and export-producing oligarchy willingly abandoned or adopted the gold standard system whenever it was to their benefit and profit.

*

Much of the discussion above has been concerned with short-run conditions and adjustment of each economy, and frequently each has been considered in isolation. In this section certain long-run features and interconnections between these economies will be noted briefly. Although the successful working of this sterling system – for that was really what the pre-1914 gold standard amounted to – did depend on the supreme international confidence in the pound, the particular institutional structure of international banking and finance which was centred in London, the acknowledged dominance of the Bank of England, nevertheless particular economic relationships played an important role in ensuring that, for Britain at least, maladjustments in the flows of international payments and receipts were never too large or too persistent to swamp the institutional structure.

When the stability of this sterling system as a whole is considered, it is important, first, to note that Britain provided a steadily growing market for the increasing supplies of primary products from the developing countries. Despite considerable fluctuations in British foreign investment and exports, the broad trend of activity showed steady growth, for (as noted earlier) in periods when the former variables were high so far as underlying trend values are concerned, domestic British investment was low, and vice versa, so that one offset somewhat variations in the other. Nevertheless, an element of instability for the primary producers especially remained because they had little influence over the world prices of their produce and hence the terms of trade of primary products for manufactures. Indeed, a sharp fall in their export prices seriously affected their well-being and could strain their adherence to stable exchange rates, especially if their foreign debt-service charges had a large element of fixed-interest payments. However, in general, the growing, assured, market afforded to these producers by Britain enabled them to earn sufficiently increased supplies of sterling to meet their debt-service charges and to increase their imports and well-being.[26]

Important, secondly, was the interlinking of the lending and borrowing countries and the responsiveness of trade flows to capital movements – especially for Britain. For British foreign investment (e.g. by means of new overseas issues on the London Stock Exchange) at times increased considerably and was transferred (in real terms eventually) without any serious strain on the balance of payments because of the influence of *ex ante* overseas investment directly and indirectly on export sales, whilst any temporary strain, as the net proceeds from borrowing were transferred out of Britain in the form of gold or sterling bills, was speedily eased by the reflux of British funds employed abroad. Furthermore, when British investment abroad declined, exports likewise declined, reducing the British current-account surplus, so that sterling did not become scarcer. Here the long-run tendency for the peaks in home investment to occur with troughs in foreign investment so that domestic activity was more stable in its growth than exports, was of especial importance in bringing about a rising demand for imports, and helping the primary producers whose production of exportables was expanding as investment projects financed from the last wave of foreign investment from Britain matured.

The following crude pattern of economic relationships between Britain and the primary producers who were on the periphery of the gold standard system suggests itself. British loans to overseas countries increased their purchases from Britain and their debt-service payments so that on the one hand they did not permanently gain much gold, nor did Britain lose much gold through the loan-transfer transactions. Secondly, when the investment projects matured, their production of exportables was expanded, for which there was a ready market in Britain. The primary producers' exports rose so that they could pay their foreign debt-service charges and dividend remittances, *and* purchase more imports, whilst because of their growing prosperity British exports expanded. Such trade flows thus contributed to the economic growth of both partners and their mutual welfare, besides providing a basis for stability.

This idyllic scheme, although perhaps realized pretty well in the long run, did give rise to particular short-run difficulties – especially for the primary producers. For, in the upsurge of foreign lending if the sums transferred were temporarily in excess of Britain's current-account surplus and caused the loss of gold, Bank Rate adjustments and the reflux of British short-term funds brought speedy relief. On the other hand, the decline in foreign lending often occurred before the investment projects had been completed and had expanded exportable production so that balance-of-payments difficulties faced the borrowers because of the added burden of extra debt-service charges on an as yet unexpanded production – especially if the ratio of debt-service charges/exports had risen sharply.[27] In this setting of crisis (and possible British fears about these countries' exchange stability or possible default on interest payments) it is dubious whether the short-term pool of credit in London helped such economies to the extent that has sometimes been suggested. Rather they were left to adjust themselves through income movements, which affected their import purchases, whether they remained on the gold standard or perforce embraced a system of flexible exchange rates.

Again, variations in the prices of primary products and in the terms of trade tended to affect these economies more sharply than Britain, for they were more heavily dependent on international trade in most cases.[28] Indeed, in the short run sharp fluctuations impeded or enhanced development, and brought in the former case balance-of-payments strain. For example, falling primary product prices between 1889 and 1896 prevented Argentine export values from rising, despite a great expansion in the volume of exportable production which foreign investment had facilitated; after 1896, however, rising prices enhanced export values, facilitated greatly her return to the gold standard in 1900 and her subsequent adherence until 1914.

In conclusion, mention must be made of one important role played by gold discoveries – they served to keep the whole gold standard system liquid enough to support a growing volume of international transactions and to provide the necessary underpinning of sterling.

Notes

1 Whale (1937).
2 Whale (1937).
3 These may be reworked in the case of an import of gold.
4 If more exportables were consumed at home at the expense of domestic savings, no contractionary income movements would result immediately – the equilibrating forces would be limited to the effects of the loss of gold on money supply, etc., as in the case of 1.

  If other countries employ the proceeds of extra loans from the country in question to buy extra goods from her (i.e. increased exports) then the loss of gold and the decline in incomes will both be arrested, perhaps after a time-lag.
5 This rise will be moderated or even eliminated in the cases where activity falls.
6 Assuming that the demand elasticities are big enough.
7 See Sayers (1936) for an interesting and revealing discussion.
8 Cf. Schumpeter (1939), vol. II, p. 673. This credit 'which was currently turned into cash to be presently reinvested almost anywhere within the gold area, responded to the Bank's slightest move very much more promptly than foreign-owned balances would have done, facilitated great capital transactions, supported foreign business, mitigated domestic stringencies. Because of its presence, tightening the open market – raising open-market rates – not only regulated, but by drawing gold, eased situations.'
9 For example, in 1913 the monetary stringencies in London led to Argentine railway companies postponing new issues until the more propitious conditions of early 1914.
10 For example, Clare (1931), p. 75, referring to the Bank of England and its measures to prevent the export of gold: 'If 5 per cent fails to arrest the export, other measures may have to be resorted to. The Reichsbank, in such a case, would possibly give exporters to understand that they must be prepared to incur the consequences of its displeasure if the withdrawals were persisted in. This the Bank (sc. of England) cannot do; nor can it put a premium on gold – like the Bank of France did before the law of June 1928 made France a free gold country.' Compare also Goschen (1905), pp. 117–19, and Withers (1916), pp. 6, 38 (especially).

  The Bank of England's own evidence before the US National Monetary Commission of 1910 is instructive: Q: 'How do you account for the fact that at times a higher bank rate in England fails to attract gold from the continent, when lower rates prevail there?' A: 'Because there is no gold market on the continent so free as the London Market and the continental markets frequently do not release gold for export until the rate in London has reached a figure which threatens disturbance to their own financial position' (US National Monetary Commission, 1910, p. 27).

11 The author's study of Argentine experience between 1880 and 1914 has convinced him of this rather arrogant claim.

12 See Goschen (1905), p. 121, referring to domestic gold circulation, 'You cannot "tap" this immense mass of sovereigns when you most want gold, except so far as there might be a slight flow towards the centre in times of very dear money. Even if the rate of interest were 8 per cent the bulk of the people would not carry less gold about then than they did before.'

13 If increased import purchases were made at the expense of savings, then the analysis of case (a) is appropriate.

14 It is the net proceeds of a loan transferred abroad in this form which affect the exchanges, not the total proceeds of a loan, for some portion of this never left Britain, being spent directly on capital goods for export to the borrower.

15 It is true that rising export sales would increase British imports as activity increased, but this point needs to be discussed with reference to long-term trends (see p. 161).

16 For a fuller discussion, see Ford (1958–9), pp. 302–8.

17 In the years of high capital export the ratio of net home investment *plus* realized foreign investment to national income is high (e.g. in 1872, 15.0 per cent and in 1913 15.2 per cent, whilst in years of low capital export it is low (e.g. in 1882, 10.4 per cent and in 1896, 9.7 per cent). With a balanced budget, these figures indicate the behaviour of the ratio of *ex post* net domestic savings to national income, and may provide some guide to *ex ante* savings. The estimates are taken from Lenfant (1951) and years of high activity have been chosen for the purposes of this comparison.

18 See White (1933). Again, if the French had not lent abroad, they might well have disrupted the system by amassing most of the world's gold.

19 Indeed, in the short run the supply of exportables and the supply of exports (for domestic consumption of exportables was inelastic with respect to price and income) were both highly inelastic, whereas the supply of imports may be taken as perfectly elastic.

20 It may be doubted whether the loss of external reserves was allowed to affect the domestic credit position in the same way as in Australia or New Zealand, where sterling balances formed both the banking system's cash reserves and the country's foreign-exchange reserves. Given fairly stable cash/deposit ratios, any loss in foreign exchange would bring about a deflationary banking policy with speed. In the 1870s also, Argentine governments preferred to authorize extra issues of paper and subsequent depreciation to the rigours of credit contraction needed to preserve specie payments in that crisis.

21 For a full treatment of this episode, see Ford (1958).

22 For example, domestic investment in the meat trade, whether in freezing plants, in ranches, or in stock, was conditioned by the behaviour of the export markets for meat. Domestic building operations also were affected by changes in the balance of payments: on the one hand the prosperity which rising foreign-currency receipts brought induced extra building, whilst the increase in the quantity of money in Argentina, following this expansion of receipts and the net import of gold, provided extra resources for the banking system to lend and lowered interest rates.

23 It should be noted that rising foreign-currency receipts (besides bringing a gold influx) would also increase the domestic demand for non-exportables via rising incomes, and so promote some slight equilibrating changes in purchases if their prices rose. It would indeed be difficult to say whether such prices rose because of such rising incomes, or because of the expansionary effects of the gold influx.

24 Because of lags in the transmission of income effects, foreign-currency payments,

although growing, would tend to lag behind growing foreign-currency receipts over a period of years so that each year a favourable balance of payments and net import of gold resulted. Once the growth in foreign-currency receipts slackened or ceased, payments would catch up, bringing a less favourable or even adverse balance of payments. Indeed any decrease in receipts would bring a sharp adverse movement in the balance of payments until payments reversed their previous trend and declined.

25 In the period 1911–14 service charges amounted to some 35 per cent of export values.

26 This is a long-run view, which applies once the investment projects (financed from abroad) have matured and expanded the production of exportables. In the short run for primary producers balance-of-payments difficulties, which strained adherence to the gold standard, did occur because frequently the debt-service charges were immediate (e.g. fixed-interest securities) and bore heavily on an unexpanded output and supply of foreign exchange. Such difficulties did not arise for Britain.

27 Fixed-interest securities, rather than equities, were a feature of British foreign lending, so that service charges were immediate. So long as lending continued, these could be met without much strain, but when lending declined, crises often arose. See Ford (1956).

28 Furthermore, even if primary product prices did move against Britain, she did benefit somewhat, for debtors could pay their service charges and dividend remittances were greater, whilst purchases of British exports rose.

References

Clare, George (1931), *A Money Market Primer*, 3rd edn, London, E. Wilson.

Extracto Estadistico de la Republica Argentina correspondiente al ano, 1915 (1916), Buenos Aires.

Ford, A.G. (1955), 'Export price indices for the Argentine Republic, 1881–1914', *Inter-American Economic Affairs* (autumn).

——(1956), 'Argentina and the Baring crisis of 1890', *Oxford Economic Papers.*

——(1958), 'Flexible exchange rates and Argentina, 1885–1900', *Oxford Economic Papers.*

——(1958–9), 'The transfer of British foreign lending, 1870–1914', *Economic History Review.*

Goschen, G.J.G. (1905), *Essays and Addresses on Economic Questions*, London, Edward Arnold.

Lenfant, J.H. (1951), 'Great Britain's capital formation, 1865–1914', *Economica*, New Ser. XVIII.

Sayers, R.S. (1936), *Bank of England Operations 1890–1914*, London, P.S. King.

Schumpeter, Joseph A. (1939), *Business Cycles*, New York, McGraw-Hill.

US National Monetary Commission (1910), *Interviews on the Banking Systems of England, Scotland, France, Germany, Switzerland and Italy*, Senate Doc. No. 405, Washington, D.C., US Government Printing Office.

Whale, P. Barrett (1937), 'The working of the pre-war gold standard', *Economica*, (February).

White, H.D. (1933), *The French International Accounts 1880–1913*, Cambridge, Mass., Harvard University Press.

Withers, Hartley (1916), *Money Changing*, 2nd edn, London, John Murray.

Part III

The interwar gold exchange standard

Introduction

The international gold standard was reconstructed at considerable cost and with great effort after World War I. The first selection in Part III, the *First Interim Report* of Britain's Cunliffe Committee, provides the definitive statement of the prevailing view of the gold standard's indispensability. Little more than a decade later, it was increasingly recognized that the interwar system was not operating as smoothly as the classical gold standard of previous years. The second selection, an extract from the *Report* of the British Macmillan Committee, describes the problems with the interwar system's operation. Heavily influenced by John Maynard Keynes and written at the height of the 1931 financial crisis, it emphasizes such destabilizing factors as wage and price rigidities, actions of central banks to offset the impact of international gold flows, and the growing tendency to hold foreign exchange as a supplement to gold reserves. The third selection, written by Ragnar Nurkse for the League of Nations, provides what remains an influential account and explanation of the interwar gold standard's collapse.

9

First interim report

Cunliffe Committee on Currency and Foreign Exchanges after the War*

To the Lords Commissioners of His Majesty's Treasury and the Minister of Reconstruction

Introduction

My Lords and Sir,

1 We have the honour to present herewith an interim report on certain of the matters referred to us in January last. In this report we attempt to indicate the broad lines on which we think the serious currency difficulties which will confront this country at the end of the war should be dealt with. The difficulties which will arise in connection with the foreign exchanges will be no less grave, but we do not think that any recommendations as to the emergency expedients which may have to be adopted in the period immediately following the conclusion of peace can usefully be made until the end of the war is clearly in sight and a more definite opinion can be formed as to the conditions which will then prevail. We propose also to deal in a later report with questions affecting the constitution and management of the Bank of England, and with the applicability of the recommendations contained in this report to Scotland and Ireland, in regard to which we have not yet taken evidence. We have therefore confined our inquiry for the present to the broad principles upon which the currency should be regulated. We have had the advantage of consultation with the Bank of England, and have taken oral evidence from various banking and financial experts, representatives of certain chambers of commerce and others

*From Cd. 9182, London, HMSO, 1918, pp. 3–7, 11–12, abridged.

who have particularly interested themselves in these matters. We have also had written evidence from certain other representatives of commerce and industry. Our conclusions upon the subjects dealt with in this report are unanimous, and we cannot too strongly emphasize our opinion that the application, at the earliest possible date, of the main principles on which they are based is of vital necessity to the financial stability and well-being of the country. Nothing can contribute more to a speedy recovery from the effects of the war, and to the rehabilitation of the foreign exchanges, than the re-establishment of the currency upon a sound basis. Indeed, a sound system of currency will, as is shown in paragraphs 4 and 5, in itself secure equilibrium in those exchanges, and render unnecessary the continued resort to the emergency expedients to which we have referred. We should add that in our inquiry we have had in view the conditions which are likely to prevail during the ten years immediately following the end of the war, and we think that the whole subject should be again reviewed not later than the end of that period.

The currency system before the war

2 Under the Bank Charter Act of 1844, apart from the fiduciary issue of the Bank of England and the notes of Scottish and Irish Banks of Issue (which were not actually legal tender), the currency in circulation and in Bank reserves consisted before the war entirely of gold and subsidiary coin or of notes representing gold. Gold was freely coined by the Mint without any charge. There were no restrictions upon the import of gold. Sovereigns were freely given by the Bank in exchange for notes at par value, and there were no obstacles to the export of gold. Apart from the presentation for minting of gold already in use in the arts (which under normal conditions did not take place) there was no means whereby the legal tender currency could be increased except the importation of gold from abroad to form the basis of an increase in the note issue of the Bank of England or to be presented to the Mint for coinage, and no means whereby it could be diminished (apart from the normal demand for the arts, amounting to about £2,000,000 a year, which was only partly taken out of the currency supply) except the export of bullion or sovereigns.

3 Since the passing of the Act of 1844 there has been a great development of the cheque system. The essence of that system is that purchasing power is largely in the form of bank deposits operated upon by cheque, legal tender money being required only for the purpose of the reserves held by the banks against those deposits and for actual public circulation in connection with the payment of wages and retail transactions. The provisions of the Act of 1844 as applied to that system have operated both to correct unfavourable exchanges and to check undue expansions of credit.

4 When the exchanges were favourable, gold flowed freely into this country and an increase of legal tender money accompanied the development of trade. When the balance of trade was unfavourable and the exchanges were adverse, it became profitable to export gold. The would-be exporter bought his gold from the Bank of England and paid for it by a cheque on his account. The Bank obtained the gold from the Issue Department in exchange for notes taken out of its banking reserve, with the result that its liabilities to depositors and its banking reserve were reduced by an equal amount, and the ratio of reserve to liabilites consequently fell. If the process was repeated sufficiently often to reduce the ratio in a degree considered dangerous, the Bank raised its rate of discount. The raising of the discount rate had the immediate effect of retaining money here which would otherwise have been remitted abroad and of attracting remittances from abroad to take advantage of the higher rate, thus checking the outflow of gold and even reversing the stream.

5 If the adverse condition of the exchanges was due not merely to seasonal fluctuations, but to circumstances tending to create a permanently adverse trade balance, it is obvious that the procedure above described would not have been sufficient. It would have resulted in the creation of a volume of short-dated indebtedness to foreign countries which would have been in the end disastrous to our credit and the position of London as the financial centre of the world. But the raising of the Bank's discount rate and the steps taken to make it effective in the market necessarily led to a general rise of interest rates and a restriction of credit. New enterprises were therefore postponed and the demand for constructional materials and other capital goods was lessened. The consequent slackening of employment also diminished the demand for consumable goods, while holders of stocks of commodities carried largely with borrowed money, being confronted with an increase of interest charges, if not with actual difficulty in renewing loans, and with the prospect of falling prices, tended to press their goods on a weak market. The result was a decline in general prices in the home market which, by checking imports and stimulating exports, corrected the adverse trade balance which was the primary cause of the difficulty.

6 When, apart from a foreign drain of gold, credit at home threatened to become unduly expanded, the old currency system tended to restrain the expansion and to prevent the consequent rise in domestic prices which ultimately causes such a drain. The expansion of credit, by forcing up prices, involves an increased demand for legal tender currency both from the banks in order to maintain their normal proportion of cash to liabilities and from the general public for the payment of wages and for retail transactions. In this case also the demand for such currency fell upon the reserve of the Bank of England, and the Bank was thereupon obliged to raise its rate of discount in order to prevent the fall in the proportion of that reserve to its liabilities. The same

chain of consequences as we have just described followed and speculative trade activity was similarly restrained. There was therefore an automatic machinery by which the volume of purchasing power in this country was continuously adjusted to world prices of commodities in general. Domestic prices were automatically regulated so as to prevent excessive imports; and the creation of banking credit was so controlled that banking could be safely permitted a freedom from state interference which would not have been possible under a less rigid currency system.

7 Under these arrangements this country was provided with a complete and effective gold standard. The essence of such a standard is that notes must always stand at absolute parity with gold coins of equivalent face value, and that both notes and gold coins stand at absolute parity with gold bullion. When these conditions are fulfilled, the foreign-exchange rates with all countries possessing an effective gold standard are maintained at or within the gold specie points.

Changes which have affected the gold standard during the war

8 It will be observed that the fall in a number of the foreign exchanges below the old export specie points which has taken place since the early part of 1915[1] is not by itself a proof that the gold standard has broken down or ceased to be effective. During the present war the depredations of enemy submarines, high freights, and the refusal of the government to extend state insurance to gold cargoes have greatly increased the cost of sending gold abroad. The actual export specie point has, therefore, moved a long way from its old position. In view of our enormous demands for imports, coupled with the check on our exports due to the war, it was natural that our exchanges with neutrals should move towards the export specie point. Consequently, the fall in the export specie point would by itself account for a large fall in our exchange rates. Such a fall must have taken place in the circumstances, even though all the conditions of an effective gold standard had been fully maintained.

9 The course of the war has, however, brought influences into play in consequence of which the gold standard has ceased to be effective. In view of the crisis which arose upon the outbreak of war it was considered necessary, not merely to authorize the suspension of the Act of 1844, but also to empower the Treasury to issue currency notes for one pound and for ten shillings as legal tender throughout the United Kingdom. Under the powers given by the Currency and Bank Notes Act 1914, the Treasury undertook to issue such notes through the Bank of England to bankers, as and when required, up to a maximum limit not exceeding for any bank 20 per cent of its liabilities on current and deposit accounts. The amount of notes issued to each bank was to be treated as an advance bearing interest at the current Bank Rate.

10 It is not likely that the internal demand for legal tender currency which was anticipated at the beginning of August 1914 would by itself have necessitated extensive recourse to these provisions. But the credits created by the Bank of England in favour of its depositors under the arrangements by which the Bank undertook to discount approved bills of exchange and other measures taken about the same time for the protection of credit caused a large increase in the deposits of the Bank. Further, the need of the government for funds wherewith to finance the war in excess of the amounts raised by taxation and by loans from the public has made necessary the creation of credits in their favour with the Bank of England. Thus, the total amount of the Bank's deposits increased from, approximately, £56,000,000 in July 1914 to £273,000,000 on 28 July 1915 and, though a considerable reduction has since been effected, they now (15 August) stand as high as £171,870,000. The balances created by these operations passing by means of payments to contractors and others to the joint stock banks have formed the foundation of a great growth of their deposits which have also been swelled by the creation of credits in connection with the subscriptions to the various war loans.[2] Under the operation of these causes the total deposits of the banks of the United Kingdom (other than the Bank of England) increased from £1,070,681,000 on 31 December 1913, to £1,742,902,000 on 31 December 1917.

11 The greatly increased volume of bank deposits, representing a corresponding increase of purchasing power and, therefore, leading in conjunction with other causes to a great rise of prices, has brought about a corresponding demand for legal tender currency which could not have been satisfied under the stringent provisions of the Act of 1844. Contractors are obliged to draw cheques against their accounts in order to discharge their wages bill – itself enhanced on account of the rise of prices. It is to provide this currency that the continually growing issues of currency notes have been made. The Banks instead of obtaining notes by way of advance under the arrangements described in paragraph 9 were able to pay for them outright by the transfer of the amount from their balances at the Bank of England to the credit of the currency note account and the circulation of the notes continued to increase. The government subsequently, by substituting their own securities for the cash balance so transferred to their credit, borrow that balance. In effect, the banks are in a position at will to convert their balances at the Bank of England enhanced in the manner indicated above into legal tender currency without causing notes to be drawn, as they would have been under the prewar system, from the banking reserve of the Bank of England, and compelling the Bank to apply the normal safeguards against excessive expansion of credit. Fresh legal tender currency is thus continually being issued, not, as formerly, against gold, but against government securities. Plainly, given the necessity for the creation of bank credits in favour of the government for the purpose of financing war

expenditure, these issues could not be avoided. If they had not been made, the banks would have been unable to obtain legal tender with which to meet cheques drawn for cash on their customers' accounts. The unlimited issue of currency notes in exchange for credits at the Bank of England is at once a consequence and an essential condition of the methods which the Government have found necessary to adopt in order to meet their war expenditure.

12 The effect of these causes upon the amount of legal tender money (other than subsidiary coin) in bank reserves and in circulation in the United Kingdom are shown in the following paragraph.

13 The amounts on 30 June 1914, may be estimated as follows:

Fiduciary Issue of the Bank of England	£18,450,000
Bank of England notes issued against gold coin or bullion	£38,476,000
Estimated amount of gold coin held by banks (excluding gold coin held in the Issue Department of the Bank of England) and in public circulation	£123,000,000
Grand total	£179,926,000

The corresponding figures of 10 July 1918, as nearly as they can be estimated, were:

Fiduciary Issue of the Bank of England	£18,450,000
Currency notes not covered by gold	£230,412,000
Total Fiduciary Issues[3]	£248,862,000
Bank of England notes issued against coin and bullion	£65,368,000
Currency notes covered by gold	£28,500,000
Estimated amount of gold coin held by banks (excluding gold coin held by Issue Department of Bank of England), say	£40,000,000
Grand total	£382,730,000

There is also a certain amount of gold coin still in the hands of the public which ought to be added to the last-mentioned figure, but the amount is unknown.

14 As Bank of England notes and currency notes are both payable at the Bank of England in gold coin on demand this large issue of new notes, associated, as it is, with abnormally high prices and unfavourable exchanges,

must have led under normal conditions to a rapid depletion, threatening ultimately the complete exhaustion, of the Bank's gold holdings. Consequently, unless the Bank had been prepared to see all its gold drained away, the discount rate must have been raised to a much higher level, the creation of banking credit (including that required by the government) would have been checked, prices would have fallen and a large portion of the surplus notes must have come back for cancellation. In this way an effective gold standard would have been maintained in spite of the heavy issue of notes. But during the war conditions have not been normal. The public are content to employ currency notes for internal purposes, and, notwithstanding adverse exchanges, war conditions interpose effective practical obstacles against the export of gold. Moreover, the legal prohibition of the melting of gold coin, and the fact that the importation of gold bullion is reserved to the Bank of England, and that dealings in it are limited have severed the link which formerly existed between the values of coin and of uncoined gold. It is not possible to judge to what extent legal tender currency may in fact be depreciated in terms of bullion. But it is practically certain that there has been some depreciation, and to this extent therefore the gold standard has ceased to be effective.

Restoration of conditions necessary to the maintenance of the gold standard recommended

15 We shall not attempt now to lay down the precise measures that should be adopted to deal with the situation immediately after the war. These will depend upon a variety of conditions which cannot be foreseen, in particular the general movements of world prices and the currency policy adopted by other countries. But it will be clear that the conditions necessary to the maintenance of an effective gold standard in this country no longer exist, and it is imperative that they should be restored without delay. After the war our gold holdings will no longer be protected by the submarine danger, and it will not be possible indefinitely to continue to support the exchanges with foreign countries by borrowing abroad. Unless the machinery which long experience has shown to be the only effective remedy for an adverse balance of trade and an undue growth of credit is once more brought into play, there will be very grave danger of a credit expansion in this country and a foreign drain of gold which might jeopardize the convertibility of our note issue and the international trade position of the country. The uncertainty of the monetary situation will handicap our industry, our position as an international financial centre will suffer and our general commercial status in the eyes of the world will be lowered. We are glad to find that there was no difference of opinion among the witnesses who appeared before us as to the vital importance of these matters.

Cessation of government borrowings

16 If a sound monetary position is to be re-established and the gold standard to be effectively maintained, it is in our judgement essential that government borrowings should cease at the earliest possible moment after the war. A large part of the credit expansion arises, as we have shown, from the fact that the expenditure of the government during the war has exceeded the amounts which they have been able to raise by taxation or by loans from the actual savings of the people. They have been obliged therefore to obtain money through the creation of credits by the Bank of England and by the joint stock banks, with the result that the growth of purchasing power has exceeded that of purchasable goods and services. As we have already shown, the continuous issue of uncovered currency notes is inevitable in such circumstances. This credit expansion (which is necesarily accompanied by an evergrowing foreign indebtedness) cannot continue after the war without seriously threatening our gold reserves and, indeed, our national solvency.

17 A primary condition of the restoration of a sound credit position is the repayment of a large portion of the enormous amount of government securities now held by the banks. It is essential that as soon as possible the state should not only live within its income but should begin to reduce its indebtedness. We accordingly recommend that at the earliest possible moment an adequate sinking fund should be provided out of revenue, so that there may be a regular annual reduction of capital liabilities, more especially those which constitute the floating debt. We should remark that it is of the utmost importance that such repayment of debt should not be offset by fresh borrowings for capital expenditure. We are aware that immediately after the war there will be strong pressure for capital expenditure by the state in many forms for reconstruction purposes. But it is essential to the restoration of an effective gold standard that the money for such expenditure should not be provided by the creation of new credit, and that, in so far as such expenditure is undertaken at all, it should be undertaken with great caution. The necessity of providing for our indispensable supplies of food and raw materials from abroad and for arrears of repairs to manufacturing plant and the transport system at home will limit the savings available for new capital expenditure for a considerable period. This caution is particularly applicable to far-reaching programmes of housing and other development schemes.

The shortage of real capital must be made good by genuine savings. It cannot be met by the creation of fresh purchasing power in the form of bank advances to the government or to manufacturers under government guarantee or otherwise, and any resort to such expedients can only aggravate the evil and retard, possibly for generations, the recovery of the country from the losses sustained during the war.

Use of Bank of England discount rate

18 Under an effective gold standard all export demands for gold must be freely met. A further essential condition of the restoration and maintenance of such a standard is therefore that some machinery shall exist to check foreign drains when they threaten to deplete the gold reserves. The recognized machinery for this purpose is the Bank of England discount rate. Whenever before the war the Bank's reserves were being depleted, the rate of discount was raised. This, as we have already explained, by reacting upon the rates for money generally, acted as a check which operated in two ways. On the one hand, raised money rates tended directly to attract gold to this country or to keep here gold that might have left. On the other hand, by lessening the demands for loans for business purposes, they tended to check expenditure and so to lower prices in this country, with the result that imports were discouraged and exports encouraged, and the exchanges thereby turned in our favour. Unless this twofold check is kept in working order the whole currency system will be imperilled. To maintain the connection between a gold drain and a rise in the rate of discount is essential to the safety of the reserves. When the exchanges are adverse and gold is being drawn away, it is essential that the rate of discount in this country should be raised relatively to the rates ruling in other countries. Whether this will actually be necessary immediately after the war depends on whether prices in this country are then substantially higher than gold prices throughout the world. It seems probable that at present they are on the whole higher, but, if credit expansion elsewhere continues to be rapid, it is possible that this may eventually not be so.

Continuance of differential rates for home and foreign money not recommended

19 It has been argued before us that during the period of reconstruction and perhaps for many years afterwards it will be possible and desirable, even though the exchanges are adverse, to keep money for home industry substantially cheaper in this country than it is abroad and yet retain an effective gold standard by continuing the present practice of differentiating between home money and foreign money. It is held that relatively low rates should be offered for home money and charged on domestic loans, while gold is at the same time prevented from going abroad by the offer of high rates for foreign money. In our judgement, so soon as the present obstacles in the way of international intercourse are removed, any attempt to maintain this differentiation must break down because it would be impracticable to prevent people from borrowing at the low home rate and contriving in one way or another to re-lend at the high foreign rate. This could only be prevented, if

at all, by the maintenance of such stringent restrictions upon the freedom of investment after the war as would, in our opinion, be most detrimental to the financial and industrial recovery of this country. Even, however, if differentiation, as a postwar policy, were practicable, it would not, in our judgement, be desirable. For the low home rate, by fostering large loans and so keeping up prices would continue to encourage imports and discourage exports; so that, even though the high rate offered for foreign money prevented gold from being drawn abroad, it would only do this at the cost of piling up an ever-growing debt from Englishmen to foreigners. It would be necessary at the same time to continue to pay for our essential imports of raw materials by borrowing in the United States and elsewhere, instead of by increasing our exports, thus imposing further burdens of foreign debt. This process could not continue indefinitely, and must sooner or later lead to a collapse. We are, therefore, of opinion that the need for making money dear in the face of adverse exchanges cannot, and should not, be evaded by resort to differential rates.

Legal limitation of note issue necessary

20 The foregoing argument has a close connection with the general question of the legal control of the note issue. It has been urged in some quarters that in order to make possible the provision of a liberal supply of money at low rates during the period of reconstruction further new currency notes should be created, with the object of enabling banks to make large loans to industry without the risk of finding themselves short of cash to meet the requirements of the public for legal tender money. It is plain that a policy of this kind is incompatible with the maintenance of an effective gold standard. If it is adopted there will be no check upon the outflow of gold. Adverse exchanges will not be corrected either directly or indirectly through a modification in the general level of commodity prices in this country. On the contrary, as the issue of extra notes stimulates the conditions which tend to produce an advance of prices, they will become steadily more and more adverse. Hence the processes making for the withdrawal of our gold will continue and no counteracting force will be set in motion. In the result the gold standard will be threatened with destruction through the loss of all our gold.

21 The device of making money cheap by the continued issue of new notes is thus altogether incompatible with the maintenance of a gold standard. Such a policy can only lead in the end to an inconvertible paper currency and a collapse of the foreign exchanges, with consequences to the whole commercial fabric of the country which we will not attempt to describe. This result may be postponed for a time by restrictions on the export of gold and by borrowing abroad. But the continuance of such a policy after

the war can only render the remedial measures which would ultimately be inevitably more painful and protracted. No doubt it would be possible for the Bank of England, with the help of the joint stock banks, without any legal restriction on the note issue, to keep the rate of discount sufficiently high to check loans, keep down prices, and stop the demand for further notes. But it is very undesirable to place the whole responsibility upon the discretion of the banks, subject as they will be to very great pressure in a matter of this kind. If they know that they can get notes freely, the temptation to adopt a lax loan policy will be very great. In order, therefore, to ensure that this is not done, and the gold standard thereby endangered, it is, in our judgement, imperative that the issue of fiduciary notes shall be, as soon as practicable, once more limited by law, and that the present arrangements under which deposits at the Bank of England may be exchanged for legal tender currency without affecting the reserve of the Banking Department shall be terminated at the earliest possible moment. Additional demands for legal tender currency otherwise than in exchange for gold should be met from the reserves of the Bank of England and not by the Treasury, so that the necessary checks upon an undue issue may be brought regularly into play. Subject to the transitional arrangements as regards currency notes which we later propose, and to any special arrangements in regard to Scotland and Ireland which we may have to propose when we come to deal with the questions affecting those parts of the United Kingdom, we recommend that the note issue (except as regards existing private issues) should be entirely in the hands of the Bank of England; the notes should be payable in gold in London only, and should be legal tender throughout the United Kingdom. [...]

Summary of conclusions

47 Our main conclusions may be briefly summarized as follows:

Before the war the country possessed a complete and effective gold standard. The provisions of the Bank Act 1844, operated automatically to correct unfavourable exchanges and to check undue expansions of credit (paras 2–7).

During the war the conditions necessary to the maintenance of that standard have ceased to exist. The main cause has been the growth of credit due to government borrowing from the Bank of England and other banks for war needs. The unlimited issue of currency notes has been both an inevitable consequence and a necessary condition of this growth of credit (paras 8–14).

In our opinion it is imperative that after the war the conditions necessary to the maintenance of an effective gold standard should be restored without delay. Unless the machinery which long experience has shown to be the only effective remedy for an adverse balance of trade and an undue growth of credit is once more brought into play, there will be grave danger of a progressive credit expansion which will result in a foreign drain of gold menacing the convertibility of our note issue and so jeopardizing the international trade position of the country (para. 15).

The prerequisites for the restoration of an effective gold standard are:

(a) The cessation of government borrowing as soon as possible after the war. We recommend that at the earliest possible moment an adequate sinking fund should be provided out of revenue, so that there may be a regular annual reduction of capital liabilities, more especially those which constitute the floating debt (paras 16 and 17).

(b) The recognized machinery, namely the raising and making effective of the Bank of England discount rate, which before the war operated to check a foreign drain of gold and the speculative expansion of credit in this country, must be kept in working order. This necessity cannot, and should not, be evaded by any attempt to continue differential rates for home and foreign money after the war (paras 18 and 19).

(c) The issue of fiduciary notes should, as soon as practicable, once more be limited by law, and the present arrangements under which deposits at the Bank of England may be exchanged for legal tender currency without affecting the reserve of the Banking Department should be terminated at the earliest possible moment. Subject to transitional arrangements as regards currency notes and to any special arrangements in regard to Scotland and Ireland which we may have to propose when we come to deal with the questions affecting those parts of the United Kingdom, we recommend that the note issue (except as regards existing private issues) should be entirely in the hands of the Bank of England. The notes should be payable in London only and should be legal tender throughout the United Kingdom (paras 20 and 21).

As regards the control of the note issue, we make the following observations:

1   While the obligation to pay both Bank of England notes and currency notes in gold on demand should be maintained, it is not necessary or desirable that there should be any early resumption of the internal circulation of gold coin (para. 23).

2   While the import of gold should be free from all restrictions, it is convenient that the Bank of England should have cognizance of all gold exports and we recommend that the export of gold coin or bullion should be subject to the condition that such coin and bullion has been obtained from the Bank for the purpose. The Bank should be under obligation to supply gold for export in exchange for its notes (para. 24).

3   In view of the withdrawal of gold from circulation we recommend that the gold reserves of the country should be held by one central

institution and that all banks should transfer any gold now held by them to the Bank of England (para. 25).

Having carefully considered the various proposals which have been placed before us as regards the basis of the fiduciary note issue (paras 26–31), we recommend that the principle of the Bank Charter Act 1844, should be maintained, namely that there should be a fixed fiduciary issue beyond which notes should only be issued in exchange for gold. The separation of the Issue and Banking Departments of the Bank of England should be maintained, and the Weekly Return should continue to be published in its present form (para. 32).

We recommend, however, that provision for an emergency be made by the continuance in force, subject to the stringent safeguards recommended in the body of the report, of section 3 of the Currency and Bank Notes Act 1914, under which the Bank of England may, with the consent of the Treasury, temporarily issue notes in excess of the legal limit (para. 33).

We advocate the publication by the banks of a monthly statement in a prescribed form (para. 34).

We have come to the conclusion that it is not practicable to fix any precise figure for the fiduciary note issue immediately after the war (paras 35–9).

We think it desirable, therefore, to fix the amount which should be aimed at as the central gold reserve, leaving the fiduciary issue to be settled ultimately at such amount as can be kept in circulation without causing the central gold reserve to fall below the amount so fixed. We recommend that the normal minimum of the central gold reserve to be aimed at should be, in the first instance, £150 million. Until this amount has been reached and maintained concurrently with a satisfactory foreign exchange position for at least a year, the policy of cautiously reducing the uncovered note issue should be followed. When reductions have been effected, the actual maximum fiduciary circulation in any year should become the legal maximum for the following year, subject only to the emergency arrangements previously recommended. When the exchanges are working normally on the basis of a minimum reserve of £150 million, the position should again be reviewed in the light of the dimensions of the fiduciary issue as it then exists (paras 40–2).

We do not recommend the transfer of the existing currency note issue to the Bank of England until the future dimensions of the fiduciary issue have been ascertained. During the transitional period the issue should remain a government issue, but new notes should be issued, not against government securities, but against Bank of England notes, and, furthermore, when opportunity arises for providing cover for existing uncovered notes, Bank of England notes should be used for this purpose also. Demands for new currency would then fall in the normal way on the Banking Department of the Bank of England (paras 43 and 44).

When the fiduciary portion of the issue has been reduced to an amount which experience shows to be consistent with the maintenance of a central gold reserve of £150 million, the outstanding currency notes should be retired and replaced by Bank of England notes of low denomination in accordance with the detailed procedure which we describe (paras 45 and 46).

We have the honour to be,
My Lords and Sir,
Your obedient Servants,
(Signed)   CUNLIFFE (*Chairman*)
C.S. ADDIS
R.E. BECKETT
JOHN BRADBURY
G.C. CASSELS
GASPARD FARRER
HERBERT C. GIBBS
W.H.N. GOSCHEN
INCHCAPE
R.W. JEANS
A.C. PIGOU
GEO. F. STEWART
W. WALLACE

Notes

1   In the abnormal circumstances at the outbreak of war the neutral exchanges moved temporarily in our favour owing to the remittance home of liquid balances from foreign countries and the withdrawal of foreign credits.

2   This process has had results of such far-reaching importance that it may be useful to set out in detail the manner in which it operates. Suppose, for example, that in a given week the government require £10,000,000 over and above the receipts from taxation and loans from the public. They apply for an advance from the Bank of England, which by a book entry places the amount required to the credit of public deposits in the same way as any other banker credits the account of a customer when he grants him temporary accommodation. The amount is then paid out to contractors and other government creditors, and passes, when the cheques are cleared, to the credit of their bankers in the books of the Bank of England – in other words is transferred from public to "other" deposits, the effect of the whole transaction thus being to increase by £10,000,000 the purchasing power in the hands of the public in the form of deposits in the joint stock banks and the bankers' cash at the Bank of England by the same amount. The bankers' liabilities to depositors having thus increased by £10,000,000 and their cash reserves by an equal amount, their proportion of cash to liabilities (which was normally before the war something under 20 per cent) is improved, with the result that they are in a position to make advances to their customers to an amount equal to four or five times the

sum added to their cash reserves, or, in the absence of demand for such accommodation, to increase their investments by the difference between the cash received and the proportion they required to hold against the increase of their deposit liabilities. Since the outbreak of war it is the second procedure which has in the main been followed, the surplus cash having been used to subscribe for Treasury Bills and other government securities. The money so subscribed has again been spent by the government and returned in the manner above described to the bankers' cash balances, the process being repeated again and again until each £10,000,000 originally advanced by the Bank of England has created new deposits representing new purchasing power to several times that amount. Before the war these processes, if continued, compelled the Bank of England, as explained in paragraph 6, to raise its rate of discount, but, as indicated below, the unlimited issue of currency notes has now removed this check upon the continued expansion of credit.

3   The notes issued by Scottish and Irish banks which have been made legal tender during the war have not been included in the foregoing figures. Strictly the amount (about £5 million) by which these issues exceed the amount of gold and currency notes held by those banks should be added to the figures of the present fiduciary issues given above.

10

Report

Macmillan Committee on Finance and Industry*

The international gold standard

35 To restore gold to its old position as an international standard of value was the avowed aim of currency policy for a period of six or seven years after the cessation of hostilities. This aim was endorsed by two International Conferences, that of Brussels (1920) and Genoa (1922). Since the restoration of the gold standard the main preoccupation of currency authorities has been with the manner in which it has worked and the extent to which, under the conditions actually experienced, it has been responsible for the present degree of international disequilibrium.

36 By an international gold standard is to be understood not identity of the currency arrangements of all the countries comprising the gold standard group but the possession by all of them of one attribute in common, namely that the monetary unit (i.e. pound sterling, dollar, franc, mark and so on) should possess a gold value prescribed by law, or, rather, a gold value within the limits of the buying and selling price of gold of the local central bank. In almost all countries gold coin has now been withdrawn from circulation and its place taken by paper representatives of the gold. The gold price of the paper representatives of gold is determined by the limits at which the central banks will give gold for paper, or paper for gold. Thus in Great Britain an ounce of standard gold, containing eleven parts of gold to one part of alloy, is legally

*From Cmd. 3897, London, HMSO, 1931, pp. 18–24, 106–14, abridged.

equivalent to £3.17s. 10½d. This is the price at which the Bank of England must sell gold in exchange for its own notes: the minimum price at which it must give its own notes in exchange for gold is £3.17s. 9d.

37 The legal determination by each of a group of countries of the gold equivalent of the monetary unit, though an essential, is not the only condition of an effective international gold standard. Something more is necessary; namely, the right freely to import gold and to tender it in unlimited quantities to the central bank; and the converse right, freely and in unlimited quantities, to draw gold from the central bank and to export the gold so obtained. During and immediately after the war there were countries which, though nominally, were not actually, on the gold standard because the rights in question did not exist. Thus in Great Britain, although the holder of Bank of England or of currency notes was legally entitled to obtain gold in exchange for notes, he was, under war conditions, unable in practice to export gold and was later by statute prohibited from exporting it except under licence. Again, in Sweden, gold importers were not free to tender gold in unlimited quantities to the central bank: the Swedish krona therefore possessed a value superior to the weight of gold which it nominally represented.

38 The right to demand gold in exchange for local purchasing power, or local purchasing power in exchange for gold, is not, however, the only guarantee of the effective working of the gold standard. It is sufficient if the local currency is exchangeable for another currency which is itself convertible into gold. It is possible indeed to classify currency systems based upon the gold standard by the extent to which the relationship between the local monetary unit and gold is proximate or remote. First there are the systems in which the monetary unit is itself a gold coin; then come currency systems in which conversion takes the form of the exchange by the central bank of gold bars into local currency or vice versa; more remote still is the connection when the conversion right takes the form of an exchange of local purchasing power into foreign currency which is itself convertible into gold bars or gold coin. Nor is it absolutely necessary that the right to convert should be conferred by statute; it suffices if the currency authority never refuses to give gold or the equivalent at a fixed rate for the local currency, and vice versa.

Primary objective of the gold standard

39 The primary object of the international gold standard is to maintain a parity of the foreign exchanges within narrow limits; this has the effect of securing a certain measure of correspondence in the levels of prices ruling all over the gold standard area. Incidentally it provides an objective test of the correspondence of local currency policy with that of the rest of the world,

whilst under it the currency mechanism itself provides the resources by which, in the event of temporary disequlibrium in the relation of one currency to another, equilibrium can be restored. But although so long as an international gold standard exists, the currency authority of any gold standard country has always a simple test of the effect of its policy constantly before it, the disequilibrium between the local currency in relation to the rest of the world leading to a loss of gold may be due to deep-seated causes which, if not corrected by measures involving a definite change in values in the country in question, would result in a permanent drain of gold, or alternatively it may be due to a merely temporary deficiency in the balance of payments, not in itself due to deep-seated currency derangements. A sudden check to exports due to the failure of a crop in an exporting country, or a sudden weakening of markets in an importing country, or pressure on the foreign-exchange market due to a demand for remittance in consequence of a rush of new long-term issues in the capital market, or the withdrawal of short-term balances from a money market in consequence of political unrest in the borrowing or lending country, or indeed, in any part of the world, are instances in point. What is necessary is the possession of some one exportable commodity, the value of which will not fall, i.e. for which the short-period price is not subject to change. Gold is such a commodity; so also is the exchange represented by a draft on a bank of the creditor country. Gold and foreign-exchange reserves are easily mobilizable assets which are available at moments of emergency, when perhaps nothing else is available. Thus, under the international gold standard, the currency system itself provides the resources by means of which equilibrium can be restored, so long as the causes by which disequilibrium has been brought about are only temporary in character, and so long as the international gold standard is itself maintained.

40 The fact that a state of temporary disequilibrium can be adjusted by flows of gold or foreign exchange does not remove from the currency authority the necessity of caution and of interpreting the situation in the light of its fundamental duty of safeguarding the international standard. What appears at first sight to be a case of purely temporary disequilibrium may prove to be a symptom of a more deep-seated lack of adjustment. Whilst gold exports need not be followed by more drastic remedial measures if the disequilibrium is temporary, they are always a warning both to the money market and to the central bank itself that further action may later be necessary. Thus, whenever gold is lost, the central bank is provided with an 'automatic' signal of the emergence of conditions which may make positive action necessary. The ultimate aim – the restoration of the international value of the currency – is clear, but the action to be taken, and the precise moment at which it should be taken, remain in the sphere of discretion and judgement, in a word with 'management'. That the sphere of 'management' in this sense is wide and

responsible is beyond doubt. For if the wrong action is taken, the state of disequilibrium which the monetary authority designs to correct may be accentuated or perpetuated. If, in a state of temporary disequilibrium, the monetary authority takes action resulting in a change in the level of values here, a new state of disequilibrium may be unnecessarily created. The sense in which the gold standard can be said to be automatic is thus very limited; it is automatic only as an indicator of the need for action and of the end to be achieved.

Secondary objectives of the gold standard

41 It may be considered a secondary object of the international gold standard to preserve a reasonable stability of international prices. The mere existence of an effective international gold standard does not, however, guarantee stability of prices as a whole either over space or over time. In the nineteenth century, indeed, price movements in different gold standard countries showed a marked tendency to move together, but the absolute level of prices showed a considerable degree of long-period instability. And in the postwar period the sympathetic movement of prices over space is subject to a much greater degree of interference than was the case before the war, whilst the trend of prices over time has shown a very marked degree of instability. These circumstances call for investigation.

42 If prices are to be kept in approximate equality over space, two sets of conditions, which must be present simultaneously, are necessary. In the first place, countries which are losing gold must be prepared to act on a policy which will have the effect of lowering prices, and countries which are receiving gold must be prepared to act on a policy which will have the effect of raising prices. In the second place, the economic structure (as distinct from the currency structure) must be sufficiently organic and sufficiently elastic to allow these policies to attain their objective. The first condition concerns central banking policy; the second limiting condition is not a question of monetary policy, but of the actual economic conditions in which such policy has to work. In practice, it may easily happen that where the first condition is present, the second is absent, and vice versa.

43 The nineteenth-century philosophy of the gold standard was based on the assumptions that (a) an increase or decrease of gold in the vaults of central banks would imply respectively a 'cheap' or a 'dear' money policy, and (b) that a 'cheap' or a 'dear' money policy would affect the entire price structure and the level of money-incomes in the country concerned. But, in the modern postwar world, neither of these assumptions is invariably valid. The growth of the practice of central banks, by which gold inflows or outflows are offset by the

withdrawal or creation of bank credit – the movement of gold not being allowed to produce any effect on monetary conditions – involves not the absence of policy, but a policy inconsistent with the rapid adjustment of relative money-incomes and prices. Thus, if at a time when gold flows freely to the United States the Federal Reserve System offsets gold imports by sales of securities, thereby preventing credit expansion, the level of American money-incomes and prices will not rise. If, at the same time, the levels of European money-incomes and prices are already higher than international equilibrium justifies, the whole burden of re-adjustment will be thrust exclusively on Europe. Again, if the level of British costs is out of line with international conditions, but gold exports are offset by the creation of fresh credit by the Bank of England, the maladjustment will continue. Both the failure of American incomes and prices to rise, and the failure of British incomes and prices to fall, may be deliberately intended, but in that case a policy of stabilizing local values has been, implicitly or explicitly, substituted for a policy of maintaining a level of values consistent with international equilibrium.

44 Moreover, the effect of the policy of a central bank is uncertain when the general economic structure is itself rigid, and more particularly so when the object of that policy is to reduce the price level and the income structure. Pressure can be brought to bear upon the users of credit by a restriction of credit or the raising of Bank Rate, but that pressure cannot be directly brought to bear upon the costs of production. If the economic structure is rigid, then the effect may be to depress wholesale prices but to leave other prices unchanged, and the process of restoring incomes and prices to an equilibrium level through gold flows and associated bank policy may be interrupted or long delayed or even completely obstructed.

45 The degree to which the price level remains stable over a period of time is again profoundly influenced by policy. If gold were the only form of currency, if there were no alternative uses for gold, and if no stocks of gold were held by central banks, the price level would be directly affected by the habits of the community on the one hand and the output of gold on the other. Actually, in the modern world, gold plays in the main only an indirect role in the determination of the price level, because the circulating media consist overwhelmingly of paper money and bank deposits; it is this volume of purchasing power which directly affects the price level and not the amount of gold which may be held in reserve. Gold itself affects the price level mainly through the decisions of the holders of gold reserves as to the amount of purchasing power which they will allow to be outstanding against a given holding of gold. Central banks and currency authorities as a whole can increase their total reserves only to the extent of the new gold supplies available each year for currency purposes. An acute competition for gold in

order to increase reserve ratios tends to a reduction of the aggregate amount of purchasing power against which the gold is held, and to a fall in prices additional to the fall which would in any case have taken place if, in a period of falling supplies of gold, a rigid relationship between gold supplies and additional supplies of purchasing power had been maintained, i.e. if reserve ratios had been left unchanged. In a period of expanding trade, production and population, a decreased gold supply, unless accompanied by a similar movement of reserve ratios, lowers prices. If, in addition, certain countries take steps to obtain gold solely for the purpose of increasing the ratio of their gold to their liabilities, the price level must fall still more. It falls more because the countries successful in the struggle do not allow their additional supplies of gold to affect their prices, and because the countries which are threatened by a loss of gold take steps to resist the loss which have the effect of lowering their prices.

Conditions necessary for the working of the gold standard

46 The international gold standard is intended to subserve the general ideal of stability – as regards the relations between currencies, and price relationships over space and time – but it does not, in and of itself, guarantee that this ideal will be realized. The international gold standard can, under appropriate conditions, enable both exchange stability and a considerable degree of price stability to be attained simultaneously, over a wide area, but, the mere fact that the standard is gold, and that it is international, will not under all conceivable conditions and varieties of policy, automatically bring about these results. In other words, there are 'rules of the game', which, if not observed, will make the standard work with undesirable, rather than beneficial, consequences.

47 It is difficult to define in precise terms what is implied by the 'rules of the game'. The management of an international standard is an art and not a science, and no one would suggest that it is possible to draw up a formal code of action, admitting of no exceptions and qualifications, adherence to which is obligatory on peril of wrecking the whole structure. Much must necessarily be left to time and circumstance. Central banks, in whose hands the working of the international gold standard has been vested, no doubt largely recognize that in many respects the purely traditional and empirical rules by which their conduct was guided in prewar days are no longer adequate as guides of action in present-day conditions, and we consider that the following principles would be generally accepted:

(i) The international gold standard system involves a common agreement as to the ends for which it exists.

(ii) It should be an object of policy to secure that the international gold standard should bring with it stability of prices as well as that it should guarantee stability of exchange.

(iii) Action by individual central banks which, by repercussions on the policy of the others, imperils the stability of the price level should, as far as possible, be avoided.

48 The direct influence of central banks upon the price level is exerted through an alteration of the volume of purchasing power brought about by changes in Bank Rate or by variations in the volume of assets held by them. But there is also an indirect influence exerted by central banks to which considerable importance must be attributed. Changes in the level of Bank Rate affect the price, and therefore the yield, of investment securities. In periods of low Bank Rate the price of fixed-interest-bearing securities tends to rise, and their yield to fall. The supply of such securities is therefore gradually encouraged because the cost of borrowing is lower whilst at the same time the demand for them is increased once confidence has returned in any degree. Long-terms funds are thereby placed at the disposal of governments and entrepreneurs and the process of real capital formation is stimulated, with the result that a rise of general prices is engendered. It may even be held that the indirect effect of easier conditions in the money market is more important as an intermediate link in the chain of events which leads from acute depression to the gradual restoration of confidence than the direct effect of attempting an expansion of the volume of purchasing power. For a central bank has no assurance that the net amount of purchasing power in existence will in fact be increased by the steps which it may take to that end. Its own operations in the market, through purchases of securities, may for instance lead to a re-payment to it of loans previously made by way of discounts; the net amount of purchasing power would then perhaps remain unchanged. The investment market, and particularly the international investment market, thus occupies a place of great importance among the agencies determining price changes. [...]

The main objectives of the monetary system

The gold standard

The recent working of the gold standard

242 Unfortunately, the anticipations of those who were responsible for our return to the gold standard in 1925 have to a large extent not been fulfilled. Whether these anticipations were justified at the time, and what other course was practically possible, are questions on which we do not all agree, but which

it would be unfruitful now to discuss. The six years since that act of policy have, for the reasons stated below, proved to be of a very abnormal character and the sacrifices which a return to gold at the old parity involved have not been compensated by the advantages of international price stability which were anticipated.

243 The accomplished fact of the restoration of our currency to the prewar gold parity and its maintenance there for a period of six years creates, however, an entirely new situation; and it by no means follows, even if the view be held, as it is by some of us, that a mistake was made in 1925, that the consequences can be repaired by a reversal of policy in 1931.

244 Apart from the more general considerations relating to the gold standard which we discuss below, there have been two sets of difficulties in the way of its working to advantage in recent years, one of which we may expect, and the other of which we may hope, to be temporary.

245 The first set of difficulties has been caused by the fact that the various gold parities established by the countries returning to the gold standard did not bear by any means the same relation in each case to the existing levels of incomes and costs in terms of the national currency. For example, Great Britain established a gold parity which meant that her existing level of sterling incomes and costs was relatively too high in terms of gold, so that, failing a downward adjustment, those of her industries which are subject to foreign competition were put at an artificial disadvantage. France and Belgium, on the other hand, somewhat later established a gold parity which, pending an upward adjustment of their wages and other costs in terms of francs, gave an artificial advantage to their export industries. Other countries provide examples of an intermediate character. Thus the distribution of foreign trade, which would correspond to the relative efficiencies of different countries for different purposes, has been seriously disturbed from the equilibrium position corresponding to the normal relations between their costs in terms of gold. This, however, has been a consequence of the manner in which the postwar world groped its way to back to gold, rather than of the permanent characteristics of the gold standard itself when once the equilibrium of relative costs has been re-established, though, even after six years, this is not yet the case.

246 The second set of difficulties has resulted from the international lending power of the creditor countries being redistributed, favourably to two countries, France and the United States, which have used this power only spasmodically, and adversely to the country, Great Britain, which was formerly the leader in this field and has the most highly developed organization for the purpose. This redistribution of lending power has been largely due to the character of the final settlement of the war debts in which this

country has acquiesced. For although Great Britain suffered during the war a diminution of her foreign assets of some hundreds of millions, she has agreed to a postwar settlement by which she has resigned her own net creditor claims, with the result, that on a balance of transactions, virtually the whole of the large annual sums due from Germany accrues to the credit of France and of the United States. This has naturally had the effect of greatly increasing the surplus of these two countries, both absolutely and relatively to the surplus of Great Britain. The diminution in Great Britain's international surplus, due to her war sacrifices remaining uncompensated by postwar advantages, has, however, been further aggravated recently by the adverse effect on her visible balance of trade of the first set of difficulties just mentioned, namely, the differing relationships between gold and domestic money-costs on which different countries returned to the gold standard.

247 This redistribution of lending power need not, however, in itself have interfered with the working of the gold standard. The difficulties have arisen through the partial failure of the two receeipients, during the last two or three years, to employ the receipts in the way in which Great Britain had always employed hers, namely, either in the purchase of additional imports or in making additional foreign loans on long-term. On the contrary, they have required payment of a large part of their annual surplus either in actual gold or in short-term liquid claims. This is a contingency which the normal working of the international gold standard does not contemplate and for which it does not provide.

248 But this set of difficulties, too, one may hope, though with less confidence, to be a temporary phenomenon. Should it not prove so, we can scarcely expect the international gold standard to survive in its present form. If for any reason, however plausible from its own point of view, a creditor country, after making all the purchases it desires, is unwilling to lend its remaining surplus to the rest of the world, there can be no solution except the ultimate destruction of the export trade of the country in question through a relative reduction in the gold costs of other countries. If there were no international standard, but each country had its own domestic currency subject to fluctuating exchanges, this solution would come about at once. For in this event the exchanges of France and the United States, for example, would by now have risen to so high a level relatively to the rest of the world that their exporters would have been driven out of business, so that their unlent surplus would have disappeared. According to the classical theory of the gold standard, the same result should ensue, though more slowly and painfully, as a result of movements of gold inflating costs in those countries and deflating costs elsewhere. But in the modern world, where, on the one hand, inflows of gold are liable to be sterilized and prevented from causing an expansion of credit, whilst on the other hand the deflation of credit set up elsewhere is

prevented by social causes from transmitting its full effect to money-wages and other costs, it may be that the whole machine will crack before the reaction back to equilibrium has been brought about.

249   Unfortunately upon these two sets of abnormal difficulties there ha supervened, starting in the United States, a business slump of a more norma type though of quite unusual dimensions, further aggravated, in the opinion o some, by being associated with the necessity for a transition from the high rates of interest appropriate to the war and postwar period back towards the lower rates which were typical before the war.

250   Naturally the total result leads some people to question the desirability of adhering to an international standard.

The question of an international standard

251   This brings us to the question whether adherence to an international standard may involve the payment of too heavy a price in the shape o domestic instability. Many countries, both today and at former times, have found that such continued adherence involves a strain greater than they can bear. But these are generally debtor countries, the trade of which i: concentrated on a narrow range of primary products subject to violen disturbances of prices. If we leave aside the position today, experience does no show that a creditor country with diversified trade is liable to suffer undue domestic strain merely as the result of adherence to an international standard We are of opinion, therefore, that we should not be influenced merely by the exigencies of the moment, if there is reason to believe that there may be important countervailing advantages on a longer view. If we need emergency measures to relieve the immediate strain, we should seek them in some other direction.

252   In the particular case of Great Britain we believe that there are such advantages. One of our most valuable sources of income, indeed one of our most important export industries, is the practice of international banking and associated services. Along with our shipping and our staple export industrie: this has been for a long period past one of our main sources of wealth. It is by no means clear that the possible advantages to our export activities from the fact that a fluctuating exchange would automatically offset the rigidity o money-incomes would balance the unquestionable loss to the first named; and we might be a poorer country on balance. It is not necessary, in order to reach this conclusion, to exaggerate the benefits which accrue to us from our international financial business. They are not so enormous as to outweigh all other considerations. For example, it is not likely that they have gone even a fraction of the way towards compensating the losses of wealth through

unemployment in recent years. It is not our case that industry should be sacrificed to finance. It is, rather, that the benefits to industry from a fluctuating exchange would be inadequate to compensate the losses in other directions. For whilst a fluctuating exchange would have undoubted advantages in certain conditions, it would often be merely substituting one form of instability for another. It would not be possible for a country so intricately concerned with the outside world as Great Britain is to escape so simply from the repercussions of instability elsewhere.

253 There is, moreover, a further reason which cannot easily be weighed merely in the balance of our own direct economic advantage and which weighs more heavily with us than any other. There is, perhaps, no more important object within the field of human technique than that the world as a whole should achieve a sound and scientific monetary system. But there can be little or no hope of progress at any early date for the monetary system of the world as a whole, except as the result of a process of evolution starting from the historic gold standard. If, therefore, this country were to cut adrift from the international system with the object of setting up a local standard with a sole regard to our domestic situation, we should be abandoning the larger problem – the solution of which is certainly necessary to a satisfactory solution of the purely domestic problem – just at the moment, maybe, when, if we were able to look a little further forward, the beginnings of general progress would be becoming visible.

254 We conclude, therefore, that we shall best serve the purpose for which we were set up, and have the greatest hope of securing a sufficient general agreement to lead to action, if we base our recommendations on the assumption, which we hold justified, that the next phase of monetary policy must consist of a wholehearted attempt to make the existing international standard work more satisfactorily. It is possible – though we believe that hard experience will teach them otherwise – that some countries may be unable or may fail to work an international standard in a satisfactory way. But this is not yet proved, and it would be unwise for us, who have so much to gain by it, to give up the attempt to secure a sound international currency.

Devaluation

255 It has been represented to us that, without in any way departing from the principle or the practice of adherence to an international standard, it is desirable for us in the national interest to do now what might have been accomplished with much less difficulty in 1925, namely, to revise the gold parity of sterling. Such a step is urged on the ground that, if we diminished the gold equivalent of the pound sterling by 10 per cent thereby reducing our gold costs automatically by the same percentage, this would restore to our export

industries and to the industries which compete with imported goods what they lost by the return to gold at a figure which was inappropriate to the then existing facts, and that it would also have the great advantage of affecting all sterling costs equally, whether or not they were protected by contract.

256 We have no hesitation in rejecting this course. It is no doubt true that an essential attribute of a sovereign state is a power at any time to alter the value of its currency for any reasons deemed to be in the national interest, and that legally, therefore, there is nothing to prevent the British Government and Parliament from taking such a step. The same may be said of a measure writing down all debts, including those owed by the state itself, by a prescribed percentage – an expedient which would in fact over a considerable field have precisely the same effect. But, while all things may be lawful, all things are not expedient, and in our opinion the devaluation by any government of a currency standing at its par value suddenly and without notice (as must be the case to prevent foreign creditors removing their property) is emphatically one of those things which are not expedient. International trade, commerce and finance are based on confidence. One of the foundation stones on which that confidence reposes is the general belief that all countries will seek to maintain so far as lies in their power the value of their national currency as it has been fixed by law, and will only give legal recognition to its depreciation when that depreciation has already come about *de facto*. It has frequently been the case – we have numerous examples of recent years – that either through the misfortunes of war, or mistakes of policy, or the collapse or prices, currencies have fallen so far below par that their restoration would involve either great social injustices or national efforts and sacrifices for which no adequate compensation can be expected. The view may be held that our own case in 1925 was of this character. The British currency had been depreciated for some years. It was obvious to the whole world that it was an open question whether its restoration to par was in the national interest and there is no doubt in our minds as to our absolute freedom at that time to fix it, if it suited us, at a lower par value corresponding to the then existing exchange. But it would be to adopt an entirely new principle, and one which would undoubtedly be an immense shock to the international financial world, if the government of the greatest creditor nation were deliberately and by an act of positive policy to announce one morning that it had reduced by law the value of its currency from the par at which it was standing to some lower value.

257 Moreover, considering the matter from another point of view, in the environment of the present world slump the relief to be obtained from a 10 per cent devaluation might prove to be disappointing. It is not certain that, with world demand at its present low ebb, such a measure would serve by itself to restore our export trades to their former position or to effect a radical cure of

unemployment. On the contrary, in the atmosphere of crisis and distress which would inevitably surround such an extreme and sensational measure as the devaluation of sterling, we might well find that the state of affairs immediately ensuing on such an event would be worse than that which had preceded it.

The prospects of the gold standard

258 The course of events in the last two years has had the effect of forcing a number of countries off the gold standard. But these are all debtor countries; and if matters continue as at present, it will be the debtor countries of the world, and not a creditor country such as Great Britain, which will be the first to find the strain unbearable. We consider that the leading creditor countries of the world should consult together to prevent matters from continuing as at present. In order that Great Britain may speak with authority in such discussions, it is essential that her financial strength should be beyond criticism. This largely depends in the near future on an increase of her surplus available for new foreign lending.

259 In this connection it may be worth while to summarize the result of certain information which we have collected. For it is of a reassuring character and goes some way to answer certain criticisms which have been made, or doubts which have been entertained, regarding one aspect of the financial position of this country. In view of the large volume of foreign issues which have been floated in recent years in London and of the common belief that, in addition, British investors have made large purchases in the United States, partly of foreign bonds initially issued in New York and partly of American securities, whilst at the same time our surplus for new foreign lending has been diminished, it has been surmised that Great Britain must have been financing some part of her new foreign investment on long term by means of an increase, and perhaps a dangerous increase, in her short-term liabilities to foreign centres. We have accordingly made it our business to collect for the first time as full a summary as possible both of foreign liquid resources in London and of British acceptances on foreign account. We take this opportunity of thanking the Bank of England, which has done the detailed work on our behalf, and the numerous financial institutions which have willingly co-operated in supplying the information, since they have enabled us to fill what was perhaps the greatest gap in our previous knowledge of the financial commitments of this country. We cannot claim that our figures are complete and they could doubtless be improved with further experience; but we believe that they may cover, in quantity, nearly the whole field. The most important item about which we have no information is the total of sterling bills held in their own custody by foreign banks, and it may be that this item is a more fluctuating one than the items for which we have obtained figures. We were prepared to find

that these totals might give some support to the fears expressed above, but in fact they are reassuring.

260 The figures may be summarized as follows:

End of year	Deposits and sterling bills held in London on foreign account[1]	Sterling bills accepted on foreign account	Net liability of London
	£	£	£
1927	419,000,000	140,000,000	279,000,000
1928	503,000,000	201,000,000	302,000,000
1929	451,000,000	176,000,000	275,000,000
1930	435,000,000	161,000,000	274,000,000
1931 (March)	407,000,000	153,000,000	254,000,000

[1] Exclusive of sterling bills held by foreign banks in their own custody.

261 We have not obtained figures prior to 1927. We think it probable that in the period between the return to the gold standard in 1925 and the end of 1927 London's net liability was increasing substantially, since the French balances abroad were mainly built up during that period. But these figures show that in the last three years, so far from there having been a large increase in London's short-term liabilities, there has been a small decrease in their amount, so far as we have been able to ascertain it.[1] The preliminary figures which we have obtained for the first quarter of the present year indicate that this tendency has been continued.

262 We have not obtained figures of British balances abroad, i.e. of British short-term claims on foreign centres (which may be quite considerable in amount), or of various other items which would be required for a complete picture. It would be desirable to obtain these, as we recommend later [in a chapter not reproduced here].

263 It seems probable, therefore, that in spite of the reduction of our surplus, the whole of our *net* purchases of foreign securities have been paid for out of our currently accruing surplus on income account. It is possible, we think, that this surplus may be somewhat larger than the usual estimate.

264 As regards the immediate situation, it is also interesting to note that the trade returns, unsatisfactory though they are, bear out the conclusion that the worst strain of a situation such as the present falls on the raw-material countries. During the first quarter of this year the quantity of our exports fell off by more than 30 per cent, whereas the reduction in the quantity of our imports was only 6 per cent. Nevertheless, as a result of the catastrophic fall of raw-material prices, the visible balance of trade has been actually less adverse

to us than in recent years, the net position in terms of money moving £5 million in our favour, so that less of our surplus under other heads (i.e. from foreign interest, shipping, etc.), is being required today to finance our imports than in 1930 or in 1929.

265 The same point can be strikingly illustrated by what has happened in the case of the single commodity wheat. At the price prevailing in December 1930, the annual cost of our wheat imports would be about £30 million less than it was in 1929, and £60 million less than in 1925. It is obvious what a large contribution this single item represents to the national cost of supporting the present volume of unemployment. It is a great misfortune both for us and for the raw-material countries that we should have a great volume of unemployment through their inability to purchase from us as a result of the fall in the price of their produce. But merely from the point of view of our balance of trade it is not to be overlooked that the latter fact not only balances the former but may even outweigh it. We conclude that the underlying financial facts are more favourable than had been supposed, and that Great Britain's position as a creditor country remains immensely strong.

Note

1 It is interesting to compare these figures with the comparable items for the United States. (The American returns also include other figures reducing their total net liability, which we have not yet been able to collect for Great Britain.)

End of year	Deposits and bills held in USA on foreign account	Dollar bills accepted on foreign account	Net liability of New York
	£	£	£
1927	637,000,000	83,000,000	554,000,000
1928	595,000,000	104,000,000	491,000,000
1929	632,000,000	171,000,000	461,000,000
1930	573,000,000	168,000,000	405,000,000

The figures of dollar acceptances are taken from the Annual Reports of the United States Department of Commerce on the Balance of International Payments of the United States and the New York Federal Reserve Bank Monthly Review. The figures issued by the American Acceptance Council are somewhat higher.

11

The gold exchange standard

Ragnar Nurkse*

Among the various schemes and proposals which repeatedly crop up in discussions of monetary reform, one that has enjoyed a wide appeal is the idea of an international currency system with exchange rates stable, as under the gold standard, but with liquid foreign balances constituting the international means of settlement and the international monetary reserves. Gold, it has been suggested, could be dispensed with in such a system not only as a means of international payment but also as a standard of value, especially if the currency or currencies in which the reserves were held were maintained reasonably stable in terms of goods and services.

Monetary history has furnished many examples of the exchange standard principle. Indeed, the practical application of this principle must find a place in any account, however condensed, of international monetary relations during the interwar period. The gold standard that was 'restored' in the 1920s was in the main a gold *exchange* standard. But an exchange standard need not be a *gold* exchange standard; the sterling area which emerged from the currency chaos of the Great Depression in the 1930s is another important example of the exchange reserve system.

*From League of Nations, *International Currency Experience*, Geneva, League of Nations, 1944, pp. 27–46, abridged.

Origin and growth

The recommendations of the Genoa Conference

The adoption of a gold exchange standard was officially recommended by the Genoa Conference, which met in the spring of 1922 to consider the problems of financial reconstruction. This recommendation was based on the view that there existed a shortage of gold, due both to a decline in current supply and to an actual or prospective increase in demand for monetary purposes. The world output of gold declined by about one-third from 1915 to 1922 (see Appendix I) as a natural result of the general rise in prices during and after the war, which entailed a rise in gold-mining costs, and which was not accompanied by a corresponding rise in the price of gold.

At the same time, it was feared that a return to the gold standard would lead to a scramble for gold, pushing up the commodity value of gold through competitive deflation.

The Financial Commission of the Genoa Conference, presided over by Sir Robert Horne, the British Chancellor of the Exchequer, therefore included the following resolution among the 'Currency Resolutions' of its final report:

Resolution 9. These steps [balancing of budgets; adoption of gold as a common standard; fixing of gold parities; cooperation of central banks, etc.] might by themselves suffice to establish a gold standard, but its successful maintenance would be materially promoted ... by an international convention to be adopted at a suitable time. The purpose of the convention would be to centralize and coordinate the demand for gold, and so avoid those wide fluctuations in the purchasing power of gold which might otherwise result from the simultaneous and competitive efforts of a number of countries to secure metallic reserves. The convention should embody some means of economizing the use of gold by maintaining reserves in the form of foreign balances, such, for example, as the gold exchange standard or an international clearing system.

In Resolution 11 of the report, various proposals were made to serve as a basis for the convention contemplated in Resolution 9. Besides stressing the need for balanced budgets, fixed gold parities, free exchange markets, etc. Resolution 11 contained the following provisions:

1. ...The maintenance of the currency at its gold value must be assured by the provision of an adequate reserve of approved assets, not necessarily gold.

2. When progress permits, certain of the participating countries will establish a free market in gold and thus become gold centres.

3. A participating country, in addition to any gold reserve held at home, may maintain in any other participating country reserves of approved assets in the form of bank balances, bills, short-term securities, or other suitable liquid resources.

4. The ordinary practice of a participating country will be to buy and sell exchange on other participating countries within a prescribed fraction of parity of exchange for its own currency on demand.

5. The convention will thus be based on a gold exchange standard.

The proposed convention failed to materialize; but the influence of the Genoa resolutions was nevertheless considerable.

Prewar antecedents of the gold exchange standard

Before proceeding to show the practical effect of these recommendations, it may be well to observe that the gold exchange system was by no means invented at Genoa. It had been practised in many cases before 1914. One example commonly quoted is the arrangement by which exchange between London and Edinburgh was regulated in the second half of the eighteenth century. Another example is the convention concluded in 1885 between the central banks of Denmark, Norway and Sweden.[1] Of greater historical importance was Russia's policy, adopted in 1894, by which exchange reserves initially acquired by loan were held abroad – at first in Berlin and later also in other centres – and the government stood ready to buy and sell bills on the centres in question at fixed rates of exchange. The success of the Russian experiment was widely noticed, and a short time later Austria-Hungary established a similar system.

Even in countries on the full gold standard, central banks prior to 1914 were in the habit of holding a certain amount of foreign exchange in addition to gold. In 1913 fifteen European central banks[2] together held about 12 per cent of their total reserves in the form of foreign exchange. In 1925 the percentage of foreign exchange in the total gold and exchange reserves of twenty-four European central banks, as shown in Appendix II, was 27 per cent; and in 1928 it rose to 42 per cent. Clearly the holding of foreign exchange by central banks was on the whole much less extensive before 1914 than it became later. It was the existence of a large *private* fund of mobile balances – it was the constant flow of equilibrating short-term capital transfers effected by commercial banks, traders and arbitrageurs in response to small changes in exchange and interest rates – which prior to 1914 created conditions similar to exchange standard arrangements and reduced the need for gold movements. After the monetary upheavals of the war and early postwar years, private short-term capital movements tended frequently to be disequilibrating rather than equilibrating: a depreciation of the exchange or a rise in discount rates, for example, instead of attracting short-term balances from abroad, tended sometimes to affect people's anticipations in such a way as to produce the opposite result. In these circumstances the provision of the equilibrating capital movements required for the maintenance of exchange stability devolved more largely on the central banks and necessitated a larger volume of official foreign-exchange holdings.

The examples just given of the pre-1914 gold exchange system were confined to Europe. But it was outside Europe that the system played its most important part. India, ever since 1898, has provided the classic instance of the working of an exchange standard. The 'Gold Standard Fund' introduced by the United States in the Philippine Islands in 1903 is also a well-known case. Argentina and Japan operated what amounted in practice to a sterling exchange system in the years before 1914. Outside Europe the application of the exchange standard principle made little further progress in the 1920s. The spread of the gold exchange standard on the lines recommended by the Genoa Conference was, in the main, a European development.[3]

Modification of central bank statutes

'Adoption of the gold exchange standard' meant, in the first instance, adoption of statutes permitting central banks to hold foreign exchange instead of gold in their legal reserves against notes in circulation or against notes and sight deposits. The first few years after the Genoa Conference were a period of great activity in central banking legislation, and the new statutes adopted were strongly influenced by the Genoa resolutions. This was true in particular of the countries that restored their currencies with the assistance of the Financial Committee of the League of Nations, such as Austria (1922), Danzig (1923), Hungary (1924), Bulgaria (1926), Estonia (1927) and Greece (1928), where the central banks were authorized to hold the whole of their reserves in foreign bills and balances convertible into gold. Italy (1927) was among the countries that took a similar course. In a number of other countries, however, and especially in the later 1920s, the statutes adopted tended to depart from this model, and required the maintenance of a certain proportion of gold in the total legal reserve of gold plus foreign exchange. The proportion was fixed at 75% in Germany (1924), 33% in Albania (1925), 75% in Belgium and Poland (1927), and 70% in Romania (1929).

Altogether, the countries whose central banks at some time during the period 1922–31 were entitled to hold their legal reserves partly or wholly in foreign exchange form quite a long list, including Albania, Austria, Belgium, Bolivia, Bulgaria, Chile, Colombia, Czechoslovakia, Denmark, Ecuador,

Egypt, Estonia, Finland, Germany, Greece, Hungary, Italy, Latvia, Peru, Poland, Portugal, Romania, Spain, Uruguay, USSR, Yugoslavia. In addition, there was a number of countries which practised an exchange standard but which had not yet established a central bank during this period: for instance, India, New Zealand, Argentina and Venezuela.

It would be misleading to overemphasize the role of central banks' legal reserve regulations in the working of the exchange standard system. Central banks which had the right to hold foreign exchange in the legal reserve did not always make use of this right and preferred sometimes to hold gold. On the other hand, banks which did not have this right sometimes held large amounts of foreign exchange outside the legal reserve. The central banks of Japan, Australia and Norway, for example, were allowed to count nothing but gold as legal cover; yet they held considerable foreign balances and were (rightly) regarded as practising the exchange standard system in fact.[4]

If the legal reserve requirements of central banks had exercised an important influence on domestic credit policies, then the legal status of foreign-exchange holdings might have made an important difference. But the practical effect of the reserve requirements upon national credit policies in the period under review was, on the whole, not very striking. On the other hand, changes in central banks' foreign assets may occasionally have influenced domestic credit policy even if they formed no part of the legal reserve.

Whatever the legal provisions, some central banks undoubtedly found it at times advantageous, in meeting temporary fluctuations in the balance of payments, to operate a foreign exchange reserve outside the legal cover, especially when it was thought that changes in the assets held as legal cover might attract undue attention and provoke undesired psychological repercussions.

In the preceding paragraphs, the question whether the central bank has the power to acquire foreign exchange at all was not even put; such power was taken for granted. The curious case of France shows that it cannot be taken for granted. Prior to 7 August 1926, the Bank of France was not entitled to purchase gold or foreign exchange at anything but the old prewar parities. A law of 7 August 1926 empowered the Bank to acquire foreign exchange and gold at market rates and to issue notes against these assets beyond the legal maximum limit of the note circulation. The depreciation of the franc reached its low point in July 1926, and a *de facto* stability was maintained from December 1926 onwards. The Bank acquired in fact enormous amounts of foreign exchange. When the legal stabilization of the franc was carried out in June 1928, the Bank was not permitted to count this foreign exchange as part of the 35 per cent minimum cover against notes and sight liabilities; and the law of 7 August 1926 was repealed, though the Bank was not prevented from continuing to hold the exchange acquired up to June 1928. France's *de facto* adherence to the international exchange standard thus lasted less than two years. The important role played by France in the breakdown of the system will make it necessary to take up her case in more detail at a later point.

Sources of central banks' exchange holdings

After the legal provisions had been made allowing a bank of issue to purchase foreign assets or to count them as part of its legal reserve, the next task was to create conditions enabling the bank actually to acquire such assets. There were several ways in which this was done.

In the first place, various countries received foreign stabilization or reconstruction loans, mainly from the United States and the United Kingdom, the proceeds of which passed at least in part into the hands of the central banks. Austria and Hungary, for example, were able to raise such loans (amounting to about $100 million and $45 million respectively) under the auspices of the League of Nations. Germany obtained a stabilization loan of $200 million under the Dawes Plan, Belgium obtained a loan of $100 million, Poland one of $50 million. Italy received a stabilization credit of $125 million from a group of central banks led by the Bank of England and the Federal Reserve Bank of New York.

Secondly, efforts were made by some countries to acquire foreign reserves by improving the current balance of payments; and in some cases this was attempted through a deflation of costs and prices. Such deflation may have tended to improve the trade balance, but its main influence on exchange reserves operated more frequently through the capital account of the balance of payments. Deflation involved high interest rates, thus tending to attract funds from abroad. Moreover, foreign capital was attracted at times by the currency appreciation which frequently accompanied the deflation preceding the legal stabilization. Especially when the monetary authorities made known their intention to stabilize the exchange at a level higher than the current market value, or when such an intention was assumed to exist, there was an incentive for bull speculation in the currency concerned. Italy, for instance, experienced a considerable capital inflow of this speculative character during the eighteen months preceding the *de jure* stabilization in December 1927, when the lira was steadily appreciating. Similar movements of speculative funds were observed in Denmark and Norway in the two or three years of exchange appreciation prior to January 1927 and May 1928 respectively, when the two countries legally restored the prewar gold parities of their currencies.

Even apart from such cases of deflation and exchange appreciation, interest differentials during the years 1925–8 generally provided a sufficient inducement for large amounts of short- and long-term capital to move, from New York and London in particular, to the countries adhering to the gold exchange standard. To the extent that the individual borrowers needed funds in domestic currency, it was the banking system in these countries that came to hold the proceeds of private foreign loans in the form of liquid foreign-exchange reserves.

A further source of foreign exchange, as demonstrated particularly in the case of France, was the repatriation of private domestic capital funds, combined to some extent with an improvement of the current balance of payments through undervaluation of the currency. The repatriation of capital to France set in as soon as the exchange depreciation was arrested; it continued after *de facto* stabilization was achieved; and it was stimulated by the 'profit' created by the devaluation on the conversion of foreign balances into domestic currency and by the fear that this 'profit' might be reduced through an appreciation of the currency.

Functioning and breakdown

Fluctuations in foreign-exchange reserves prior to 1931

The operation of the gold exchange system is illustrated in Appendix II showing the year-to-year changes in central banks' foreign exchange and gold holdings in twenty-four countries during the period 1924–32. The last two years of this period are marked by a wholesale liquidation of foreign-exchange reserves, reflecting the complete collapse of the gold exchange standard. The liquidation period will be dealt with later. For the moment we may briefly note certain features of the system in the earlier and more 'normal' years.

One feature worth noting is the number of countries where the gold stock was kept unchanged, and where consequently changes in the balance of payments so far as they affected the central bank showed themselves exclusively in the foreign-exchange reserve. In Finland, as may be observed from Appendix II, the gold stock remained constant throughout the period 1924–32, while the foreign-exchange reserve, which was much larger than the gold stock, underwent wide fluctuations. A constant gold stock and a varying exchange reserve may also be observed in Lithuania (up to 1930), in Portugal (from 1926 to 1931), and in Latvia and Norway (up to 1931). This fact is particularly remarkable in the case of Norway and Lithuania, where foreign assets were not eligible as cover against note circulation or sight deposit liabilities. Of certain other countries such as Sweden, Bulgaria and Yugoslavia, though their gold reserves did not remain absolutely unchanged, it is likewise true to say that the fluctuating portion of their international monetary reserves was made up predominantly of foreign liquid assets.

In the Netherlands and in Greece, as shown in Appendix II, a part of the gold stock was converted into foreign exchange in 1925 and 1928 respectively.

In other cases, however, such substitutions as occurred were mostly in the opposite direction. As early as 1925, Germany shifted a large part of her reserves from foreign exchange into gold. Hungary did the same in 1926. This tendency away from the gold exchange system was reinforced in 1928, when Italy and Poland converted some of their foreign exchange into gold. Even where such large or sudden shifts did not take place, the proportion of foreign exchange in the total reserves was in some cases allowed gradually to decline, as in Austria (from 1925), Czechoslovakia (from 1927) and Yugoslavia (from 1924 onwards).

In Germany, it will be remembered, the central bank was not legally qualified to hold more than one-fourth of its statutory reserve in the form of foreign exchange. Foreign assets held outside the statutory reserve accounted for most of the fluctuations in the bank's foreign-exchange holdings. The share of foreign exchange in the statutory reserve fell indeed far below 25 per cent in the years after 1926. In 1928 the proportion of *all* foreign assets of the Reichsbank to its total gold and exchange holdings fell to the low level of 16 per cent, compared with 61 per cent in 1924. This sharp drop was only partly due to the conversion of foreign balances into gold in 1925. When the bank's total reserve increased in 1926, that increase was taken exclusively in the form of gold; when an outflow occurred in the following year, the reduction affected exclusively the foreign-exchange reserve. The proportion of foreign exchange declined further in the spring of 1929. When after the signature of the Young Plan a temporary resumption of the capital influx occurred in the second half of 1929, the bank took advantage of this to replenish its foreign exchange holdings not only within but also outside the statutory reserve, and so to recover a margin of free play between the fluctuations of the balance of payments and the internal currency supply.

But the size of the international monetary reserve in the hands of the Reichsbank was not only a function of the balance of payments. It depended largely also on the behaviour of the private money market in Germany and particularly on the behaviour of the commercial banks. These banks, as a result of Germany's foreign borrowing, kept substantial liquid resources abroad as working balances. Variations in their preference for foreign balances as against domestic central bank funds – determined by changes in interest differentials and exchange rates, by fluctuations in trade activity or by the state of confidence – were an important factor influencing the movement of the Reichsbank's exchange reserve and the size of the domestic credit base. Similar conditions prevailed in other European countries that were borrowing heavily in New York and elsewhere during the period under review.

The striking increase in Italy's central exchange reserve in 1926 and 1927 was largely due, as mentioned before, to a speculative inflow of funds induced by the upward tendency in the value of the lira. After the stabilization in

December 1927, the exchange reserve was steadily reduced. A part of the decline, however, was due to purchases of gold, especially in 1928.

In spite of the wide fluctuations observed in individual countries, the proportion of foreign assets in the total central-bank reserves of twenty-three European countries, excluding France, was surprisingly steady in the six years prior to 1931. As may be seen from the last line of table 11.1, the ratio varied only slightly between 35 and 40 per cent. It is the inclusion of France that produces the wide fluctuations in this ratio as calculated for a total of twenty-four countries.

France on the gold exchange standard

At the end of 1928, France alone accounted for more than half of the total of central-bank exchange holdings shown in the first line of table 11–1. The role of France in the rise and decline of the gold exchange standard clearly demands a more detailed consideration.

For several years prior to July 1926, France experienced a flight of capital, which depreciated the exchange far below the level corresponding to domestic costs and prices. There were practically no gold exports, the Bank of France preferring to keep its relatively modest gold reserve intact. It was the surplus in the current balance of payments which arose as a result of the exchange depreciation that provided the means by which the real transfer of the flight capital was accomplished.

Table 11.1 Foreign exchange and gold reserves of European central banks ($ million)

End of:	1924	1925	1926	1927	1928	1929	1930	1931	1932
Total (24 countries)									
Foreign exchange	845	917	1,159	2,145	2,520	2,292	2,300	1,216	505
Gold	2,281	2,367	2,568	2,903	3,490	3,841	4,316	5,273	5,879
Total	3,126	3,284	3,727	5,048	6,010	6,133	6,616	6,489	6,384
Foreign exchange as % of total	27	28	31	42	42	37	35	19	8
Total excluding France (23 countries)									
Foreign exchange	831	904	1,043	1,295	1,233	1,271	1,273	374	329
Gold	1,571	1,656	1,857	1,949	2,236	2,208	2,217	2,574	2,622
Total	2,402	2,560	2,900	3,244	3,469	3,479	3,480	2,948	2,951
Foreign exchange as % of total	35	35	36	40	36	37	37	13	11

In July 1926, drastic measures were initiated to balance the budget and to restore confidence. The value of the franc recovered from less than $2\frac{1}{2}$ US cents in July to nearly 4 US cents in December 1926, at which level it was stabilized, at first *de facto* and later, in June 1928, *de jure*.

In August 1926, as mentioned earlier, the Bank of France was granted the right to purchase gold and foreign exchange at market rates. During the next four or five years, in order to prevent the franc from appreciating above the level established in December 1926, the Bank had to purchase enormous amounts of gold and foreign assets. From August 1926 to the date of the legal stabilization – 25 June 1928 – the Bank's foreign-exchange acquisitions, amounting to over 26,000 million francs (or over $1,000 million at the current rate of exchange), by far exceeded its purchases of gold, amounting to about 10,000 million francs. After that date, its gold stock rose steadily up to 1932. Under the monetary law of 25 June 1928, the Bank was no longer permitted to buy foreign exchange. Just before the legal stabilization, the Bank had bought large amounts of foreign exchange for forward delivery. These forward contracts matured in the second half of 1928, raising the total foreign-exchange holdings of the Bank to 32,800 million francs (or nearly $1,300 million) at the end of the year. There was some doubt as to whether, under the law just mentioned, the Bank was justified in thus increasing its holdings. The amount in question was therefore converted into gold, and the foreign-exchange reserve fell back to the previous level of 26,000 million francs in June 1929. At that level it remained virtually unchanged for over two years, that is until the second half of 1931, when the Bank started the liquidation process which practically wiped out its foreign-exchange reserve in the two following years.

It is necessary to distinguish clearly between the two principal sources of the gold and exchange holdings acquired by the Bank after August 1926, even though the data permit of no sharp separation in the actual statistics. There was, in the first place, the 'repatriation of capital'. The desire of French investors to repatriate their funds was natural, in view of the temporary and abnormal character of the preceding capital export. In fact, however, in the then existing condition of the balance of payments the 'repatriation' meant essentially that the total of foreign assets held by the French public and banking system remained unchanged, but that an increasing proportion of this total was transferred from the hands of private banks and capitalists into the ownership of the Bank of France.

The second factor at work tended to increase the *total* of French foreign assets: it was the 'undervaluation' of the franc, the function of which, prior to July 1926, had been to effect the real transfer of flight capital abroad. This undervaluation, though appreciably reduced through the recovery of the franc in the latter half of 1926, persisted in a substantial degree after December 1926, creating as it were an automatic export of capital through a surplus in the current balance of payments. Having lost a large part of her long-term foreign assets through the Russian Revolution, France was not prepared to resume foreign long-term investment on any considerable scale, and so the current surplus went in the main simply to increase the country's gold reserves and liquid foreign balances.

A third source may have operated at certain times to swell the gold and exchange holdings of the Bank of France: namely, imports of foreign speculative funds. But these do not, in retrospect, seem to have been nearly as important as they appeared to certain contemporary observers (including the authors of the Bank's annual reports for 1927 and 1928). Most of the speculative positions built up by foreigners during the months preceding the legal stabilization were rapidly and easily liquidated after June 1928.[5]

Foreign speculation played, however, an important part in the reasons given by the Bank for converting some of its foreign exchange into gold. In its annual reports for 1927 and 1928, the Bank argued that its purchases of foreign balances and bills created an abnormal condition of liquidity in the centres where they were held; that it thus itself provided the funds used for speculative purchases of francs; and that only the conversion of its foreign assets into gold could stop the vicious inflationary circle.

But in so far as the Bank's foreign-exchange purchases represented 'repatriation of capital' they constituted in fact simply a redistribution inside France in the ownership of foreign assets. The fact that bills or bank deposits in London, for example, passed from the ownership of a private Frenchman into the ownership of the Bank of France cannot have had appreciable effects, if any, on market conditions in London. It is difficult to see, more particularly, how it could have increased the financial facilities for exchange speculation in London. True, if the private Frenchman's foreign assets consisted of long-term securities, then – since the only foreign assets the Bank of France was prepared to hold were short-term bills and bank balances – the 'repatriation' of French capital would have meant a shift of funds from the long-term to the short-term market in London; but the resources of the London market as a whole could hardly have been substantially affected. Besides, the private French assets in London or New York were in fact mostly held in a highly liquid form, as they had come there in search of security rather than profit.

To the extent that the Bank of France's purchases of foreign bills and balances reflected the 'automatic' capital export resulting from the under-valuation of the franc, there was likewise a change in the ownership of short-term bills and bank deposits in, say, London; but this time from *British* ownership into the ownership of the Bank of France. How this could have had an inflationary effect in London is difficult to see. The effect is more likely to have been deflationary, especially in the case of bank deposits passing from the active domestic circulation into the inactive holding of the Bank of France.

The French funds that had taken flight and were temporarily held abroad represented an amount of finite magnitude. Their transfer to the Bank of France – the process of 'repatriation' – was bound to come to an end sooner or later. There was no such definite limit to the current surplus in the balance of payments arising from the undervaluation of the franc. How long this surplus was to continue depended on the speed and strength of the corrective forces tending to restore equilibrium in the balance of payments. One equilibrating factor, indeed, was to some extent neutralized. The increase in the gold and exchange reserve of the Bank of France was in part offset by a reduction in the Bank's domestic assets and an increase in its deposit liabilities to the government, so that the growth of the gold and foreign-exchange reserve did not produce an equivalent expansion in the note circulation and in private sight deposits at the Bank. The adjustment of a country's balance of payments, however, does not depend solely on changes in the quantity of domestic currency and credit in accordance with changes in international currency reserves; it also depends largely on changes in income and effective demand directly connected with the balance of payments. Briefly, the low exchange value of the franc tended to divert expenditure of Frenchmen as well as foreigners from foreign goods and services to French goods and services, and this led to an increase in aggregate income and demand in France tending to bring the international accounts into balance. In fact the French surplus in current transactions disappeared after 1930; the franc ceased to be undervalued. The effect of the undervaluation on economic conditions had been favourable in France, but unfavourable abroad; the French balance of payments no doubt contributed, though probably to a minor degree, to the forces making for depression in the rest of the world at the turning-point of the business cycle in 1929–30.

After June 1928, as stated before, the Bank of France was no longer entitled to buy foreign exchange. In its annual reports for 1929 and 1930, written at a time when it was no longer possible to justify the purchase of gold in place of foreign exchange by a desire to curb speculative and inflationary tendencies abroad, the Bank referred to its gold imports as a natural result of the automatic gold standard mechanism. In the latter part of 1931, the Bank began to liquidate its foreign bills and balances. It should be noted that nearly half of the reduction shown in the Bank's foreign assets during 1931 represents the exchange loss incurred on its sterling assets. In 1932 the conversion of foreign exchange into gold continued at an accelerated pace. In 1933 the foreign-exchange reserve was reduced to an insignificant amount; but in that year the gold stock also suffered a reduction, the first of a long series of reductions.

In its annual reports for 1931 and 1932 the Bank declared that ever since 1928 its desire and intention had been to convert its foreign assets into gold, and that it had refrained from doing so only out of regard for the 'monetary difficulties of other countries'.[6] This indeed was the essence of the French position: from the outset, France was a reluctant member of the gold exchange system; she regarded her partial adhesion to it as an essentially temporary makeshift and longed to give her currency 'an exclusively metallic foundation'.[7]

The breakdown of the gold exchange standard

The fate of the gold exchange standard was sealed when France decided in 1928 to take nothing but gold in settlement of the enormous surplus accruing to her from the repatriation of capital and from the current balance of payments. The French gold imports certainly aggravated the pressure of deflation in the rest of the world and especially in London. In London, the pressure became unbearable in the end, and the gold parity of the pound was abandoned. When in the summer of 1931 French capitalists and commercial banks became nervous about their sterling assets and anxious to 'repatriate' them, the Bank of France could not take over these assets and hold them in its exchange reserve; they had to be turned into gold. Even without the law of June 1928 it may be that the Bank, sharing the public's nervousness, would still have demanded gold. In certain other countries which were also repatriating their sterling balances at that time, central banks were legally free to acquire these balances, but in fact preferred gold to sterling. Hence the heavy gold losses of the Bank of England in the three months preceding the suspension of the gold standard on 21 September 1931.

The breakdown of exchange stability led in turn to a further scramble for gold through the liquidation of previously accumulated foreign-exchange reserves of central banks, since the possibility of losses arising from exchange-rate fluctuations rendered the holding of foreign balances risky. Indeed the withdrawal of balances from the United Kingdom after September 1931 was often imposed on central banks by their statutes, requiring them to hold their exchange reserves exclusively in gold standard currencies. To remain eligible as legal cover, these balances therefore had to be converted into gold or into a gold standard currency. As the dollar was also under pressure, a number of countries – especially in eastern and south-eastern Europe – transferred their reserve balance from London to Paris. Paris, in fact, became for a time a minor gold exchange centre for such countries as Poland, Czechoslovakia and Bulgaria, especially after April 1933 when the dollar, too, ceased to be eligible for reserve purposes.

The crisis of September 1931 was followed by a withdrawal of balances from the United States as well as from the United Kingdom. In the two years 1931 and 1932, the monetary gold stock of the United States was reduced from $4225 to $4045 million, or by $180 million. In the United Kingdom, the net reduction amounted to $125 million (from $718 to $583 million), making a reduction of $315 million for the two countries together during these years. Over the same period, however, the combined gold reserves of six creditor countries, namely France, Belgium, Italy, the Netherlands, Sweden[8] and Switzerland, rose by as much as $1929 million (from $2943 to $4872 million). Thus only a small part of the gold absorbed by these countries came from the two centres where most of their foreign-exchange reserves were held. Where did the remainder come from? Though some of it came from current gold production, it is clear that to a certain extent the pressure resulting from the collapse of the gold exchange system was passed on from London and New York to the world's debtor countries, mainly through the abrupt cessation or even reversal of capital movements and through the fall in prices of primary commodities.[9]

If we separate the twenty-four countries of Appendix II into two groups – creditors and debtors – we see at once that the conversion of foreign-exchange reserves into gold was confined to the six creditor states. From the end of 1930 to the end of 1932 their gold reserves, as shown in table 11.2, increased by $1929 million, while their foreign-exchange holdings declined by $1331 million. The tendency to replace foreign assets by gold in this group of countries had already become apparent in 1928/29.

The eighteen debtor states, as shown in table 11.2, suffered a heavy reduction in gold reserves as well as in foreign exchange, though the proportionate decline was considerably greater in foreign exchange than in gold. They lost $366 million of gold in 1931 and 1932. Debtor countries outside Europe lost about $260 million of gold in this period.

Table 11.2 Central banks' foreign exchange and gold reserves ($ million)

End of:	1928	1929	1930	1931	1932
Total of 6 creditor countries					
Foreign exchange	1,878	1,604	1,679	1,024	348
Gold	1,987	2,430	2,943	4,214	4,872
Total	3,865	4,034	4,622	5,238	5,220
Foreign exchange as % of total	49	40	36	20	7
Total of 18 debtor countries					
Foreign exchange	642	688	621	192	157
Gold	1,503	1,411	1,373	1,059	1,007
Total	2,145	2,099	1,994	1,251	1,164
Foreign exchange as % of total	30	33	31	15	13

While most of the gold reserves lost by the debtor countries were in effect passed on to creditor countries converting their dollar and sterling balances into gold, the foreign-exchange reserves lost by the debtor countries were largely used to repay short-term credits called in by the reserve centres themselves (i.e. mainly New York and London). Just as the granting of private short-term credits by New York and London had supplied the central banks of debtor countries with a large part of their dollar and sterling reserves in the 1920s, so the withdrawal of those credits in the early 1930s tended to wipe out these reserves. It is clear that when debtor countries used up their foreign-exchange reserves for payments to the centres in which the reserves were held, there occurred an extinction and not simply a transfer of central banks' international currency reserves.

Thus the breakdown of the gold exchange standard involved a sharp reduction in the aggregate of international currency reserves not only through the conversion of exchange reserves into gold but also through the absorption of exchange reserves by payments to the reserve centres. The total foreign-exchange reserves of the twenty-four countries included in Appendix II declined by $1800 million in 1931 and 1932 – that is, by an amount far in excess of the $1000 million of gold which came into central bank reserves in the world as a whole from current production and other sources in these two years.

Merits and defects of the system

The liquidation of the gold exchange standard and the scramble for gold which it implied – more especially the large-scale absorption of gold by the countries that later came to be known as the 'gold bloc' – gave added strength to the forces of deflation throughout the world. It was chiefly to avoid deflation that the gold exchange standard was recommended at Genoa. As events turned out, the deflation was only postponed; the principle of 'gold economy' was abandoned when it was most needed, at a time, namely, when other factors making for depression were coming into play in any case.

The gold exchange standard was often accused of tending to breed inflation.[10] In actual fact, of course, no general rise in prices occurred in the period from 1924 to 1928 when the gold exchange standard was in fairly extensive operation; on the contrary, prices of primary commodities showed a falling trend from 1926 onwards. Yet the charge was perhaps true in a sense, but it betrayed a misconception of the primary object of the system. The gold exchange standard was *intended* to be an anti-deflationary device and therefore in that sense 'inflationary'. Without it, the shortage of international currency might have led to a general deflation which would have 'corrected' the situation through a reduction in the value of international transactions and an increase in the output of new gold. With it, the gold shortage was made good by exchange reserves; gold production could remain lower than it otherwise would have been, and there was thus an 'economy of gold' even in the sense of an economy of productive resources engaged in gold-mining.

One serious weakness of the gold exchange system was the great variability in the degree to which central banks relied on exchange reserves as against gold. To understand the causes of this variability it is necessary to consider the motives that led individual countries to adopt the gold exchange standard and to adhere to it. The principal motive should have been a realization of the common interest or, in negative terms, the fear of a worldwide deflation. But individual countries were inclined to neglect the external repercussions of their actions; and the threat of a world deflation was, to each of them, a remote and ineffective sanction.

Countries in need of foreign capital could be induced to observe the exchange standard rules by various means of persuasion and pressure exerted by the lending centres. Especially in the countries where postwar monetary reconstruction was carried out with outside assistance, the advice given and the desires expressed by the experts and financiers of the lending countries played an important role in the practical working of the gold exchange standard.

On the other hand, this factor tended to discredit the system in the eyes of certain creditor and also certain debtor countries. The holding of foreign balances instead of gold in the central monetary reserve came to be regarded as damaging to the prestige of a great or even a moderately great nation. It is largely for this reason that the countries whose balances were in absolute amount the most important – including, for instance, France, Germany, Italy and Poland – did not regard their own use of the gold exchange standard as anything but a transitory expedient.[11]

Moreover, in certain quarters the gold exchange standard was regarded as merely a British 'fad',[12] or even as a device invented and sponsored by Great Britain to make it easier for her to return to the prewar parity without the necessary internal adjustments in costs and prices, and to retain her gold reserves. It has been observed[13] that at the Genoa Conference the exchange standard doctrine was propounded mainly by the British delegation.

The only tangible bait offered by the gold exchange standard to its adherents was the interest return obtainable on foreign-exchange reserves as opposed to gold. The 'heavy expense of the gold standard system'[14] in terms of the interest forgone was supposed to render the gold exchange method particularly attractive to the poorer countries. That may have been so; but the argument did not appeal to the national pride of the less poor countries, even though it may have appealed to the accountants of their central banks. In the profit-and-loss returns of central banks interest receipts from foreign bills and balances played sometimes indeed a very prominent part. Thus in 1929 they provided the Bank of France with 65 per cent of its gross profits. How drastic a change the liquidation of its exchange holdings entailed in the Bank's profit-and-loss account may be seen from the following comparison of the position in 1929 with that in 1934 when receipts from foreign assets had fallen to 3 per cent of gross profits:

Francs (million):	*1929*	*1934*
Receipts from foreign assets	1250	20
Receipts from domestic assets, commissions, etc.	684	547
Total gross profits:	1934	567

The 1920s were a period of relatively high interest rates. In the leading financial centres, 4 per cent, 5 per cent or even more could be obtained from three-month bank bills and similar short-term investments. In 1929 the Bank of France earned an average of 4.6 per cent on its foreign bills and bank balances. Just as the high level of money rates in the 1920s may have contributed in some degree to the spread and the maintenance of the gold exchange standard, so the sharp decline that took place in 1930 may have tended to weaken people's attachment to it. In London and New York rates of discount on bank drafts or acceptances dropped from over 5 per cent in the summer of 1929 to about 2 per cent in the second half of 1930. In 1931, however, with the onset of the international liquidity crisis, money rates shot up again; yet the inducement of higher interest was powerless to stop the general flight from the gold exchange standard.

Interest returns became a wholly secondary consideration when stability of exchange rates and confidence in such stability broke down. The depreciation of a currency in which foreign-exchange reserves were held meant that these reserves lost some of their value as means of settlement in relation to other countries, even though their power to purchase commodities or to discharge financial obligations in the country in which they were held was not necessarily impaired by the exchange depreciation. The fear of exchange losses was in fact an overpowering motive for the liquidation of foreign reserves and rendered the operation of an exchange standard quite impossible. Besides, the statutes of most central banks, as mentioned before, expressly required that if any exchange standard were practised at all, it should be a *gold* exchange standard; and the liquidation of foreign-exchange reserves became at least in some measure compulsory as soon as the currency of a reserve centre ceased to be convertible into gold at a fixed parity.

One criticism which has figured prominently in discussions of the gold exchange standard has still to be considered. It has been asserted that movements in foreign-exchange reserves do not operate in the same reciprocal fashion as gold movements. Under the gold bullion standard, according to the traditional view, the country losing gold is forced to deflate and the country gaining gold is induced to inflate, so that the burden of any necessary adjustment is shared and therefore eased. Under the gold exchange standard, it is argued, a country that is gaining or losing foreign-exchange reserves may well be obliged to effect the appropriate expansion or contraction of credit; but in the country where these reserves are held nothing happens that would bring into play a reciprocal tendency towards contraction or expansion. This argument calls for three brief comments.

In the first place, whether the country where the reserves are held is or is not directly affected by changes in their volume depends to some extent on the form in which they are held. If they were held in the form of sight deposits with the central bank, such changes would have a strong effect analogous to gold movements, since they would involve additions to or withdrawals from the amount of central-bank funds available for the domestic credit base. If the reserves were held in the form of deposits with commercial banks, as was more commonly the case, they would involve shifts of deposits from the active domestic circulation to the inactive holding of the foreign central bank, or vice versa; their effects, though in the 'right' direction, would obviously be much weaker.[15]

But even if it were true that changes in foreign holdings made no difference to credit conditions in the reserve centre, the contrast that is supposed to exist between the effects of gold movements on the one hand and movements in foreign liquid reserves on the other rests largely on a preconceived opinion as to the effects that gold movements ought to have, rather than on an empirical study of the effects they did have in the period under review. There was a strong tendency for countries to insulate their internal money supply from the influences of the balance of payments. More often than not, gold movements were offset or 'neutralized', not always deliberately by any means, but often 'automatically'; not always owing to the action but frequently owing to the inaction of the central bank. The adjustment of the balance of international payments does not depend as closely as has sometimes been thought on changes in the domestic money supply in the various countries.

Thirdly, the common theoretical charge of a lack of reciprocal adjustment in the gold exchange system loses its force under certain conditions which happened to prevail in reality. Suppose two countries (A and B) hold their reserves in a third (C). If one of them (A) loses reserves to the other (B), there is obviously full reciprocal action between the two, just as if gold had moved; provided of course that the 'rules of the game' are observed and that the movement is not neutralized. It may be objected that this is rather a special assumption to make. But it is an assumption that corresponds to the facts. The gold exchange system was not an agglomeration of countries indiscriminately holding each others' currencies. There was a distinct tendency for reserves to be held in a central nucleus (C), even though the nucleus consisted not of one but of two or three countries. In such a system, full reciprocal adjustment of credit and prices can take place between the member countries *inter sc.*[16] It is true that between the member countries on the one hand (A, B) and the centre country on the other (C) the adjustment, on the present assumptions, will tend to be unilateral instead of reciprocal. (If prices in the member countries are on the whole appreciably lower than in the centre country, their aggregate foreign reserves and hence their domestic credit base will expand; and vice versa.) But this is as it should be. It is part of the centre country's responsibility in such a system to keep its level of prices and employment reasonably stable; it is for the member countries to keep themselves attuned to that level.

Within the area over which the system operates, and so long as it operates, the centre country need have no anxiety about its own international liquidity, since its own currency is accepted and used as a means of international settlement by the countries adhering to the system. In return, it is of vital importance for the centre country to keep up its demand for imports and/or its foreign lending, so as to maintain the liquidity of the member countries. The decline of economic activity in 1929–32 was far greater in the United States than in the rest of the world, and was reflected in a sharp drop in United States imports which, together with the cessation of long-term lending and the recall of short-term credits, severely depleted the dollar reserves of most of the member countries.

In fact, however, the nucleus of the gold exchange system consisted of more than one country; and this was a special source of weakness. With adequate co-operation between the centre countries, it need not have been serious. Without such co-operation it proved pernicious. In addition to the variability of the member countries' exchange holdings as compared with gold, reserve funds were liable to move erratically from one centre to another, from London, for instance, to New York and vice versa, and each centre was subject to risks and disturbances on that account. Gold had to be immobilized in these centres as cover against such transfers, and the desired economy of gold was to that extent nullified. When one of the member countries – France – desired to become a gold centre herself, these difficulties were further increased. By and large, however, it was not until the suspension of the gold parity by the United Kingdom that transfers of funds in search of security set in on a really devastating scale from one centre to another.[17] How the breakdown of exchange stability and the cumulative liquidation of the gold exchange system acted and reacted on one another was indicated earlier in this chapter. Here it may be remarked that, given the existence of several centre countries, it is exchange stability as between these centres that is of primary importance for the working of an exchange standard. When the comparative prospects of the various centre currencies become subject to discussion, sudden and disruptive shifts of reserve funds will be difficult to avoid. The problem does not arise in a system with only one centre, and an occasional alteration of exchange rates between a member country and that single centre is unlikely to have serious consequences for the functioning of the system as a whole.

Appendix I Gold supply

[in millions of US dollars of old gold parity ($20.67 per fine ounce)]

	World output[a]	Eastern dishoarding[b]	Central reserves[c]	Change in central reserves	Industrial consumption[d]
1914	448		5,345		
1915	472		6,241	+ 896	
1916	455		6,630	+ 389	
1917	421		7,147	+ 517	
1918	384		6,816[e]		
1919	358		6,805[e]		
1920	333		7,255[e]		
1921	330		8,044[e]		
1922	320		8,417		156
1923	369		8,651	+ 234	153
1924	385		8,976	+ 325	146
1925	384		8,997	+ 21	152
1926	395		9,233	+ 236	142
1927	394		9,593	+ 360	124
1928	390		10,057	+ 464	119
1929	397		10,336	+ 279	
1930	432		10,944	+ 608	102
1931	461	146	11,323	+ 379	63
1932	498	224	11,933	+ 610	36
1933	525	152	11,976	+ 43	40
1934	570	152	13,050	+1,074	39
1935	625	102	12,990	− 60	49
1936	688	77	13,600	+ 710	46
1937	730	40	14,400	+ 800	47
1938	780	34	15,300	+ 900	30

a Source: US Bureau of Mint. The estimates include the USSR.
b Source: Bank of International Settlements.
c Source: Federal Reserve Bulletin, September 1940. Reported gold reserves of central banks and governments (excluding in particular certain stabilization funds, such as the British Exchange Equalization Account).
d Source: US Bureau of Mint. Gross estimates, including not only the new gold but also the scrap and coin used in the arts. The net consumption, excluding scrap and coin, has been estimated at an annual average of $100 million during the five years 1925–9 (see *Interim Report of the Gold Delegation*, League of Nations 1930, p. 90).
e Excluding Russia's reserve, not reported in those years: reported at $666 million in 1917 and at $3 million in 1922.

Appendix II Foreign exchange and gold reserves of central banks

[in US $ (thousands)]

Key: A: Foreign exchange. B: gold. C: total. D: foreign exchange as % of total

End of:		1924	1925	1926	1927	1928	1929	1930	1931	1932
Austria	A	67	79	96	105	102	93	113	20	8
	B	2	2	7	12	24	24	30	27	21
	C	69	81	103	117	126	117	143	47	29
	D	97	98	93	90	81	79	79	43	28
Belgium	A	6	6	62	73	79	85	135	—	—
	B	52	53	86	100	126	163	191	354	361
	C	58	59	148	173	205	248	326	354	361
	D	10	10	42	42	39	34	41	—	—
Bulgaria	A	7	4	5	8	20	8	6	2	1
	B	8	8	8	9	10	10	11	11	11
	C	15	12	13	17	30	18	17	13	12
	D	47	33	38	47	67	44	35	15	8
Czecho-slovakia	A	20	36	62	72	74	68	72	31	30
	B	27	27	27	30	34	37	46	49	51
	C	47	63	89	102	108	105	118	80	81
	D	43	57	70	71	69	65	61	39	37
Danzig	A	6	5	8	7	8	8	9	5	3
	B	—	—	—	—	—	—	—	4	4
	C	6	5	8	7	8	8	9	9	7
	D	100	100	100	100	100	100	100	56	43
Denmark	A	13	24	7	26	31	24	27	4	−1
	B	56	56	56	49	46	46	46	39	36
	C	69	80	63	75	77	70	73	43	35
	D	19	30	11	35	40	34	37	9	—
Estonia[a]	A	1	1	1	3	7	6	4	4	1
	B	3	3	3	3	2	2	2	2	4
	C	4	4	4	6	9	8	6	6	5
	D	25	25	25	50	78	75	67	67	20
Finland	A	14	31	27	32	19	17	24	16	19
	B	8	8	8	8	8	8	8	8	8
	C	22	39	35	40	27	25	32	24	27
	D	64	79	77	80	70	68	75	67	70
France	A	14	13	116[b]	850[b]	1287	1021	1027	842	176
	B	710	711	711	954	1254	1633	2099	2699	3257
	C	724	724	827[b]	1804[b]	2541	2654	3126	3541	3433
	D	2	2	14	47	51	38	33	24	5

Appendix II (continued)

End of:		1924	1925	1926	1927	1928	1929	1930	1931	1932
Germany	A	310	243	230	113	126	194	182	−29	−29
	B	181	288	436	444	650	544	528	234	192
	C	491	531	666	557	776	738	710	205	163
	D	63	46	35	20	16	26	26	—	—
Greece	A	36	30	32	34	48	32	32	14	13
	B	12	13	14	14	7	8	7	11	8
	C	48	43	46	48	55	40	39	25	21
	D	75	70	70	71	87	80	82	56	62
Hungary	A	35	61	43	36	17	14	12	4	3
	B	7	10	30	34	35	29	29	18	17
	C	42	71	73	70	52	43	41	22	20
	D	83	86	59	51	33	33	29	18	15
Italy	A	21	64	156	398	317	271	228	114	69
	B	221	221	223	239	266	273	279	296	307
	C	242	285	379	637	583	544	507	410	376
	D	9	22	41	62	54	50	45	28	18
Latvia	A	9	6	6	10	15	11	8	3	2
	B	5	5	5	5	5	5	5	6	7
	C	14	11	11	15	20	16	13	9	9
	D	64	55	55	67	75	69	62	33	22
Lithuania	A	6	3	4	5	5	8	9	3	2
	B	3	3	3	3	3	3	4	5	5
	C	9	6	7	8	8	11	13	8	7
	D	67	50	57	63	63	73	69	38	29
Netherlands	A	45	99	75	67	88	88	99	35	29
	B	203	178	166	161	175	180	171	357	415
	C	248	277	241	228	263	268	270	392	444
	D	18	36	31	29	33	33	37	9	7
Norway	A	14	19	24	16	11	18	19	6	8
	B	39	39	39	39	39	39	39	42	39
	C	58	58	63	55	50	57	58	48	47
	D	26	33	38	29	22	32	33	13	17
Poland	A	49	1	24	100	80	59	46	24	15
	B	20	26	27	58	70	79	63	67	56
	C	69	27	51	158	150	138	109	91	71
	D	71	4	47	63	53	43	42	26	21
Portugal	A	18	18	10	8	16	17	9	21	20
	B	11	11	9	9	9	9	9	13	24
	C	29	29	19	17	25	26	18	34	44
	D	62	62	53	47	64	65	50	62	45

Appendix II *(continued)*

End of:		1924	1925	1926	1927	1928	1929	1930	1931	1932
Romania	A	—	—	—	—	—	40	10	2	3
	B	48	48	49	51	49	55	56	58	57
	C	48	48	49	51	49	95	66	60	60
	D	—	—	—	—	—	42	15	3	5
Spain	A	7	6	7	7	18	19	16	54	55
	B	489	490	493	502	494	495	471	434	436
	C	496	496	500	509	512	514	487	488	491
	D	1	1	1	1	4	4	3	11	11
Sweden	A	36	54	56	70	58	71	105	13	57
	B	64	62	60	62	63	66	65	55	55
	C	100	116	116	132	121	137	170	68	112
	D	36	47	48	53	48	52	62	19	51
Switzerland	A	37	43	43	38	49	68	85	20	17
	B	98	90	91	100	103	115	138	453	477
	C	135	133	134	138	152	183	223	473	494
	D	27	32	32	28	32	37	38	4	3
Yugoslavia	A	74	71	65	67	45	52	23	8	4
	B	14	15	17	17	18	18	19	31	31
	C	88	86	82	84	63	70	42	39	35
	D	84	83	79	80	71	74	55	21	11
Total (24 countries)	A	845	917	1159	2145	2520	2292	2300	1216	505
	B	2281	2367	2568	2903	3490	3841	4316	5273	5879
	C	3126	3284	3727	5048	6010	6133	6616	6489	6384
	D	27	28	31	42	42	37	35	19	8
Total excl. France (23 countries)	A	831	904	1043	1295	1233	1271	1273	374	329
	B	1571	1656	1857	1949	2236	2208	2217	2574	2622
	C	2402	2560	2900	3244	3469	3479	3480	2948	2951
	D	35	35	36	40	36	37	37	13	11

[a] 1924–7: Bank of Estonia and Treasury.
[b] Estimated (largely held under 'sundry assets').

Notes

1 Each of these banks was authorized by its statutes to hold balances with the two others, and to count these balances as part of the reserve on which the issue of notes was based. The convention of 1885 provided *inter alia* that 'each of these three banks shall open a current account with each of the others; on this account they may issue cheques payable at sight, even if this involves an overdraft; all sums may be paid in to their respective credits. No interest will be charged on credit or debit

balances.... Debit balances must be paid up at the request of the creditor bank.' See Janssen (1922), p. 6.

2 Austria-Hungary, Belgium, Bulgaria, Denmark, France, Germany, Greece, Italy, Netherlands, Norway, Romania, Russia, Spain, Sweden, Switzerland.

3 Cf. Brown (1940), p. 748.

4 In Japan the foreign-exchange transactions of the authorities were conducted, and the foreign balances held, not by the bank of issue but by the Yokohama Specie Bank.

5 Even after the *de facto* stabilization, from December 1926 to June 1928, the chance that the franc might in the end be legally stabilized at a level higher than the current market value was by no means negligible. There were many politicians and financiers strongly advocating such a course. There were in consequence recurrent waves of bull speculation in the franc, the last of which – in May 1928 – was particularly violent.

6 Cf. Bank of France (1932), p. 9: the Bank 'deemed it preferable not to increase through its actions the monetary difficulties of other countries. By conserving the major part of the foreign assets – notably of the pounds sterling – that it held, the Bank has contributed in a very large measure, during the last three years, to maintaining the stability of the British currency.'

7 Bank of France (1933), p. 5.

8 Sweden, as a creditor country, is included in this group, even though she was not one of the gold-absorbing countries; her gold reserve actually declined in 1931. However, the inclusion or exclusion of Sweden does not appreciably affect the totals given in the text.

9 Cf. Brown (1940), pp. 849 ff.

10 Apart from numerous French writers, mention may be made of Mlynarski (1929) who sharply attacked the gold exchange standard on this ground.

11 Cf. Brown (1940), p. 789.

12 Cf. Royal Institute for International Affairs (1931), p. 91.

13 By Sir Otto Niemeyer (1931), p. 90.

14 League of Nations (1932), p. 55.

15 Apart from the question of the effects of changes in reserve balances on credit conditions in the reserve centre, it would have been highly desirable in any case to hold such balances at the central bank. Thus the Preparatory Commission of Experts (1933, p. 16) recommended that in order to secure 'a system more centralized and subject to more effective control... foreign exchange holdings in Central Banks should be invested with or through the Central Bank of the currency concerned or with the Bank of International Settlements. This is all the more important, because it is, in our opinion, imperative that Central Banks should have a complete knowledge of all the operations of other Central Banks on their markets.'

16 Cf. Keynes (1930), vol. I, p. 353.

17 Cf. Hawtrey (1939), p. 267.

References

Bank of France (1932), *Annual Report for 1931*,
———— (1933), *Annual Report for 1932*,
Brown, Jr, William Adams (1940), *The International Gold Standard Reinterpreted, 1914–1934*, New York, National Bureau of Economic Research.

Hawtrey, R.G. (1939), *The Gold Standard in Theory and Practice* (1st edn, 1927), London, Longmans, Green.

Janssen, A.E. (1922), *A Note on the Plan for an International Clearing House*, Geneva, League of Nations, Provisional Economic and Financial Committee.

Keynes, J.M. (1930). *A Treatise on Money*, London, Macmillan.

League of Nations (1932), *Report of the Gold Delegation*, Geneva, League of Nations.

Mlynarski, F. (1929), *Gold and Central Banks*, New York, Macmillan.

Niemeyer, Sir Otto (1931), 'How to economize gold', in Royal Institute for International Affairs, *The International Gold Problem*, London, Oxford University Press, 84–94.

Preparatory Commission of Experts (1933), *Draft Annotated Agenda* for the Monetary and Economic Conference, Geneva, League of Nations.

Royal Institute for International Affairs (1931), *The International Gold Problem*, London, Oxford University Press.

Part IV

Bretton Woods and after

Introduction

The Bretton Woods System established after World War II can be seen as a form of gold exchange standard. Milton Gilbert presents an analysis of the operation of Bretton Woods written from this perspective. Gilbert also warns of sources of instability inherent in the system's design and predicts the possible demise of Bretton Woods three years before the fact. In the final selection, Richard Cooper first describes and then appraises recent proposals to re-establish the gold standard.

12

The gold-dollar system: conditions of equilibrium and the price of gold

Milton Gilbert*

This essay was written in the summer of 1967; its purpose was to explain the nature of the international monetary system and how it functioned up to mid-1967 as a background to the consideration of various possible improvements in the system. Hence, it deals with the system as it has been – not as it might become. While I have made drafting changes and clarifications, I have deliberately not extended the paper to cover the events of the past year so as to avoid discussion of matters about which there are differences in official views. My objective is to analyse the system and not to enter into the political problems of its future evolution.

More specifically, the essay aims to distinguish between difficulties arising from inadequate adjustment policies of individual countries and difficulties arising from a disequilibrium[1] in the system as a whole, which concerns the relationship between gold and the dollar. The analysis is focused on the persistent deficit in the balance of payments of the United States and is designed to bring out its underlying and transient causes.

The gold-dollar system

The present system is usually called the gold exchange standard. As it emerged from Bretton Woods and as it has functioned in the postwar period, however, it is more to the point to call it the gold-dollar system.

*From *Essays in International Finance*, no. 70, Princeton, Princeton University Press, 1968, pp. 1–20, 46–7, abridged.

It may seem curious that economics textbooks do not provide an analytical model of the system. Indeed, there is not really a formal theory of the gold exchange standard, comparable to the theory of the gold standard. This may be, partly, because the system has not been static but has been developing under the changing conditions of the last two decades. However, it is also because the system does not lend itself easily to presentation by a simplified model, as does the gold standard, since central banks do not constitute a homogeneous universe and do not act according to a set pattern of economic considerations.

The absence of an accepted theory of the gold-dollar system has made for much confusion in public discussion. Economists and officials do not start with a generally agreed conception of how the system works or ought to work, such as they have, say, in dealing with problems of demand management. They do not have a model for the equilibrium of the system or a common view on the respective roles of gold and the dollar. In these circumstances, very diverse, and often contradictory, proposals have been offered to solve the problems of the system and the deficit of the United States. In the main, these proposals are either unconvincing as prescriptions for establishing equilibrium in the framework of the present system, or they involve changes so fundamental as to constitute a new system. It is hardly surprising that the political authorities have not been able to find their way out of the maze.

Basic principles and behaviour characteristics of the system

The system rests on a series of basic principles and behaviour characteristics which determine its mode of operation. These derive from law, from international agreements, from the policy aims of central banks and governments and, in some respects, from technical necessity. It is, of course, an evolving organism, which was different thirty years ago and which will, no doubt, be different thirty years hence. The concern here, to repeat, is with the system as it has existed during the past two decades.

Fixed exchange rates

1   Fundamental to the system is the aim of monetary authorities to adhere to fixed rates of exchange. Maintenance of the rate has a high priority with all countries and other objectives are often sacrificed to it. It is apparent that fixed rates have overwhelming support from the business and financial community also.

2   To say that we have a fixed-rate system raises the question of what the rates are fixed to. Under the IMF Articles, a country may declare its par value

in terms either of gold or of the dollar of the gold weight and fineness in effect on 1 July, 1944. There is only a minor technical difference between these two standards.

However, the operative standard for most countries is the dollar as such, and central banks in practice intervene in the market when necessary by buying or selling dollars against their own currencies to keep the dollar exchange rate within agreed limits. The cross rates with other currencies are kept in line by market arbitrage. There are exceptions, of course, such as the countries of the sterling area, which peg their currencies to sterling and rely on the Bank of England to maintain the fixed rate between sterling and the dollar. But, generally, central banks operate directly on the market for dollars *vis-à-vis* their own currency, and it is the market rate on the dollar that is significant for their international competitive position – irrespective of the legal gold content of the dollar.

3   The exception in the system is the dollar itself, which both in law and in fact is fixed in terms of gold – at \$35 an ounce. The United States is not obliged to intervene in the exchange market; it has only to be prepared to buy and sell gold at \$35 and can leave it to the intervention of other central banks to maintain fixed rates to the dollar. The United States has intervened in the market at times in recent years, both spot and forward, but the purpose was to avoid losses of gold from temporary movements of funds rather than to keep rates in line.

Reserves

1   To maintain fixed rates the monetary authorities must hold reserves so that they are in a position to iron out fluctuations in supply and demand in the foreign-exchange market. Reserves consist of liquid international assets, readily available for intervening in the market, and are almost entirely confined to gold and to foreign-exchange assets in dollars and sterling.

However, while sterling is important to the international economy as a trading currency, it is active as a reserve currency only in settlements between the United Kingdom and sterling-area countries. Hence, it is a regional reserve currency and quite different from the dollar, which is the reserve currency of the system. To simplify matters I will discuss only dollars, thus treating the sterling area (and, likewise, any other monetary area) as a unit which holds reserves in gold and dollars.

It will be seen, therefore, that the system is a gold-dollar system for two reasons: first, currencies are fixed either to the dollar or to gold and, secondly, the reserves of the system are gold and dollars.

2   Each central bank is free to determine the composition of its reserves as between gold and dollars. Its policy in this respect is in its own hands, because

it can sell or buy gold against dollars at the US Treasury. If there is any constraint on such exchanges, even psychological or political, the convertibility of the dollar at its fixed relationship to gold comes into question. In practice, there is a wide range among the countries in the ratio between holdings of gold and dollars, indicating that central banks give different weight to the benefits to themselves of the two categories of assets.

3   Dollars are held almost entirely in money-market instruments and time deposits, as these are liquid assets that earn interest. Gold, on the other hand, produces no revenue. It is important to realize that, if central banks could not earn interest on dollars, their reserves would be almost entirely in gold. Some central bankers have stressed that they are not primarily concerned with interest earnings in determining the composition of their reserves. This may be true of marginal changes in reserves; but the point is that, if the United States did not permit central banks to invest dollars at interest, they would never have acquired the dollars in the first place; they would have acquired gold.

Hence, the first requirement for a currency to become a reserve currency is that there must be an open money market in which foreign central banks can freely invest in short-term paper. In addition, the money market must be capable of absorbing large central-bank transactions, and the convertibility of the currency at a fixed rate must be rather secure. It is because New York and London are the only two open money markets of any size that the dollar and sterling are the only two significant reserve currencies. And it is because exchange rates between sterling and other currencies have not been secure that the dollar, supported by large gold reserves, supplanted sterling as the reserve currency of the system.

Other currencies have not become reserve currencies either because the central bank discourages placements of funds at interest by foreign central banks or because their convertibility at a fixed rate does not seem reasonably assured over the longer run. Continental European countries have not wanted to become reserve centres; they are reluctant to have their markets and reserves disturbed by large-scale operations of foreign central banks and some, also, see no point in their country bearing the interest burden attached to having their currency held as reserves.

It has been said that dollars are kept in reserves primarily as a matter of convenience, since dollars can be used directly in the exchange market whereas gold must first be converted into dollars for the purpose of market intervention. However, dollars held in money-market paper or on fixed-term deposit must equally be converted into cash to be available for market intervention, and there is no great difficulty in converting gold into cash.

While a variety of developments went to make the dollar the reserve currency of the system, the United States took no initiative in the matter; its action was only permissive.

4   With respect to its reserves, also, the United States is an exception. While other countries are free to hold their reserves in any combination of gold and dollars they wish, including 100 per cent in dollars, the United States must hold its reserves essentially in gold. This is because there is no other currency besides the dollar that can be used for general intervention in the exchange market; hence, any foreign currencies held by the United States cannot be used for general support of the dollar in the way that other countries use the dollar as a general support for their currencies. The United States can generally use foreign-exchange holdings only for bilateral settlements. To underline the importance of this point, France could hold all its reserves in dollars if it were so minded, but the United States could only hold a quite small fraction of its reserves in French francs.

The foreign-exchange assets that have appeared in the reserve statistics of the United States in recent years were always acquired for specific purposes. For example, there may be a temporary holding of D-Marks which were acquired in the market in anticipation of repaying D-Mark Roosa bonds to the Bundesbank. Or, there may be small holdings of Swiss francs to be fed into the market when the dollar is under pressure so that the Swiss National Bank will not have to acquire the excess of dollars which it might then want to convert into gold.

The only currency that the United States has held in large amounts has been sterling. These holdings arose mainly because American assistance to the Bank of England was given in the form of swaps of dollars against sterling – rather than as simple advances. The sterling, of course, could not be used at the same time by the United States to meet its own deficit or to avoid gold losses and, therefore, was not 'reserves' in the ordinary sense of immediately marketable assets. To count such sterling assets in reserves is about as appropriate as it would be, say, for a business firm to include its accounts receivable in its cash.

5   Since the United States is the only country obliged to hold its reserves in gold, the function of gold as a 'discipline' against excessive money creation is primarily applicable to the United States. Other countries are subject to balance-of-payments discipline, but the discipline lies in the loss of any reserves – whether dollars or gold. Even so, a loss of gold makes a much greater impression on public opinion in many countries than a loss of foreign-exchange reserves or foreign borrowing by the central bank. If other countries entirely stopped acquiring gold, the discipline of gold on the United States would become rather theoretical. This is particularly so because increases in its liabilities to foreign official institutions seem to have exerted little discipline on the United States.

6   Why do central banks, apart from the United States, hold non-interest-bearing gold at all and what determines the proportion between their holdings of gold and dollars? Several considerations are involved, to which the various countries attach different importance.

(a) Gold is unique in that the asset of the holding country is not a liability of another country. For dollar assets, on the other hand, there must be a liability in the United States – either money-market paper or bank deposits. Hence, the disposition of gold is entirely in the hands of the holding country, while the use of dollars may require the acquiescence of the United States. However remote it may seem, countries take account of the possibility that exchange balances may be blocked in times of political trouble, such as war, and they hold some gold over which they are the sole masters. This is the 'war-chest' motive and it is often said that holding gold is an aspect of sovereignty. Gold-buying by China in 1965 and 1966 probably reflected this motive, and one sees its influence frequently in times of political stress. The war-chest motive is sometimes disparaged by writers who look upon gold as anachronistic, but it is evident that every major country gives it some weight in its reserve policy. Apart from the fact that gold reserves have been drawn upon in past wars, their existence supports a country's credit standing in such troubled times. It is a fact also that foreign-exchange balances have been blocked for political reasons.

(b) The exchange risk to a central bank on its gold reserves is limited to a possible fall in the price of gold or to an appreciation of its own currency *vis-à-vis* gold. On dollar reserves there is the additional risk of its own currency appreciating *vis-à-vis* the dollar as a result of a rise in the dollar price of gold while its own price of gold remains unchanged. When sterling depreciated in 1931, some central banks had large balance-sheet losses on their sterling holdings by the change in exchange relationships. The small group of central banks that hold almost all of their reserves in gold are concerned primarily to avoid such risk to their balance-sheet position. They do not consider it a primary function of the central bank to earn interest on its reserves; they took their increases of reserves in gold even when there seemed to be no possible threat to the convertibility of the dollar, because they knew, if the risk should arise, there might be practical limitations to conversion of dollars into gold. Having their reserves in gold, they believe, gives them greater independence of action in the event of a future monetary crisis; that is, if the United States should reduce the gold content of the dollar, they would be free to fix their exchange rate with the dollar on prospective balance-of-payments considerations alone – without the complication of a possible loss in the domestic-currency value of their reserves.

In holding gold, of course, a central bank must have confidence in the intrinsic value of gold in terms of its own currency. But, then, they all do – and that is putting it mildly.

(c) Another consideration in reserve policy is the possibility of a universal rise in the price of gold. A central bank which held only dollars in that event would not take any loss on its reserve holdings, but it would not have the benefit of the marked-up value of reserves that gold-holding countries would have. I know of only one central bank which calculated years ago that the book profit from a possible rise in the gold price was too uncertain to set against realizable interest earnings; it, therefore, made the decision to hold a minimum in gold, to take its interest earnings on dollar holdings, and to stick to this policy even if a rise in the gold price became more of a possibility. But many other central banks have not been that unwavering. Besides, some feel themselves open to internal political criticism when their ratio of gold reserves gets much out of line with that of neighbouring countries.

(d) A large number of central banks have a very low gold ratio. These are mainly capital-importing countries. They have not given much weight to the exchange risk because they expect to maintain a fixed rate with the reserve currency under almost any circumstances. Furthermore, they look upon their reserves partly as overborrowing by their country from abroad, and they see their interest earnings as a partial offset to the interest payments which have to be made abroad. Some central banks, also, have little scope for earnings on domestic operations and it is only interest receipts on their reserves that allow them some independence from the government.

(e) A few central banks have always considered it an obligation to take at least part of any increase of reserves in gold so that the 'discipline of gold' should be a reality for the United States. Likewise, some have continued to buy some gold from the United States to maintain the principle of the convertibility of the dollar, even after it became impractical to exercise the right of convertibility to the limit. They have felt it necessary to resist full acceptance of a dollar standard and have been strengthened in this view by what they consider to be an inadequate priority which the United States gives to correction of its payments deficit. As one official put it, if we accept a full dollar standard, it would be like having a country with two central banks – sometimes working at cross purposes.

(f) In several countries the law requires the central bank to maintain reserves in gold as backing for the domestic currency. This legal provision is a leftover from the days when gold coins were in active circulation and has little relation to present-day conditions. It is the only motive for central banks holding reserves in gold that is entirely traditional.

Given this variety of motives, it is apparent that the comparative benefits of holding gold relative to dollars cannot be calculated. In other words, central banks cannot know what reserve policy will make their country better off – and, perhaps, they cannot even define precisely what being 'better off' is. What many do, therefore, is work to some rule of thumb. A few years ago, for example, there were several central banks that aimed to have about a 50–50 ratio between gold and dollars, whereas others held mostly gold and still others mostly dollars. Reserve ratios generally are not set once for all, however, but are subject to change according to circumstances – particularly to changes in the degree of certainty regarding the gold convertibility of the dollar at its fixed price.

7   Besides reserves, IMF facilities are available in the system to assist countries that encounter balance-of-payments difficulties. The amount any country may draw is originally fixed by its quota, which broadly reflects its size and economic strength. In establishing its quota, each country as a rule pays 25 per cent to the IMF in gold and 75 per cent in its own currency and agrees that its currency may be drawn upon in case of need to finance other countries' drawings. The Fund may also finance drawings partly by selling gold in order to acquire the needed currencies.

The right of a country to draw on its gold subscription is practically automatic; so also is its right to draw on any credit balance it may have built up by having had its own currency drawn upon. These two amounts have come to be called a 'reserve position in the Fund'. If a country draws on its quota above its reserve position in the Fund, it is taking credit and its right to this credit is conditional upon the IMF judging that its policies are likely to correct its external deficit.

From the standpoint of meeting a deficit, therefore, a Fund reserve position is equivalent to a country's own reserves. But it differs from reserves in three respects:

(i)   A drawing on the 25 per cent gold tranche of its quota carries repayment obligations.

(ii) Public confidence in a currency depends more on the size of reserves than on the country's reserve position in the Fund.

(iii) A Fund reserve position – except for credits under General Arrangements to Borrow (GAB) – does not yield interest like dollar reserves, nor does it have the characteristics that induce countries to hold non-interest-bearing gold; thus, when surplus countries supply resources for drawings by deficit countries, they do so as an act of co-operation rather than an act of investment for its own sake.

There has been one instance of a country making a deposit with the IMF; the consideration involved was that the deposit was covered by a full gold guarantee, in contrast to the normal gold-value guarantee incorporated in the IMF Articles. Hence, it is not an arrangement with large possibilities of expansion, because the IMF could not assume the risk on the price of gold.

The credit tranches of a country's quota are not comparable to reserves; they are conditional facilities and any credit obtained carries definite repayment obligations and interest charges.

Some high officials have had the hope that drawings on the IMF would become fairly routine central-bank operations – like the use of bank credit by a business firm to supplement its working capital. Thus far, however, this idea has not been realized; drawings on the IMF have been indicative of a strained or crisis situation in which the IMF is called upon as a rescue organization. In fact, countries have at times emphasized drawing on the IMF so as to gain public support for necessary corrective policy actions.

Since the IMF was established in 1944, there have been two general increases in countries' quotas, by 50 per cent in 1959 and by 25 per cent in 1966, as well as special increases for particular countries. Also, the General Arrangements to Borrow was agreed to by the Group of Ten industrial countries in 1962, whereby they could lend additional resources to the Fund to help meet large drawings by members of the Group. The need for this arrangement arose because the Fund's stock of convertible currencies could be inadequate to meet large drawings under conditions when a balance-of-payments deficit of the United States limited the Fund's use of its dollar holdings or when the United States itself wanted to make a large drawing on the Fund. In either of these cases, therefore, the Fund could have a problem of liquidity; in fact, in the Bretton Woods' arrangements it was probably not contemplated that the Fund's dollar holdings might not be freely usable because of a large deterioration in the reserve position of the United States.

It should be noted that transactions under the GAB are covered by a full gold guarantee.

8 In addition to the IMF, short-term central-bank credit facilities have been arranged among a number of countries. These may be used on an *ad hoc* basis and are designed essentially to help meet reversible movements of private funds and to relieve the pressure on the reserves temporarily while the character of the demand for foreign exchange is being appraised. Such assistance is provided on the credit standing of the central bank, in which the size of the reserves is an essential consideration. They are not conditional in the sense of IMF credit facilities, since the borrowing central bank cannot make commitments about the adjustment policies of its government.

9 Besides reserves and official credit facilities, extensive use is made of foreign commercial-bank credit and other private liquid funds to meet strains on the exchange market. Central banks may do this on their own account, or they may arrange matters so that it is done by their own commercial banks. The scope for such operations has been much enlarged by the development of the Euro-dollar market and the market has in recent years been drawn upon by several countries for quite large amounts. Private credit facilities are certainly a flexible supplement to official resources and are likely to be of growing importance. It would be going too far, however, to consider them a substitute for monetary reserves, especially since a country with inadequate reserves is not likely to have a high credit rating with private banks.

The adjustment process: countries in deficit

1 A country with a balance-of-payments deficit can for a time hold its exchange rate by drawing on reserves and available borrowing facilities. As these are limited, however, and as drawing on them too much may make matters worse by leading to a flight from the currency, the authorities must sooner or later take action to get out of deficit. When this adjustment is not brought about, and the exchange parity depreciates, economic and financial policy are considered by the general public to have failed. Whether maintaining the rate is a reasonable objective in given circumstances, however, depends on whether the authorities can take sufficient policy action to eliminate the deficit.

2 The policy actions available to eliminate a deficit and some limitations on them are, briefly, as follows:

(a) Fiscal and monetary restraint on total domestic demand so as to limit imports and, possibly, encourage exports. After a bout of inflationary pressure, the curtailment of demand to restore external balance often results in a short period of domestic recession. But the Bretton Woods experts did not expect countries to subject themselves to prolonged stagnation in order to maintain the fixed exchange rate of the currency. While this does happen, of course, it is the country itself which sets the priorities among its objectives.

(b) Monetary restraint to raise interest rates relative to rates abroad so as to improve the net external balance on short- and long-term capital account. This instrument, too, has limitations because it will cause domestic recession and stagnation if pushed too far – though the limits can be widened by compensatory fiscal action.

(c) Long-term borrowing abroad by the government or by other authorities of the public sector. This is easier for some countries than for others.

(d) Reduction of government expenditures abroad, in cases where such expenditures are relatively large. The limitations on this technique are political but, none the less, real.

(e) Direct controls on imports and invisibles. Import controls are subject to severe limitations by international agreement and their use by an industrial country implies a rather desperate situation. Indeed, as the major purpose of a fixed rate is to encourage liberal trading practices, there is not much sense in maintaining the rate by restrictions on trade. The limitations on controls over invisibles are less severe, but such controls are used much more for protection than for balance-of-payments purposes.

(f) Direct controls on capital exports. Such controls are not limited by international agreement and may be used freely, not only by deficit countries, but even by countries in surplus, without any sanctions being available to other countries. In fact, a country with a balance-of-payments deficit attributable to a deficit on capital account is not normally supposed to be eligible for IMF assistance. Many countries maintain controls on capital movements, either for balance-of-payments or for domestic reasons; others have little need of them because the combination of monetary and fiscal policies they follow leads to market conditions which limit capital outflows anyhow.

Hence, in adhering to the principle of no direct capital controls until a few years ago, the United States was almost alone among the convertible-currency countries. Because of its high per capita income and the huge volume of savings generated by its economy, the United States would have been the dominant capital market in the world in any case. But this position was reinforced by the controls and policies maintained in other countries.

In the last few years the United States has imposed direct capital controls to limit its gold losses. Most other industrial countries find this course perfectly natural and desirable. Indeed, some seem to believe that the deficit of the United States, apart from the effects of the Vietnam War, could be cured by stringent enough capital controls. This view, to my mind, does not take sufficient account of all the links there are between the capital and current accounts, or of the shifts that take place between the various categories of capital outflow and inflow when controls are applied.

3 The force of these instruments can be very substantial when they are used vigorously and there have been many instances in the postwar period of countries emerging successfully from a period of deficit by means of them – without undergoing deep recession or prolonged stagnation. However, cases can and do arise in which they are unable to restore external balance – usually because domestic inflation has brought internal prices and costs too far out of line. Hence, the aim of maintaining a fixed rate cannot be considered absolute.

A deficit position which requires a change in the exchange parity to bring about correction is called a 'fundamental disequilibrium' and it is provided in the IMF Articles that a country in such a situation may change its rate without sanctions. There is no legal definition of fundamental disequilibrium, but in practice countries do not apply to the IMF for a change in rate before the situation is perfectly obvious; they have always obtained approval. A country that resorts to extensive exchange restrictions in such a situation instead of adjusting the rate is not supposed to be eligible for IMF assistance, though, if the truth be told, some countries have got away with murder. It is far from pleasant for the IMF to insist that a country devalue as a condition to drawing IMF credit.

While the evidence of fundamental disequilibrium in some cases is unmistakable, the distinction between transitory and basic imbalance is difficult to make in others. There is no computer program by which the precise equilibrium rate of exchange can be determined, and, even if there were, no country would change its rate to correct a small disadvantage in the structure of exchange rates. There are several reasons which justify this attitude. First, to depreciate the rate by, say, 3 per cent or 5 per cent would be likely to do more harm than good, because of the distrust in the currency that it would engender. Secondly, the policy instruments available for maintaining external balance are sufficient to prevent prolonged reserve losses in such cases, without undue sacrifice of other objectives, for example, by rather small changes in the capital account. And thirdly, there is an adjustment process constantly at work which tends to correct small imbalances, particularly when it is helped along by appropriate demand policy and when it is not negated by continual wage inflation. This adjustment process takes place both within the given country and in the world economy on the outside; its reality is evident from the fact that reasonably well-managed countries are able to maintain fixed rates over long time spans.

Thus, the existence of fundamental disequilibrium is a matter of degree and to specify it in any given case is a matter of judgement. Such a judgement is particularly hazardous when external imbalance is accompanied by excess domestic demand and when there is likely to be some flight of capital contributing to the imbalance. For example, there were observers who considered that the lira had become overvalued in 1963, but this was proven to be a misjudgement as soon as the domestic inflation was brought under control. On the other hand, all competent analysts considered the French franc to be in fundamental disequilibrium in 1957 – and they were right.

4 For the generality of countries in deficit, the availability of a change in rate, which improves the competitive position of exports relative to imports, means that a balance in external payments can always be restored. In fact, it always is restored. When a country delays action until it runs out of reserves

and runs out of credit, it must in the end devalue. It may hide this fact from itself by tying its economy into knots with extreme exchange restrictions and multiple exchange rates and by turning its eyes from the black market which always springs into life in such circumstances. But, then, the currency has effectively been devalued *de facto*, if not *de jure*.

Consequently, there is nothing wrong with the adjustment process when it is viewed as including a change in exchange rate as the ultimate policy instrument. We have seen it work perfectly adequately in case after case. Where the external deficit was due merely to excess domestic demand, as in the Netherlands in 1956–7, Italy in 1963–4, or Germany in 1965–6, the deficit disappeared when effective monetary and fiscal measures were taken to restrict internal demand. And where such action would not do, because there was a fundamental disequilibrium, as in France in 1956–7, or Spain in 1957–9, the deficit disappeared when appropriate devaluation was undertaken in combination with restricting excess demand, which was the cause of the imbalance in the first place.

It would be far more satisfying, of course, if the monetary and economic behaviour of countries were always such that they avoided falling into fundamental disequilibrium. But if they do not, it is no reflection on the system. And if they choose to suffer the distortions and stagnation of an overvalued currency instead of adjusting to an equilibrium exchange rate, it is on their own responsibility as sovereign nations.

5 Here again, however, the United States is a significant exception because as a practical matter it cannot act directly on exchange rates. This follows to some degree from the fact that the dollar is fixed to gold, rather than to any particular currency. But it is a consequence even more of the weight of the United States in the world economy and the significance of the dollar in the international monetary system. Suppose the United States decided that its balance-of-payments deficit could not be corrected by acceptable adjustment policies, and that it had gone the limit in using its gold reserves and taking IMF and central-bank assistance. It could then either raise the dollar price at which the Treasury buys and sells gold or simply suspend gold sales by the Treasury without fixing a new price for the time being. Whether any changes would then be made in exchange rates *vis-à-vis* the dollar would depend upon the reaction of other countries. In the first case they could maintain their fixed parities to the dollar, with the result that the price of gold would be higher in all currencies. In the second case, also, they could intervene in the exchange market to maintain the peg to the dollar and let the price of gold in their own currencies be free to move with market forces.

I leave until later the question of what they might do under various conditions and here wish only to stress two points: the first is that the process available to the United States for removing a persistent deficit is different than for other countries; the second is that the equilibrium of the dollar involves the equilibrium of the whole system in a way that is different than for other currencies and is necessarily related to the price of gold. The difference between the dollar and other currencies in this regard may seem to be a difference of degree, but it is so large as to constitute a difference in kind.

6 This position of the dollar is what lies behind the official insistence on improvement of the adjustment process. There is not great concern about the adjustment process in general, because other countries cannot avoid adjustment. And even if they have to adjust by means of a change in exchange rate, it is largely a local affair which does not involve the system as a whole. The key target of the demand for better adjustment is the persistent deficit of the United States because it is likely to involve the stability of the system as a whole. There has been a strong feeling that somehow its deficit has reflected misbehaviour on the part of the United States – even when the United States was clearly not having excess demand, when the margin of unemployed resources was unnecessarily large, and when it could not be convincingly shown by what combination of policy measures the United States could meet the demand to eliminate its deficit. However, there have been very few in official circles bold enough to draw the apparently logical conclusion that the dollar was in fundamental disequilibrium; very few have felt that their exchange rate *vis-à-vis* the dollar ought to have been revalued. For its part, the United States took refuge in the idea that the trouble was with lack of adjustment by the surplus countries – and the charges back and forth left matters more or less at a standstill.

For the past several years, also, criticism of the adjustment process has been directed at the United Kingdom. However, the United Kingdom was having substantial excess demand, domestic inflation, and overfull employment. And at the same time it was asking for very large assistance from abroad to finance its external deficit. Hence, the grounds for complaint were quite different than in the case of the United States before the start of the Vietnam inflation.

7 A final point with regard to deficits. Given the nature of the policy instruments available for correcting a significant deficit position, it will be apparent that the process of adjustment is necessarily a relatively short-term affair. When it does not take place fairly quickly, it simply means that the authorities have not taken the appropriate measures – either deflation and capital controls, if the imbalance is not fundamental, or devaluation, if there is fundamental disequilibrium. And when the exchange rate is significantly overvalued, there is no way to adjust other than by changing the exchange rate.

Governments are often reluctant to accept this proposition because of the stigma usually connected with a change in the exchange rate; so they think up all sorts of pseudo-measures for the long-run correction of the deficit. In recent times, however, there is not a single successful case of long-run adjustment of a sizeable balance-of-payments deficit – apart from the special cases of reconstruction of war damage to the productive potential of the economy. And even those cases did not take very long. In former times, when stagnation of the economy led to declining wages and prices, such adjustments often occurred. In our day of downward rigidity of wages and prices and of the high priority given to full employment, however, such an adjustment can take place only through wages in the deficit country rising less than in the outside world – and the margin of correction that has been possible by this process has proven relatively small.

The United States, in particular, has had a long-term programme to restore balance for seven years and yet the goal is as elusive as ever. Failure to face up to this reflects political attitudes – not economic analysis.

The adjustment process: countries in surplus

1 It is often said, from the standpoint of the system as a whole, that both surplus and deficit countries must share the responsibility for achieving balance in international payments. However, the primary responsibility, and the active role in the adjustment process, falls in fact on deficit countries because it is their exchange rates that are in jeopardy. When a country is in surplus, the central bank can feel free to concentrate on domestic objectives of full employment and growth. But when the country is in deficit, it cannot. Thus, there is a natural bias toward being in surplus, since the surest way to avoid any risks to the exchange rate is to stay on the right side of the line. When a country is in moderate surplus, therefore, it will not take deliberate action to reduce the surplus and, even when the surplus is fairly large, deliberate corrective action is rather limited. The co-operative actions taken by surplus countries have been confined largely to facilitating the financing problem – such as prepayment of long-term debt, provision of special facilities to the banks to acquire foreign-exchange assets, and accepting special exchange-guaranteed assets instead of gold. Several countries also have used special techniques to limit the inflow of funds from abroad.

2 Besides the general aim of protecting the exchange rate, several more specific factors militate against an active adjustment policy by surplus countries:

(a) The basic objectives of economic policy are usually stated as full employment, stable prices, and external balance. Now, reasonable judgements can be made about full employment and price stability, but external balance is too hazy a concept to serve as a guide to operating policy. It needs a lot of interpretation. It is a normative, longer-run idea, whereas policy is made for a shorter run in which true 'equilibrium' can hardly ever be said to exist. The authorities are acutely aware that the external position may change rapidly and are inclined to expect that a surplus this year may disappear or be smaller next year. The relative cyclical position of the country may favour a sizeable surplus at the moment, but it is likely that both the cyclical position and the surplus will be different a year from now. The surplus may reflect other temporary influences which can always change and probably will change, such as an inflow of liquid funds or unusual imports of long-term capital. Appraisal of the underlying situation is often difficult because of changes in the foreign position of the banking system. Exports may be quite favourable, but there is the possibility that wage increases may erode the country's competitive position. And so on.

When the European countries were receiving Marshall aid, the external position was always appraised with the aid apart – quite sensibly, too, because if the aid had not been looked upon as temporary how would the countries have ever arrived at a position in which aid was no longer needed? Similarly, American military expenditures in Europe tended to be regarded as a temporary factor in the balance of payments – quite different from a country's own exports as a means of earning a foreign-exchange surplus. In sum, to the extent that surplus countries aim at adjustment, they tend to discount what they regard as temporary elements of the surplus.

(b) A somewhat similar influence arises from countries' objectives with regard to the structure of the balance of payments. This affects their willingness to pursue adjustment policies, the policy instruments they use, and the view they take of the position of the currency in the structure of exchange rates. The point may be illustrated by contrasting Canada and the Netherlands.

Both countries devote about the same percentage of GNP to gross investment and there is not a significant difference in their per capita real output. Yet, no doubt largely for historical reasons, their balance-of-payments aims are quite different.

Canada looks upon itself as a developing country with a capital requirement that cannot be fully met by internal savings. It expects the current account of its balance of payments to be in deficit and to be compensated by net capital imports. Thus, while Canada aims to avoid a deficit in its overall payments position, its use of fiscal and monetary policy is conditioned by the view that net capital imports are normal. When Canada fixed a lower rate of exchange in 1962, the obvious purpose was to reduce the deficit on current account. But obviously, also, the rate chosen, of 0.93 Canadian to the US dollar, was not intended to secure current-account balance but allowed for continuing capital imports.

The Netherlands, on the other hand, considers itself among the relatively well-off countries of the world and thinks that it should have a surplus on current account to allow for foreign aid and net capital exports – particularly to finance the foreign investment of Dutch international enterprises. Hence, it uses fiscal and monetary policy to secure a volume of domestic savings, including savings in the public sector, that exceeds domestic investment, and it generally manages to do so. If this aim is frustrated, say by an inflow of foreign direct investment or foreign purchases of Dutch securities, the authorities are unwilling to allow the current account to adjust to this situation. The result is an increase in official reserves or improvement in the external position of the banking system. When the Netherlands followed Germany in revaluation of the currency in 1961, it was certainly not with the idea that the current-account surplus would be wiped out.

This view of balance-of-payments aims is characteristic of many continental countries; that is, they aim at being in surplus on current account and some even extend the objective to the trade account. They consider it inappropriate to allow adjustment of their current-account surplus to compensate for capital exports by the United States. They could, and do to some extent, arrange their 'policy mix' or relax controls so as to obtain some offset by exports of domestic capital funds. But this often poses difficulties in the domestic sphere – political and other. They think it is mainly up to the United States to take action against its 'excessive' capital exports.

Since the imposition of direct controls on capital exports by the United States, there has been a sizeable volume of international issues on the Euro-bond market which has tended to increase Europe's net capital exports. In addition, some countries have arranged capital exports by public-sector institutions, including the central bank, to help absorb a current-account surplus. But it would take a great change of attitude indeed for the European countries to allow these techniques to expand enough to deteriorate their reserve positions, and this would not be a sustainable situation in any case.

(c) Finally, the tolerance for surpluses is influenced by the fact that international transactions have a strong upward trend. It is recognized, therefore, that reserves must increase also if they are to remain adequate to defend fixed rates against balance-of-payments fluctuations. The growth in reserves and transactions may not need to be at the same rate, since policy action may become more effective in narrowing balance-of-payments fluctuations. Also, a country's reserves for the moment may be more than adequate, so that their growth could be allowed to slide for several years without causing trouble. But after a time their upward trend would have to be resumed. This is true for individual countries and for all countries taken together. Furthermore, as an increase in reserves comes about by having an external surplus, one must say that the norm is for countries to be in surplus. Hence, equilibrium for an individual country, and for all countries together, is not simply a situation of balance between external receipts and payments; there must on average be surpluses. A country that fails to achieve a reasonable growth in reserves is bound to meet with difficulties on external account and declining confidence in its currency. Sterling is a striking example of a currency falling into this kind of situation. Since the early 1950s the United Kingdom authorities have wished to secure an upward trend in their reserves to provide better support for the sterling-area system. But the aim was constantly being crowded out by other objectives – economic and political – with the result that sterling has been subjected to repeated exchange difficulties.

The mercantilist flavour of official attitudes toward the balance of payments comes from recognition that a surplus approximates equilibrium in a growing world better than does a constant level of reserves. And, of course, economists have stressed the need for global reserves to rise. The Netherlands central bank formerly set a quantitative target for the growth of its foreign reserves and tried to arrange domestic liquidity creation so that the target would be met. Other central banks are influenced by the same idea, if in a less precise fashion.

3 While a reasonable, or even moderately large, surplus may be in the vicinity of equilibrium, cases arise of persistent extreme surplus. This is a situation in which, after total demand has been pushed to a full-employment level, the surplus does not fall to reasonable proportions. In the conventions of international co-operation, there is no obligation on surplus countries to pursue inflationary demand policies in order to bring down the surplus.

The only provision in the Fund Articles for such cases is the 'scarce currency' clause. It has never been called upon and, indeed, was expected only to be applicable to the United States. A country declared to have a 'scarce currency' would not have to do anything itself, but other countries would have a right to discriminate against it in their trade and payments regulations.

To be parallel with devaluation in cases of fundamental disequilibrium, countries in extreme surplus ought to revalue their currencies. But the high priority on fixed rates holds for currency appreciation as well as devaluation, and revaluation is a rare occurrence. The only recent case was the revaluation in 1961 of the German mark and the Dutch florin by 5 per cent.

However, revaluation must be recognized as the ultimate policy weapon available to countries that want to stop the inflationary consequences of an extreme surplus. The surplus is an inflationary force because, in pegging the rate, the central bank has to buy the excess of dollars offered in the market against domestic currency and there are practical limits to the extent to which the authorities can neutralize this increase of domestic currency by other policy actions. The revaluation of the Deutsche Mark was undertaken precisely on these grounds.

Two other cases show that the authorities do have the power to act against an extreme surplus when they feel that it constitutes an intolerable danger to internal monetary stability. Canada adopted a floating rate in 1950 to combat a huge inflow of investment funds from the Unites States; the Canadian dollar appreciated between 5 and 8 per cent and a balance was achieved in the market with a less inflationary inflow of funds from abroad. Switzerland, for some years after the war, also allowed its rate to float for most transactions other than trade and a part of tourism, when faced with an unmanageable inflow of funds from abroad. The Swiss franc on the free market appreciated as much as 30 per cent to the dollar, against the par of 4.37. It should be noted that both Canada and Switzerland could have converted their dollar inflows into gold in those days without any reproach from Washington. But it was the large surplus they did not want – even in gold.

Although rare, these instances of revaluation are significant from two standpoints. First, they show that the United States cannot foist any amount of dollars on the rest of the world; beyond a certain point other countries would sever their fixed ties to the dollar. The fact that they have not done so indicates that they have not considered their currencies to be undervalued. Secondly, the system provides countries in extreme surplus with a remedy, if they care to use it. If they do not, it is on their own responsibility. The saving grace from the standpoint of other countries is that an extreme surplus tends to be eroded by internal inflation.

4 By comparison with any previous time, there has been a high degree of international monetary co-operation in these postwar years. It must be recognized, however, that every country gives priority to its own basic interests and that the demands on co-operation cannot violate those interests. As the world is made up of sovereign states, ultimate responsibility both for the convertibility of each currency and for the control of inflation within each country is a national responsibility. [...]

Deterioration of the system

Since the eruption of the market price of gold in 1960, there has been a steady deterioration in the operation of the system and a change in its character. I summarize the main aspects of this deterioration from the review of developments already recounted.

1 The standing of the dollar as the reserve currency of the system has become compromised as there is less readiness to hold dollars freely. To minimize conversion of dollars to gold under these circumstances, the United States has resorted to giving guarantees on various of its external liabilities.

2 The United States has used moral suasion to prevent dollars being converted to gold. It is no secret that such conversions are considered to be at least uncooperative, and in some cases unfriendly. Some foreign central banks have refrained from demanding gold for dollars so as not to rock the boat. Hence, central banks no longer have full freedom over the composition of their reserves; nor is it quite right to say that the dollar is still freely convertible *de facto*.

3 After the rise of the market price of gold in 1960, the principal central banks formed the gold pool in order to keep control over the price. At the start, the assumption of the pool was that there would normally be an excess of market supply over demand – which may include buying by central banks that are not members of the pool. By 1967 the pool had to supply not only the deficit of gold for private demand but the market demand of nonmember central banks as well. The residual supplier, of course, was the United States, since the other pool members could offset their gold losses to the pool by purchases from the United States.

4 The threat overhanging gold has restricted its use in official settlements; except in desperate circumstances or for political ends, central banks try to meet temporary difficulties by other means.

5 While gold losses act as a discipline on the United States, they have become an uncertain guide for judging its balance-of-payments performance. At one moment the authorities expressed a firm intention to balance the external accounts. When they realized that this unilateral undertaking was impossible, they said that the surplus countries must carry a fair share of the burden of adjustment – without specifying what a fair share for the United States would be. The latest posture seems to be a resigned attitude towards the balance-of-payments deficit, with its persistence and size being attributed to the war in Vietnam. One can only conclude that the authorities of the United States have not formulated a set of standards for judging whether its responsibilities for the reserve currency of the system are being fulfilled. In fact, of course, with the shortage of new gold anything like as severe as it is at present, it cannot be done.

6 With the growing tightness of the system, it has become a matter of high priority to prevent any excitement on the exchange markets and to resort to extreme means to gain market confidence. One aspect of this is a fear of changes in exchange rates and a belief that almost any change in rates

constitutes a threat to the stability of the system. This is in the face of the necessity for rates to be much more finely adjusted in conditions of a gold shortage than would be needed with an adequate flow of gold.

7 Owing to limitations on the growth of reserves through gold and dollars, the system no longer has a built-in mechanism for the increase in reserves. As a consequence, the growth of reserves has depended to a large extent on special credits negotiated to finance deficits. Such arrangements are often influenced by political considerations, to the general detriment of strictly monetary and financial standards in the system. And, as the repayment of such credits would require a substantial contraction of global reserves, it is not easy to visualize their orderly liquidation.

The changes in the system that have occurred since 1960 are often presented as an evolution and strengthening of the system. While there have been innovations of permanent value, the essence of the matter has been a series of shoring-up operations to accommodate to a basic disequilibrium of the system. Far from the system being strengthened, it has been disintegrating. This can hardly be considered an evolution of the gold-dollar system, since it consists of replacing both gold and dollars with quite different instruments for the growth of reserves. The past six years have been transitional, and it is evident that the pattern of gold and credit financing followed in those years cannot be repeated in the next six years. If ways are found in the years ahead to suppress the official demand for gold, it will mean that a basically new system has come into being.

Note

1 My use of the terms 'equilibrium' and 'disequilibrium' to characterize concrete situations in the real world seems to unbalance the editorial equanimity of Fritz Machlup, who has long and resolutely maintained that these terms should be used only with reference to theoretical models with all variables fully specified. For want of more suitable terms, I shall continue to use the proscribed ones in their real-world meanings.

13

The gold standard: historical facts and future prospects

Richard N. Cooper *

Gold is a hardy perennial. It provides a psychological and material safe haven for people all around the world, and its invocation still produces deep-seated visceral reactions in many. It is not surprising, then, that when economic conditions are unfavourable, proposals to strengthen the role of gold in the monetary system find an audience much wider than the 'gold bugs' who have always seen the demise of the gold standard as the negative turning point in Western civilization.

The early 1980s is one of these periods. A number of proposals have been put forward to reinstitute some monetary role for gold, varying from window-dressing to a full-fledged revival of the gold standard. These proposals are being treated with a seriousness that would have been astonishing twenty, ten, or even five years ago. An official examination of the subject was undertaken by the Gold Commission, which was established by President Reagan in June 1981 and issued its contentious report in March 1982; and several bills have been submitted to Congress with the objective of reviving a monetary role for gold.[1]

This paper provides an examination of the leading proposals for reviving gold at the present time and addresses problems with and consequences of their implementation. Since interest in reviving gold lies primarily in a desire to eliminate inflation and preserve a non-inflationary environment – a point on which the historical gold standard offers little comfort – a final section of the paper considers other proposals for commodity standards that go beyond reliance on the single commodity, gold, to stabilize the general level of prices.

*From *Brookings Papers on Economic Activity*, I, 1982, pp. 1–3, 25–45, abridged.

Before turning to these matters, however, I examine briefly the stated and sometimes implicit objectives of those who advocate an important monetary role for gold. The primary emphasis, as noted above, is the restoration and maintenance of price stability; it is this motive, I believe, that gives gold such wide support. If the monetary side of the economy is somehow restrained by gold, the argument runs, the economy cannot inflate and prices will be stabilized. That is ultimately an empirical question, which can be addressed scientifically. But there seem to be other motivations as well. Some see restoration of gold as a way to re-establish fixed exchange rates among major currencies. To accomplish this result, all the relevant countries would have to restore a monetary role to gold in the required fashion. Action by the United States alone would not accomplish this objective; currencies could float against the US dollar even if it were tied to gold.

Finally, and perhaps most fundamentally, many advocates want greater automaticity in management of the economy, and especially monetary policy, as an objective in its own right even if the automaticity results in greater economic instability. Such underlying philosophical differences in preferences do not readily lend themselves to economic or other empirical analysis, although they derive in part from a supposed association of large government discretion in economic (and other) management with a loss of individual freedom. I am not aware, however, that this last association has been made in arguing for a return by the United States to a gold standard, at least since Americans have once again been permitted to buy and sell gold freely.[2] But to the extent that such philosophical views govern, historical evidence on economic performance under the gold standard is of secondary importance, if that. [...]

Contemporary proposals for restoring gold to a monetary role

Proposals for reinstituting a monetary role for gold cover a wide range, from re-establishing gold backing for the currency at an official price to full-fledged restoration of a gold currency. I will discuss these proposals under two broad headings: gold backing of all kinds without convertibility; and proposals calling for some form of gold convertibility, ranging from foreign monetary authorities' holdings to all holdings of dollars. I address only proposals for the United States, although as noted above, a desire to restore fixed exchange rates represents part of the interest in gold, and that requires other countries to reintroduce gold as well. But so far there has been little interest from other countries in moving toward gold convertibility.

It is worth recalling at the outset that the United States had full gold convertibility for the dollar from 1879 to 1933 (with export restrictions imposed briefly during World War I); gold convertibility for foreign monetary authorities from 1934 to 1971; and gold backing for the currency from 1879 to 1968.[3] The only country that maintains any formal monetary role for gold (apart from holding gold among central bank assets) is Switzerland, about which more will be said later.

Gold reserve requirements

The idea behind gold backing without convertibility is to limit the growth in the supply of money and presumably also to bolster psychological support for the currency by those who still attach a monetary significance to gold and do not fully comprehend that, ultimately, money is a social convention.

The most limited proposal for gold backing calls for stipulating that the currency in circulation must be backed by the existing official gold stock of the United States at its current official price of $42.22 an ounce, and that the allowable growth in outstanding currency should be limited to 3 per cent a year after a transition period, assured by revaluing the existing gold stock by 3 per cent a year.[4] For the indefinite future, this proposal amounts only to a monetary rule in thin disguise; gold plays no essential role. One might just as well back the currency with the Washington Monument or the Statue of Liberty, endowing each with an initial value and stipulating that the value should increase at the fixed rate of 3 per cent a year. Such a proposal will not be considered further here.

Gold backing for all or some portion of the money supply could also be required at a fixed price of gold, or at the market price of gold, which fluctuates substantially. If the gold backing requirement does not bind – that is, if the value of the monetary gold exceeds the requirement for gold reserves, we would be in the realm of discretionary monetary policy, as at present. When the reserve requirement does bind, the monetary authorities would have to buy gold in order to increase the money supply. Unlike under a regime of convertibility, the purchase would be at the discretion of the monetary authorities.

This kind of arrangement poses difficult but not insuperable technical problems over the valuation of monetary gold, because in general the market price must deviate from the official price if orderly monetary growth is to be maintained (otherwise the permissible monetary base would fluctuate – wildly, in recent experience – with the market price of gold). For example, the Treasury could buy gold necessary for increasing the money supply at market prices, and resell it to the Federal Reserve Banks at the fixed official price, absorbing the difference as an expenditure (or, if the official price were above the market price, as a receipt).

But the key point is that this would be a discretionary regime, not an automatic one, unless in addition a rule governing monetary growth were also imposed. It would involve extra discipline only in so far as directors at the Office of Management and Budget and their superiors balk at budgeting for gold when market prices are considerably higher than the official price, or the Secretary of the Treasury balks at the balance-of-payments implications of gold purchases. A rough idea of the magnitudes is suggested by the fact that a 4 per cent growth in the official US gold stock – implying a 4 per cent growth in that component of the money supply covered by gold reserves, if the reserves are binding – would involve a gross expenditure of $4.2 billion if the market price were $400 an ounce, and a net expenditure on the budget of $3.75 billion if the gold were resold to the Federal Reserve at the present official price. If the official price were increased, say, to $200 an ounce (with a corresponding increase in the required gold reserve to keep it binding), the gross expenditure by the Treasury for 4 per cent growth would be the same, and the net expenditure would be reduced to $2.1 billion. Obviously official US purchases of the 10.6 million ounces a year required for 4 per cent annual growth, amounting to 35 per cent of current world gold production, would very likely drive up the market price of gold considerably.

In short, gold backing by itself does not provide monetary discipline. The United States had backing for many years, and during most of that period the gold reserve requirements were not binding. The gold reserves would have permitted much more rapid growth than what actually took place. On the occasions when the reserve requirement became binding, it was lowered, and eventually removed. The national debt ceiling provides an analogous restraint on US government borrowing; it is there in principle, but in practice it is regularly overridden by other considerations, even by 'conservative' Congresses.

Switzerland is the only country that currently requires gold backing for its bank notes, in a ratio of 40 per cent. (Switzerland ceased to provide for convertibility of those notes into gold in 1954, the year the London gold market reopened.) Swiss official gold holdings grew only 7 per cent during the inflationary decade of the 1970s, but the Swiss money supply grew by 65 per cent. How was this possible? Switzerland entered the period with ample gold holdings relative to the required backing, more than double the legal requirement in 1970. The ratio fell steadily through the decade to 53 per cent in 1981, still well above the required 40 per cent. The restraint in Swiss monetary expansion has been discretionary, not conditioned by a binding gold reserve requirement.

What will happen when the reserve requirement becomes binding? Switzerland would have two options, apart from relaxing the requirement itself. It could raise its official price of gold (which still stands at 4,596 Swiss francs a kilogram, about $80 an ounce at current exchange rates), which is well below the market price, and which can be changed by simple government decree (after consultation with the Swiss National Bank). Or Switzerland could buy sufficient gold at market prices, something that country could probably do without greatly affecting the market price of gold. Either action would be discretionary in nature.

Gold convertibility

Gold convertibility exerts its discipline in quite a different way. The proposals involving convertibility vary, some calling in effect for full convertibility of all Federal Reserve notes and 100 per cent gold money thereafter. Bank notes could be issued by private banks, but they would in effect be depository receipts for gold.[5] Others are more limited, for example, calling for restoration of the pre-1971 gold convertibility for foreign monetary authorities.[6]

Although the *modus operandi* would vary substantially from one proposal to another, the underlying idea is the same: whenever some substantial group of dollar holders became dissatisfied with monetary developments and unsure about the future value of the dollar, they could and presumably would convert their dollars to gold. These conversions in turn would require the Federal Reserve to defend its gold reserves by tightening credit conditions or otherwise persuading the relevant public that gold conversions were unwarranted. The system in principle would be symmetrical: as gold reserves increased, the money supply would expand; this feature has not been emphasized by most proponents of gold convertibility. Moreover, historically, central banks have often offset ('sterilized') the expansionary effects of gold inflows, as the United States did during the late 1930s and again during the late 1940s.[7] Sterilization obviously would not be possible when gold (or gold certificates) is the sole form of money.

Since new gold production is small relative to outstanding gold stocks, the requirement for convertibility, it is argued, will automatically limit the rate of money creation, hence inflation, since there is a natural limit to how rapidly gold reserves can grow. Too rapid monetary growth would lead to conversion, which in turn (to preserve convertibility) would necessitate monetary retrenchment.

Note that most proposals for convertibility – those that fall short of a move to 100 per cent gold money – provide for some elasticity to the supply of money, so long as the relevant public is not of a disposition to convert dollars into gold. This feature indeed could conceivably be a source of instability, since in periods of high 'animal spirits' in the business and financial community outstanding Federal Reserve credit could rise substantially, only to be sharply reduced as the buoyant spirits give way to pessimism and a period of heavy conversion sets in, leading to a drop in Federal Reserve credit below its historical trend under the regime.

There is no doubt that a regime of gold convertibility could be made to function technically. But could it function politically? That is, could the political authorities resist the pressures they would be under to take countervailing action in periods of distress, either too rapid expansion or too rapid contraction? That would depend in part on how serious the distress was, which in turn would depend in part on the credibility of the monetary regime itself: expectations of long-run price stability will reduce the inertial character of inflationary impulses to the US economy, and hence improve the ability of the economy to absorb both monetary and real shocks with reduced cost in terms of lost output and employment. The argument, in short, is that a constrained monetary standard will dissuade the government and the public alike from believing they can 'inflate' out of economic difficulties, and a gold standard would provide a constrained monetary standard.

Or would it? Can convertibility be credibly established? Or would the public believe that a restored gold standard is bound to be a fair-weather vessel, likely to capsize and be abandoned in the first serious storm?

One difficulty with the credibility of a requirement for convertibility of US dollars into gold is the already huge volume of liquid dollar assets around the world. Federal Reserve liabilities at the end of 1980 were $158 billion; the US money supply was $415 billion (M1) or $1656 billion (M2); foreign monetary authorities held an estimated $240 billion in liquid dollar claims ($157 billion directly in the United States and the remainder in various 'Euro dollar' centres around the world), and other foreigners held an additional $700 billion, give or take several tens of billions, in dollar deposits (other than European interbank deposits) outside the United States. US gold reserves, by contrast, amounted to only $11.1 billion at the official price of $42.22 an ounce, and $111 billion at $422 an ounce (which has no virtue beyond being ten times the US official price and roughly equal to the market price at the end of 1981; the market price fell substantially below that in early 1982).

Full convertibility would hardly be credible, given the relation of assets to potential claims. Of course, not all outstanding liquid dollar claims would formally be convertible into gold; presumably the convertibility requirement would strictly apply only to Federal Reserve liabilities. But that provides no comfort, since the financial system functions on the supposition that all liquid dollar claims can, on short notice, be converted into claims on the Federal Reserve, either federal funds or currency. To deny or repudiate this more general convertibility is tantamount to a breakdown in the financial system, both domestic and international. Moreover, a major strength of the international financial system at present is that for large holders (that is, leaving aside bank notes) it is a closed system, so funds can be moved around in it but cannot be withdrawn from it, except by the Federal Reserve System. This feature served the international economy well in 'recycling' the large OPEC surpluses during the last decade; it would be altered by gold convertibility, which would provide a potential leakage to the system at the initiative of dollar holders, and thus could threaten the system as a whole with a convertibility crisis, as in 1931.

With too little gold relative to the potential for conversion, a gold convertibility system would be seen as a fair-weather system; expectations about future economic developments would not be changed radically; and the real costs of monetary adjustment would continue to be high, casting further doubt on the political sustainability of a gold convertibility regime.

A straightforward way to deal with these problems is to set a price of gold sufficiently high that there cannot be any doubt about the ability of the United States to sustain even large-scale conversion, at least for some time. If $422 an ounce will not be persuasive, perhaps $844 an ounce would be, and $1288 an ounce certainly should be (the last figure would result in a valuation of $333 billion on the existing US gold stock).

But with a much higher price, another, equally acute, problem arises: not only would new gold production increase substantially, but sales from the large existing gold stocks and hoards would take place. The US authorities would find themselves flooded with gold. Consider the privately held stocks first. Much of the estimated 1500 million ounces of privately held gold no doubt is held for traditional reasons, partly for ornament, partly as precautionary protection against untoward political or economic events. But much of it, especially during the 1970s, was also acquired as an investment. With a credibly high official price of gold, the prospect for further capital gains on these investments would vanish, and gold as an investment would lose its lustre, except to a small degree for portfolio diversification against remote contingencies. Thus there would be large-scale dishoarding. Even some central banks might sell their gold under these circumstances, and for similar reasons: prospective earnings on alternative assets would be much higher.

It is unclear what the supply schedule is for new production, although it is presumably upward sloping with respect to the price of gold in terms of other goods and services. In any case, as noted above, production is not determined simply by marginal costs today, but rather is subject to oligopolistic manipulation by the two major suppliers, South Africa and the Soviet Union, which are large enough to face a downward sloping demand schedule for gold. With a high and credible US official price of gold, in contrast, the demand schedule becomes perfectly elastic even for large producers, and there would then be no reason for them not to produce as much gold as it is economical to produce.

Thus there would be a flood of gold into the United States, on a more modest scale if convertibility were limited to foreign monetary authorities, on a vast scale under full convertibility. What should the United States then do? To monetize the gold would be strongly expansionary.[8] This expansion would presumably endure until the price level had risen sufficiently to reduce new gold production to the point at which it just satisfies the secular growth in demand for gold. That prolonged adjustment hardly satisfies the expectation of price stability sought by advocates of gold convertibility. The monetary authorities could sterilize the monetary impact of the additional gold, as they did at various times past. But then that would mean a return to a world of discretionary monetary policy much as that which prevailed from 1934 to 1971, a period during which reliance was placed on the monetary authorities, not gold convertibility, for monetary restraint.

With large holdings of (sterilized) gold in official hands, there would be ample room for monetary expansion without threatening convertibility, and when that room was exhausted many years later, people would rightly wonder why suddenly this constraint of gold supply, which had not been operative for many years, should induce a rush to convert, provoking a restrictive monetary policy. They would simply remove it.

Is there a price that just balances these conflicting considerations – too low a gold stock to make continued convertibility credible, or such a high gold stock that it would exert no monetary discipline and *de facto* would be a regime of discretionary management? Conceivably there could be such a price, one that would persuade hoarders to disgorge enough gold such that a combination of the higher price and the enlarged quantity of monetary gold would make the system credible but not too undisciplined. But my guess is that there is no such price. The relevant public would be sceptical about continued convertibility up to quite a high price, and only then would be won over; but the price that would be persuasive would be too high to provide the discipline.

Whether there is such a price is irrelevant, however, because there is no way of finding it. Any guess, however well informed or rationalized, would obviously be seen to be a conscious policy choice. And therein lies the problem of a restored gold standard as a source of discipline and automaticity: once the price is recognized as a discretionary variable, the discipline that a gold standard could conceivably exert would be lost.

One proposal deals directly with the difficulties of choosing a price by allowing the market to determine the price in the first instance, and then allowing the price to change (again, determined by the market) in periods of great stress. In particular, the starting official price would be the average market price in the five days preceding restoration of convertibility, following six months' notice of the intention to introduce a regime of convertibility. The official price would then be fixed indefinitely at this level, unless gold reserves dropped below 25 per cent of the target level of gold reserves (set by the ratio of gold reserves to Federal Reserve liabilities on the day before resumption of gold convertibility) or rose above 175 per cent of the target level. In either of these events, a 'gold holiday' would be declared for ninety days to allow the private market to set a new price. During gold holidays the government would not engage in either purchases or sales of gold, nor would the Federal Reserve be permitted to alter the monetary base by more than 1 per cent.[9] Within 50 and 125 per cent of this target, monetary policy would be discretionary, but the degree of discretion would be reduced as the outer limits were approached. For instance, if gold reserves are above 125 per cent of target, the monetary base must be increased by 1 per cent a month, and this rises to 2 per cent a month if reserves are above 150 per cent of target. Below 50 per cent of target, the monetary base must be reduced by 1 per cent a month.

This scheme, like the adjustable-peg system of exchange rates, would provide strong incentives to speculate for or against gold as the highly visible reserve level approached the critical boundaries, which, combined with the mandatory adjustments in monetary base, would introduce a strong source of instability into the monetary system. Moreover, while the method for choosing the official price would ensure that the 'market' accepted that price at the outset, the same method would lend itself to manipulation by large holders of gold, and in particular to manipulation by South Africa and the Soviet Union, the principal sources of new gold. They would have a strong interest in as high an official US price as possible, and therefore would surely take all possible steps to withhold new gold supplies from the market during the critical six-month period after the announcement. Although the price of gold is primarily an asset price because it is the price that persuades the public to hold existing stocks of gold throughout the world, even relatively small changes in the stock relative to changes in demand can have a substantial impact on price. Thus, at the margin, withholding supplies would raise the price. Expectations by the public concerning future sales by these countries would have no influence on current market prices, since after resumption day the United States would provide a perfectly elastic demand at the indicated price, so such sales would not be expected to depress future market prices.

Finally, shifts in market sentiment about gold or the dollar could under this regime trigger prolonged monetary contractions or expansions. With no distinction among different sources of disturbance, this feature could result in greater monetary instability rather than achieving its stated purpose of greater stability. For instance, another disturbance in the oil market resulting in much higher oil prices would require severe monetary contraction if either the public or the oil-exporting countries decided to acquire gold, but no contraction if they did not decide to acquire gold, and that decision in turn would be heavily influenced by the political circumstances surrounding the disturbance, not merely (or even mainly) by monetary conditions in the United States. This proposal would certainly not offer the prospect for long-run price stability that many proponents of the gold standard desire, and that Laffer ('price stability would return in short order') claims for it.[10]

Another approach may be possible to deal with the excess of outstanding dollar holdings over existing US gold reserves, and the difficulties that poses for determining an appropriate price for gold. Some of the outstanding dollars might be 'locked up' in a substitution account under the auspices of the International Monetary Fund to reduce the contingent claims on US gold. If enough dollars were converted to SDR (special drawing rights) claims on the substitution account, usable only to finance payments deficits, perhaps US gold valued at, say $422 an ounce would represent a credible reserve.

There are two difficulties with this idea. First, most of the outstanding dollars outside the United States are in private rather than official hands and could not be placed into a substitution account without first driving them into official hands, presumably by creating prospects for a weak dollar. Such an exercise would itself be hazardous and would threaten the objective of monetary stability that motivates consideration of a restored gold standard.

Second, at present, for a variety of reasons, many official holders of dollars would be reluctant to exchange them for SDR-denominated claims in a substitution account, even claims that provide considerable liquidity to each holder in case of balance-of-payments need. The terms of the substitution account would have to be very attractive to induce many developing countries to participate in the scheme. The process of negotiation over these terms and even the negotiated outcome would very likely cast doubt on the determination of the community of nations to restore global monetary stability or to help the United States restore the stability of the dollar.

I conclude this discussion of gold convertibility regimes by noting that neither history nor logic offers compelling reason to expect gold convertibility to lead to stable prices. Exchange rates could be stabilized only if other countries also introduced gold convertibility and if maintaining that convertibility became (as it was in the late nineteenth century) the principal objective of policy. But if countries were willing to do that, they could do it without the intermediation of gold.

There is another disadvantage to reinstituting gold in a monetary role that is in any way linked to the market for gold, directly or indirectly. As has already been noted, the principal producers of gold in the world, together accounting for nearly 80 per cent of world production, are South Africa and the Soviet Union. Both countries exercise considerable discretion in the amount of gold they actually put onto the market rather than allow competitive market incentives to prevail. Both are, in very different ways, at political odds with other members of the community of nations. Restoring gold convertibility would provide a windfall of considerable magnitude to those two countries. They could sell all they wished without depressing the market, and every $100 per ounce in the price is worth about $1 billion annually to the Soviet Union on its current estimated gold production and $2.2 billion to South Africa. For the reasons given above, a credible regime of gold convertibility would require a substantial increase in price above the current market level. An ill-conceived attempt to avoid this price increase and to rely on new supplies to provide for limited monetary growth would place the monetary system of the United States hostage to political decisions in one or both of these countries.

No escape from discretion

The choice of a price for gold plays a central role in the viability of any restoration of gold to a monetary role. Yet the choice of a price, while crucial, is unavoidably arbitrary and is known to be arbitrary. So long as this is so, a rule based on a supposedly fixed price of gold cannot be a credible rule. If gold were to become unduly constraining, its price could be changed, and that would be widely known – indeed, it is intrinsic to the process of setting a price in the first place. In this respect, the situation today is fundamentally different from the situation in the nineteenth and early twentieth centuries. Then the dollar price of gold was historically given and not open to question (except for minor adjustments on several occasions to preserve the relation to silver). The price was not conceived as a policy variable. Now it is, indeed must be. Yet gold ceases to provide monetary discipline if its price can be varied. So long as the price of gold is a policy variable, a gold standard cannot be a credible disciplinarian. It provides no escape from the need for human management, however frail that may seem to be.

Other commodity standards

The failure of the gold standard to achieve price stability was well understood by many who lived through it, and provoked thought about what arrangements might produce greater stability. Most of the public debate in the nineteenth century focused around the alternative of silver (which conceptually had the same disadvantages as gold), of bimetallism, and of using paper currency elastically to supplement gold in periods of stringency. In the twentieth century serious proposals have arisen for broadly based commodity money, for a 'tabular' standard that alters the definition of money according to the movement of some commodity price index, and for monetary policy to be keyed formally and directly to a price index. Each of these ideas had nineteenth-century antecedents.

Bimetallism and symmetallism

Bimetallism endows two metals, gold and silver, with full monetary status at a fixed price. Because variations in supply and in non-monetary demand are unlikely to be perfectly correlated, this system can generally be expected to provide greater price stability in the long run than monometallism, provided the monetary authorities do not run out of either metal – that is, provided they hold reserves large enough to maintain the fixed price between the metals so that both of them stay in circulation. Variations in the relative supply of gold and silver plagued bimetallism over the years. It was Newton's overpricing of gold at the English mint that failed to retain the recently reminted silver coins and inadvertently placed Britain on the gold standard. The gold value of the US dollar was adjusted in 1834 to correct for the previous undervaluation of gold, and overdid it (the silver–gold mint ratio was changed from 15:1 to 16:1), leading to an overvaluation of gold and the export of silver. Generally speaking, French coinage was sufficiently important during the nineteenth century to keep the price of silver relative to gold around France's official mint ratio of $15\frac{1}{2}$:1, but this was after the Nevada discoveries of 1859 and the decision of Germany to switch from silver to gold in 1871, followed by Scandinavia. France was unable to hold the ratio and abandoned unlimited coinage of the silver five-franc piece in 1874.

Alfred Marshall pointed out the difficulties in maintaining a fixed price between any two commodities over time, and suggested that 'true bimetallism' should define the currency in terms of fixed quantities of the two metals, leaving the relative price free to vary. Marshall favoured a symmetallic standard, as Edgeworth called it, over a monometallic one. At first he shied away from actually recommending it on the grounds that a change in the monetary standard would be too disruptive to justify the modest gains from it, but as agitation over the standard mounted, he began to advocate it.[11]

Commodity reserve currency

A logical extension of Marshall's proposal would be to enlarge the list of commodities, fixed in quantity, in which the monetary unit is defined and against which it is issued. This was done by Benjamin Graham and his unrelated namesake, Frank Graham, in the 1930s. Benjamin Graham proposed that the dollar be defined in terms of a fixed-weight bundle of twenty-three commodities (reduced to fifteen in his international variant) and that the Federal Reserve issue notes against warehouse receipts for the bundle thus defined.[12] His proposal was to supplement the existing monetary system with commodity money. Frank Graham would have included a much longer (but unspecified) list of commodities in his commodity bundle, and he would have substituted commodity money for all other forms of money, at least in terms of future growth. At the margin, he favoured what was called 100 per cent money; in effect all new currency and demand deposits would represent warehouse receipts for the commodity bundles. He recognized that this preferred variant was not realistic and he was willing to settle for less.[13]

Benjamin Graham selected his proposed commodities on the basis of their economic importance and their storability. Commodity production was monetized under the scheme, but the relative prices of commodities were left free to vary; only the average price level was held constant in terms of dollars. Graham was motivated in large measure by anti-depression considerations; he felt that support for primary commodity prices in times of economic slack would help stabilize overall economic activity. By the same token, release of commodities (demonetization) would help to limit booms, both by supplying commodities out of stocks and by contracting the money supply. His scheme in effect would provide perfectly elastic demand for the commodities (taken as a bundle) included in the monetary unit in times of depressed economic activity, and perfectly elastic supply (so long as physical stocks lasted) in times of boom.

Stabilizing the price level of a limited bundle of storable commodities will stabilize the general price level only if the terms of trade between the commodities in question and manufactured goods (and services, if the 'general' price level is taken to be the consumer price index) are unchanging over time.[14] Apart from both the improbability of satisfying this condition and the resources tied up in the monetized commodities (reckoned by proponents to be about 3 to 4 per cent annually of the value of the stored commodities) – a factor that also applies to gold, although on a smaller scale – it is unclear why there has not been more enthusiasm for commodity-reserve proposals. Such proposals have found little interest beyond intellectuals. I suspect that conservatives really want gold, for reasons of history and sentiment, whereas non-conservatives prefer managed money.[15] Also, the schemes are basically too complicated to appeal to a wider public.

Benjamin Graham pointed out in 1961 that between the Commodity Credit Corporation and the strategic stockpile, the US government during the 1950s acquired enormous reserves of both agricultural and non-agricultural commodities valued at $16 billion (over 10 per cent of the money supply in 1960). Part of these acquisitions were even monetized through the federal budget deficit and the Federal Reserve's acquisition of Treasury bills. So the costs were incurred anyway, but in the name of other objectives and sometimes with a destabilizing rather than a stabilizing influence on price movements.[16]

The idea of a commodity currency was revived in 1964 in an international context by Albert Hart, Nicholas Kaldor, and Jan Tinbergen. They proposed an International Commodity Reserve Currency (ICRC) in lieu of an increase in the price of gold or reliance on a world fiduciary money as a solution to the problem of growing reliance on the US dollar as a reserve currency and increasing dissatisfaction with that arrangement.[17] They were flexible on the composition of the ICRC, suggesting thirty commodities for illustrative purposes only. The commodities should be chosen for their importance in international trade, and with that in mind the composition of the ICRC should be reviewed and if appropriate altered at five-year intervals. (They do not address the question of the *relative* price changes that would occur when individual commodities are greatly increased or reduced in importance following these reviews, and are consequently purchased or sold from stocks.) This scheme is not designed to stabilize national price levels because countries are free to pursue autonomous monetary and exchange-rate policies, but rather is intended to stabilize the 'real value' of the international unit of account. Curiously, their proposal also includes parallel treatment of gold, which would not be included in the ICRC bundle. The International Monetary Fund was thus to be left the task of stabilizing the price of gold in terms of the ICRC, reminiscent of bimetallism. Given sponsorship of the proposal by the United Nations Conference on Trade and Development, one can assume that it was designed to appeal to developing countries by providing demand for primary products in the bundle; but, as with the Graham proposal, relative prices are left free to vary, so there is no perfectly elastic demand for any particular commodity.

Indexation

The complexities of a multiple-commodity standard can be avoided by the simple expedient of indexing all dollar-denominated contracts by a suitably broad price index, provided the supply of money is limited. The basic idea goes back at least to Joseph Lowe, who suggested in 1822, long before price indexes were constructed, that contracts be adjusted for changes in the general value of commodities. The idea was promoted a decade later by George Poulett Scrope, who is sometimes credited with inventing the 'tabular standard', since he mentions the possibility of adjusting the legal tender as well as contracts. Writing in 1875, Jevons proposed that indexation of contracts be adopted on a voluntary basis at first, but that later it might be made compulsory for all contracts in excess of three months, indirect evidence that the real value of deferred payment was not preserved under the gold standard. He argued that indexation would represent an easy change; all that was necessary was a dispassionate government office to collect and collate the price information, publishing its results fully so they would be subject to public review and criticism.[18] Marshall also advocated indexation, and urged the Royal Commission on the Depression of Trade and Industry to attend to developing a purchasing-power index, or government unit, as he called it. He believed that once it was understood it would be popular in contracts; unlike his proposal for symmetallism, about which he was somewhat diffident, he considered indexation on the urgent and active agenda for reform.[19] In fact, the British government did not publish a consumer price index until 1914, nearly thirty years later; the US government did so in 1919.

The tabular standard

Indexation can be carried a step further, to include money itself, along with some link to the supply of money. This is known as the tabular standard, and is alluded to by Scrope in 1833, described by Jevons in 1875, advocated by Irving Fisher in 1920, and recently revived by Robert Hall.[20] Fisher proposes that the definition of the dollar in terms of gold (he was writing during the gold standard period) should be indexed to the cost of living. Contracts would be written in terms of dollars, without indexation, but indexation would be automatic by adjusting the dollar. If, for example, the relevant price index fell, the number of grains of gold that defined the dollar as a unit of account would be reduced by a corresponding amount. In other words, for purposes of settling debts, the goods value of the dollar would be preserved, since more gold would be required to settle a given debt denominated in dollars. The reverse adjustment would take place if the relevant price index rose.[21]

This scheme amounts to full indexation of all contracts, including gold-convertible paper money, against changes in the real value of gold, with gold remaining the formal basis of the dollar. In addition, Fisher would have adjusted the gold money supply in parallel with adjustments in the gold value of the dollar. If prices fell, for instance, the gold content of the dollar would be reduced, that is, the dollar price of gold would be raised, and gold would flow into the Treasury (against the issuance of gold certificates) from private hoards, from abroad, and eventually from new production. The reverse would occur if prices rose. Fisher would have reinforced this natural influence by issuing new gold certificates against the capital gains on existing Treasury stocks of gold, or retiring gold certificates in the event of rising prices, although this was not an essential part of his proposal.[22]

Robert Hall has recently revived the ideal of a tabular standard (without endorsing it), but he would substitute for the role of gold in Fisher's standard a weighted average of four commodities (ammonium nitrate, copper, aluminium, and plywood, ANCAP for short) whose price index has tracked very closely the US consumer price index over the past thirty years.[23] The dollar would be defined in terms of a specified combination of physical quantities of these commodities, and they would be legal tender in settlement of debts. Fiat money would presumably disappear, and bank notes could be issued freely, fully redeemable in ANCAPs. When the consumer price index rose, the dollar would be redefined to contain more ANCAPs. In this way, contracts with deferred payment written in terms of dollars would involve repayment that was constant in terms of purchasing power, as measured by the consumer price index. Unlike the Grahams, Hart–Kaldor–Tinbergen, and Fisher, Hall would not require or even permit the government to engage in purchases or sales of the commodities comprising ANCAP. The government would simply define the dollar in terms of ANCAPs and would endow them with the attribute of legal tender, so that private and government debts in effect would be settled in ANCAPs or paper claims to them. Private arbitrage, which would involve some physical storage of the commodities in ANCAP, would ensure that a paper dollar or dollar demand account remained equal in value to the current ANCAP definition of the dollar.

Hall suggests that this would be a perfectly workable arrangement, but sees no advantage in it over a well-managed fiat money. He prefers a system whereby monetary policy would be keyed to deviations of the consumer price index from its target values (ultimately, after a transition period, zero change): for each per cent the consumer price index is above its target the Federal Reserve would engage in open-market sales with a view to raising the Treasury bill rate by 0.1 per cent; and it would act similarly each month that the consumer price index exceeded its target, so the effect would be cumulative.[24]

Conclusions

Consideration of the gold standard involves three quantities: gold; paper money (including demand deposits) called dollars; and some composite of goods and services in which members of the public are directly interested, for example those used to construct the consumer price index, a composite that we can call goods. There are three 'prices' linking these three quantities: the dollar price of goods, the dollar price of gold, and the gold price of goods, or the commodity terms of trade between gold and other goods. Because any one of these relative prices can be derived from the other two, only two of them are independent: (dollar/goods) = (gold/goods) × (dollar/gold) or ($/G) = (A/G) × ($/A), where G stands for goods and A stands for *aurum* (or ANCAP). Inflation involves the first of these three prices, $/G. In attempting to limit inflation, advocates of the gold standard would fix the third price, the dollar price of gold (or, equivalently, the gold content of the dollar). This can be done if the government has a sufficiently large stock of gold relative to the stock of dollars outstanding and if, when necessary, it devotes control of the supply of dollars to that objective. Alternatively, it can be done by going to a pure metallic currency, in which 'dollars' *are* gold. These advocates contend that by fixing the dollar price of gold, $/A, they will stabilize the dollar price of goods, $/G. Both history and logic refute this contention, however, because in general the relative price between gold and other commodities, A/G, is variable over time. To be sure, there is some feedback from A/G to the supply of gold, because this price influences the cost of extracting gold. But this influence occurs only with long lags, and even then it is weak because gold is an exhaustible resource, not in perfectly elastic long-run supply. It would be necessary to argue that in the long run both discovery and technical change adapt so as to assure fixed terms of trade between gold and goods. Certainly this price, A/G, in fact showed great variation in the nineteenth century, and it also showed a great change during the 1970s when gold prices rose much more than goods prices did (A/G fell by about 80 per cent). In short, A/G is too variable to permit $\$/G$ to be stabilized by fixing $\$/A$.

The Graham and the Fisher and Hall schemes seek to control the dollar price of goods directly. The Graham plan would do so by buying and selling a bundle of goods against dollars at a fixed price, with a sufficiently broadly defined bundle so that its price is highly correlated with all goods. Even so, it is necessary to be concerned with long-run divergences in the relative price between their suggested composites and goods more generally. Frank Graham would also control tightly the quantity of dollars by making commodity bundles the exclusive source of (additional) money.

The tabular standard of Fisher and Hall would define the dollar as some commodity or composite commodity, then would adjust the definition of the dollar at regular intervals to ensure dollar price stability of a large bundle of goods and services, such as consumer price index: $\$/G$ can be stabilized (to be sure, as Hall points out, not always without economic hardship) by adjusting $\$/A$ to offset exactly changes in the real price A/G, which under a commodity standard is the sole source of instability in the general level of prices.

In summary, if stabilizing the dollar price of commodities is the objective, fixing the dollar price of gold is not the way to achieve it. Direct action on the dollar price of goods is more likely to be successful. But as was noted at the beginning of this paper, an objective – perhaps the dominant one – of the advocates of a restoration of gold is to reduce greatly or even eliminate discretion in the hands of the monetary authorities. It is noteworthy that all of the commodity-based proposals except that of Benjamin Graham sharply reduce or eliminate altogether discretion in monetary management.[25]

Seen this way, these proposals, taken together, raise the interesting philosophical question of why one should think that experts are more clever at devising operational, non-discretionary monetary regimes than they are at monetary management within a discretionary regime. If the desire for a non-discretionary regime is really simply another way – misguided, as shown above, in the case of gold – of assigning priority above all others to the objective of price stability in the management of monetary policy, that can be done directly by instructing the Federal Reserve unambiguously to take whatever action is necessary to ensure price stability. If collectively we are ambivalent about that priority, that is the principal source of the problem, not the nature of the regime.

Notes

1 Establishment of the Gold Commission was not at President Reagan's initiative, however. He was responding to a statutory requirement to study US policy on the role of gold in the domestic and international monetary systems. In 1980 President Carter signed an act to increase US quotas at the International Monetary Fund, to which this requirement had been added as a rider by Senator Jesse Helms.

   With much disagreement among its members, the Gold Commission recommended against restoration of any formal monetary role for gold. In its one positive recommendation, the majority of the commission favoured issuance of gold coins by the US Mint, denominated by weight, sold at market prices, and exempt from capital-gains taxation. See Gold Commission (1982).

2 The point was made explicitly twenty years ago by Arthur Kemp, however, who observed that the ability to carry wealth, especially gold coins, has provided individuals with the opportunity to escape from political tyranny throughout history. See Kemp (1962), pp. 137–54, especially pp. 152–3. This volume, incidentally, offers an excellent sampling of the debate twenty years ago on sound versus unsound money and the desirable degree of discretion to leave in the hands of the monetary authorities – with a heavy majority of the contributors being against much, if not any, discretion.

3 In 1933 the gold coins and gold certificates in the hands of the public were all called in. The Banking Act of 1934 established the requirement that the Federal Reserve Banks should hold 35 per cent in gold against their deposit liabilities and 40 per cent against outstanding notes. In 1945 these requirements were reduced to a uniform 25 per cent against both deposits and notes. In 1965 the reserve requirement against deposits was eliminated, and in 1968 the reserve requirement against notes was eliminated.

4 Weintraub (1981), pp. 21–4.

5 See H. Res. 391, a bill submitted to Congress by Representative Ron Paul in January 1981.

6 I leave aside suggestions that gold convertibility be re-established only for residents of the United States on the grounds that it would always be possible for foreigners to arbitrage around such restrictions in the absence of a comprehensive set of exchange controls.

7 Offsetting actions by central banks, in periods of contraction as well as periods of expansion, even took place often in the heyday of the historical gold standard. See Bloomfield (1959).

8 It is for this reason that Sir Roy Harrod over the years favoured an increase in the official price of gold. See, for example, Harrod (1965), ch. 3.

9 See 'Gold Reserve Act of 1981', pp. S22–6. The basic idea derives from a proposal by Laffer (1980) who likens his proposal to that made by the United States in 1972 for the management of exchange rates around target levels of international reserves.

10 Laffer (1980). He makes much of the analogy between his proposal and the official US proposal of 1972, described in the *Economic Report of the President, January 1973*, concerning an exchange-rate regime. But the underlying purposes of the two proposals are completely different. The 1972 proposal was designed to introduce greater symmetry of adjustment between countries in deficit and those in surplus into a system that presupposed national autonomy in monetary policy and was designed to accommodate that autonomy as much as possible, while still preserving the alleged advantages of temporarily fixed exchange rates. The Laffer–Helms

proposal, in contrast, is designed to impose severe limits on autonomy in national (at least US) monetary policy.

11 Marshall (1926), pp. 14–15, 30–1.

12 Graham's short list comprised wheat, corn, cotton, wool, rubber, coffee, tea, sugar, tobacco, petroleum, coal, wood pulp, pig iron, copper and tin. At 1937 prices, coal and wheat were the most important (over 13 per cent each), tea and tin the least (2.1 per cent each). See B. Graham (1937), and (1944), p. 45. The scheme was originally proposed by Graham in 1933. W. Stanley Jevons suggested a 'multiple legal tender' that could be interpreted as a commodity standard in the same vein, but he actually proposed indexation of contracts by a commodity price index, without distinguishing between the two. See Jevons (1875), p. 327.

13 See F. Graham (1942).

14 In the United States the price of crude materials – including oil – rose by 201 per cent between 1947 and 1980; wholesale prices of finished manufactures, by 265 per cent; and prices of services (in the consumer price index), by 429 per cent.

15 It is of interest, though, that F.A. Hayek viewed commodity money favourably; see Hayek (1943), pp. 176–84.

Keynes and Friedman both opposed it. Keynes, though highly supportive of stabilization schemes for individual commodities, opposed a commodity-reserve currency on the grounds that it would have the same disadvantages as a gold standard in failing to persuade organized labour that they should keep their demands for money-wages in line with the increase in efficiency-wages (that is, productivity). He considered the risk of excessive money-wage demands as one of the major obstacles to maintenance of a full-employment economy. See Keynes (1943), pp. 215–17.

Milton Friedman also opposed a commodity-reserve currency on the grounds that a full commodity-reserve currency, lacking the mystique and historical legitimacy of gold, would in time become financially burdensome because of the real costs associated with it. This in turn would result in dilution of the concept, through various economies, which would lead in effect to discretionary policy, which he also opposed. A full commodity-reserve currency is therefore dominated both by a gold standard, with its mystique, and by a properly managed fiat money which Friedman favours (1951, pp. 204–50).

16 See B. Graham (1962), pp. 185–214.

17 See Hart, Kaldor and Tinbergen (1964), pp. 131–77; also Hart (1976), pp. 1–32.

18 Jevons (1875), p. 331; characteristically, Jevons also discusses Lowe, Scrope and other antecedents. See also Fetter (1965), p. 139; and Schumpeter (1954).

19 Marshall (1926), p. 12.

20 See Jevons (1875), Fisher (1920) and Hall (1982).

21 Fisher (1920) observes in the preface that most of his ideas were conceived before World War I, in other words during the heyday of the gold standard. Some of Fisher's comments on the disasters of the gold standard can be found on p. 117.

22 ibid., appendix I. To avoid the problem of constant reminting, Fisher would have retired all gold coins and moved to a convertible gold bullion standard. According to him, 'gold' in circulation was overwhelmingly in the form of gold certificates, yellowbacks, with most of the monetary gold already in the hands of the Treasury.

23 Hall (1982).

24 Hall (1981). To work, this proposal assumes that the response of the price level to changes in the supply of money is reasonably rapid; long response lags could lead to explosive oscillation of both money and prices. Hall's proposal was anticipated in 1832 by Charles Jones, who 'advocated a policy of price stabilization by a national

bank of issue through open market operations, buying public debt when a twenty-commodity price index fell, and selling public debt when the price index rose'. See Fetter (1965), p. 139.

25 In this respect, the proposal of Helms and Laffer is a compromise; it retains discretion in monetary management within a range, but increasingly limits that discretion as the official supply of gold continues to shrink or to rise. In doing so, it gives gold a major signalling or thermostatic function, but thereby ignores the function of gold as a commodity and the false signals that it might send.

References

Bloomfield, Arthur I. (1959), *Monetary Policy under the International Gold Standard: 1880–1914*, New York, Federal Reserve Bank of New York.

Fetter, Frank W. (1965), *Development of British Orthodoxy, 1797–1875*, Cambridge, Mass., Harvard University Press.

Fisher, Irving (1920), *Stabilizing the Dollar*, New York, Macmillan.

Friedman, Milton (1951), 'Commodity-reserve currency', *Journal of Political Economy*, 59 (June), reprinted in his *Essays in Positive Economics*, Chicago, University of Chicago Press, 1953.

Gold Commission (1982), *Report to the Congress of the Commission on the Role of Gold in the Domestic and International Monetary Systems*, Washington, D.C., US Government Printing Office.

'Gold Reserve Act of 1981', s.6, submitted to Congress by Senator Jesse Helms, in *Congressional Record* (daily edn), 5 January 1981.

Graham, Benjamin (1937), *Storage and Stability*, New York, McGraw-Hill.

——(1944), *World Commodities and World Currency*, New York, McGraw-Hill.

——(1962), 'The commodity-reserve currency proposal reconsidered', in Yeager (1962).

Graham, Frank D. (1942), *Social Goals and Economic Institutions*, Princeton, Princeton University Press.

Hall, Robert E. (1981), 'A free-market policy to stabilize the purchasing power of the dollar', unpublished MS.

——(1982), 'Explorations in the gold standard and related policies for stabilizing the dollar', in R.E. Hall (ed.), *Inflation: Causes and Effects*, Chicago, University of Chicago Press, 111–22.

Harrod, Sir Roy (1965), *Reforming the World's Money*, London, St Martin's Press.

Hart, A.G. (1976), 'The case as of 1976 for International Commodity-Reserve Currency', *Weltwirtschaftliches Archiv*, 112, no. 1.

Hart, A.G., Nicholas Kaldor and Jan Tinbergen (1964), 'The case for an International Commodity Reserve Currency', in Nicholas Kaldor, *Essays on Economic Policy*, 2, New York, Norton.

Hayek, F.A. (1943), 'A commodity reserve currency', *Economic Journal*, 53 (June – September).

Jevons, W. Stanley (1875), *Money and the Mechanism of Exchange*, New York, D. Appleton.

Kemp, Arthur (1962), 'The gold standard: a reappraisal', in Yeager (1962).

Keynes, J.M. (1943), letter to Benjamin Graham, reprinted as an appendix to Graham (1962).

Laffer, Arthur B. (1980), 'The reinstatement of the dollar: the blueprint', Los Angeles, A.B. Laffer Associates, 29 February.

Marshall, Alfred (1926), *Official Papers by Alfred Marshall*, London, Macmillan.

Schumpeter, Joseph A. (1954), *History of Economic Analysis*, New York, Oxford University Press.

Weintraub, Robert E. (1981), 'Restoring the gold certificate reserve', appendix to a study by the Subcommittee on Monetary and Fiscal Policy of the Joint Economic Committee, *The Gold Standard: Its History and Record Against Inflation*, 97 Cong. 1 sess., Washington, D.C., US Government Printing Office.

Yeager, Leland B. (ed.) (1962), *In Search of a Monetary Constitution*, Cambridge, Mass., Harvard University Press.

Further reading

Full details of works mentioned here are to be found in the References at the end of the Introduction (pp. 32–5).

The reader wishing to pursue the issues addressed in this volume is forced to cast his net widely. There is no single work providing comprehensive coverage of the theory, history or doctrine of the gold standard, much less all three. This guide provides suggestions of where to begin a search for further information.

The definitive surveys of doctrine on the gold standard remain Viner (1937) and Fetter (1965). For a more recent analysis the reader may wish to refer to Bordo (1984).

Theoretical models of the price-specie-flow mechanism can be found in many international economics textbooks. However, the literature contains few treatments of the gold standard which incorporate in a unified analytical framework the roles of interest rates, capital flows, and changes in output and spending in the gold standard adjustment mechanism. Although many of these effects can be found in the models of Meade (1951), it is difficult to pick out their individual effects. Two recent treatments are Dornbusch and Frenkel (1984) and Eichengreen (1984). Dornbusch and Frenkel design a model of a small country to analyse the role of interest rates and deposit banking in the short-run adjustment process, while Eichengreen develops a two-country model of the gold standard designed to analyse the short-run interaction of central banks.

Hawtrey (1927) provides a lively introduction to the origins of the gold standard in England and to its spread throughout the international economy in the final decades of the nineteenth century. On the development of central banking, individual bank histories should be consulted, starting with histories of the Bank of England by Clapham (1944) and Sayers (1976) and of the Bank of France by Ramon (1929). The role of the Bank Charter Act of 1844 in helping to establish the Bank of England's public role is analysed by Horsefield (1944), Whale (1944) and Sayers (1957).

Since it is sometimes argued that the classical gold standard functioned under unusually favourable circumstances, the reader may wish to consult an international economic history of the period such as Lewis (1978). As introductions to the international monetary system of the years 1880–1914, Bloomfield's (1959, 1963) studies remain unsurpassed. Many of the issues analysed by Bloomfield are subjected to statistical analysis by Morgenstern (1959) and by the contributors to Bordo and Schwartz (1984). Morgenstern will be preferred by those interested primarily in the statistical properties of the data, Bordo and Schwartz by those with a taste for tests of formal economic models.

Contemporary descriptions of the operating procedures of central banks can be found in the interviews conducted by the US National Monetary Commission (1910). Central bank operations have been analysed by historians using both descriptive and quantitative approaches: for example, on discount rate policy see Goodhart (1972), Dutton (1984) and Pippinger (1984); on the gold devices Sayers (1936); and on the practice of holding foreign-exchange reserves Lindert (1969). The operation of the gold standard at the periphery is considered by Ford (1962) and de Cecco (1974).

Readers interested in the interwar gold standard have a varied menu from which to choose. Histories of the international economy between the wars are provided by Lewis (1948) and Kindleberger (1973). Reconstruction of the international monetary system in the 1920s is considered by Clarke (1973). Britain's return to gold in 1925 has been extensively studied, notably by Sayers (1970) and Moggridge (1969, 1972). Stabilization of the French franc has attracted less attention, but see Kemp (1971). Central bank management of the system is described by Clarke (1967).

The literature on the malfunctioning of the interwar gold standard is extensive. The operation of the gold market is analysed in League of Nations (1932). Keynes's views as incapsulated in the Macmillan Committee *Report* are further spelt out in Keynes (1930). Contemporary analyses of the collapse of the system are many: for a British perspective see Gregory (1932), a European perspective Cassel (1936), and an American perspective Fraser (1933). The definitive historical analysis of the period remains the monumental study of Brown (1940). More recent perspectives on American and British developments can be found in Friedman and Schwartz (1963) and Cairncross and Eichengreen (1983).

The origins of the Bretton Woods System are described by Gardner (1956) and Horsefield (1969). An interpretation of Bretton Woods as a form of gold exchange standard appears in Dam (1982). Triffin's (1960) critiques of Bretton Woods are trenchant for their analysis of the potential for instability and prescient for their predictions of its demise. Kenen (1969) describes proposals for reform of the relationship between gold and the dollar as they were viewed toward the end of the period.

On recent proposals to restore a form of gold standard, the reader should survey the range of conflicting opinion in the US Gold Commission *Report* (1982) and its appendices. The *Minority Report*, which makes the case for the gold standard, is conveniently available as Paul and Lehrman (1982). A strongly worded defence of recent arguments favouring gold, which includes a response to the criticisms of Cooper, is Reynolds (1983). These proposals are analysed on a practical level by Fellner (1981) and Cagan (1982), and from a theoretical perspective by Flood and Garber (1984).

Index